TALKING
ABOUT
IDENTITY

TALKING
ABOUT
IDENTITY
ENCOUNTERS IN RACE, ETHNICITY, AND LANGUAGE

EDITED BY
CARL E. JAMES
AND
ADRIENNE SHADD

BETWEEN THE LINES
TORONTO, CANADA

Talking about Identity

© 2001 by Carl E. James and Adrienne Shadd

First published in Canada in 2001 by
Between the Lines
720 Bathurst Street, Suite #404
Toronto, Ontario
M5S 2R4

National Library of Canada Cataloguing in Publication Data

Main entry under title:
    Talking about identity : encounters in race, ethnicity, and language
Previously published under the title: Talking about difference.
Includes bibliographical references.
ISBN 1-896357-36-9

1. Multiculturalism — Canada.   I. James, Carl, 1952- .   II. Shadd, Adrienne L. (Adrienne Lynn), 1954- .   III. Title: Talking about difference.
FC105.M8T35 2001   306.44'6'0971   C2001-930001-8
F1035.A1T35 2001

Cover design, cover illustration, and text design by Margie Adam, ArtWork
Page preparation by Steve Izma
Printed in Canada by Transcontinental Printing

Between the Lines gratefully acknowledges assistance for its publishing activities from the Canada Council for the Arts, the Ontario Arts Council, and the Government of Canada through the Book Publishing Industry Development Program.

Canadä

THE CANADA COUNCIL | LE CONSEIL DES ARTS
FOR THE ARTS | DU CANADA
SINCE 1957 | DEPUIS 1957

ONTARIO ARTS COUNCIL
CONSEIL DES ARTS DE L'ONTARIO

CONTENTS

Acknowledgements ix

Introduction: Encounters in Race, Ethnicity, and Language 1
   Carl E. James

Part I: Who's Canadian, Anyway? 9

"Where Are You Really From?" Notes of an "Immigrant"
   from North Buxton, Ontario 10
   Adrienne Shadd

What's Your Background? 17
   Kai James

Jewish, Canadian, or Québécois? Notes on a Diasporic
   Identity 20
   Susan Judith Ship

Québécitude An Ambiguous Identity 28
   Guy Bédard

I Want to Call Myself Canadian 33
   Katalin Szepesi

Hello . . . My Name Is 35
   Katalin Szepesi

Part II: Growing up "Different" 37

My Mother Used to Dance 38
   Valerie Bedassigae Pheasant

Zebra: Growing up Black and White in Canada 44
   Lawrence Hill

"I Am Canadian but My Father Is German" 51
   Lori Weber

Present Company Excluded, of Course . . . Revisited 60
Stan Isoki

Part III: Roots of Identity, Routes to Knowing 73

Revealing Moments: The Voice of One Who Lives with
Labels 74
Didi Khayatt

German-Japanese-American-Canadian: Chapters in a
Twentieth-Century Life 89
Gottfried Paasche

It Was Always There? Looking for Identity in All the (Not) So
Obvious Places 104
howard ramos

The Elusive and Illusionary: Identifying of Me, Not by Me 115
Camille Hernández-Ramdwar

Is It Japanese Artist or Artist Who Is Japanese? 122
Lillian Blakey

Corridors: Language as Trap and Meeting Ground 133
Angèle Denis

A Black Canadian Woman of Diverse Ethnic Origins 146
Marlene Jennings

Part IV: Race, Privilege, and Challenges 149

"I've Never Had a Black Teacher Before" 150
Carl E. James

White Teacher, Black Literature 168
Leslie Sanders

Whiteness in White Academia 177
Luis M. Aguiar

Learning from Discomfort: A Letter to My Daughters 193
Barb Thomas

The "Race Consciousness" of a South Asian (Canadian, of
Course) Female Academic 212
Arun Mukherjee

There's a White Man in My Bed: Scenes from an Interracial
Marriage 219
Pui Yee Beryl Tsang

Part V: Confronting Stereotypes and Racism 229

"I Didn't Know You Were Jewish" . . . and Other Things Not
to Say When You Find Out 230
Ivan Kalmar

But You Are Different: In Conversation with a Friend 241
Sabra Desai

Ties That Bind and Ties That Blind: Race and Class
  Intersections in the Classroom 250
  Paul Orlowski
"We Are All the Same — Just Because You Are Black Doesn't
  Matter" 267
  Gifty Serbeh-Dunn and Wayne Dunn
Can Blacks Be Racist? Reflections on Being "Too Black and
  African" 277
  Henry Martey Codjoe
"Why Are Black People So Angry?" The Question of Black
  Rage 291
  Adrienne Shadd
Interrogations 301
  Stephen Patel
References 305
Contributors 323

ACKNOWLEDGEMENTS

First, we want to extend our sincere thanks to all of the contributors of *Talking about Difference: Encounters in Culture, Language and Identity* (1994), the first version of this book. Without your honest and thought-provoking essays, this new edition would not have been possible. Because of its readership and continued use in many Canadian studies and social science courses, particularly courses in race and ethnic relations, we were presented with the opportunity to republish. In this regard we must also express our appreciation to you, the readers, for your continuing interest and support over the years.

In this new edition we have reprinted some of the engaging and illuminating articles from the first book and have added new contributions. In some cases, contributors from the first edition have written interesting and insightful addenda or afterthoughts with the benefit of six years' reflection on the issues. We therefore acknowledge all the contributors to this new book. We think it will be as instrumental as the first in engaging the debates and provoking discussion related to issues of difference and identity.

In any effort of this nature there is much administrative and support work to be done. We are grateful to Elma Thomas and Nola James of the Faculty of Education, York University, for their hard work and assistance in this regard. Thanks also to Robert Clarke, whose valuable editing questions and suggestions helped to strengthen the manuscript. We are deeply indebted to Paul Eprile of Between the Lines. It was Paul's suggestion some years ago that encouraged us to think about this new version of our original work; and Paul has been of great assistance in facilitating the process and bringing about the final product. Finally, we are indebted to Kai and Marishana. Without you, our continuing interest in the questions raised by the book would have less immediacy and less magnitude. Our work is first and foremost dedicated to you.

Introduction:
Encounters in Race,
Ethnicity, and Language

••••••••••••••••••••

Carl E. James

"Where are you from?"
"What is your nationality?"
"You have an accent."
"But, I never think of you as . . . "
"I didn't know you were . . . "
"You're different."
"I'm not racist, but . . . "
"It's just a joke."
"Some of my best friends are . . . "

Questions and comments like these are so much a part of our every-day world that some of us rarely give them a second thought when we hear them or say them. And for some people, particularly the speakers, such questions and comments may be regarded as innocent, neutral, and reflective of a genuine desire to engage in conversation or "get to know the person." For some recipients, though, they are reminders of their identities — reminders of race, ethnicity, and immigrant and/or minority status — yet another occasion of "othering" and/or a reflection of the speaker's ignorance or insensitivity.

We have all had our share of moments — some embarrassing, some enlightening — with such questions and statements. As recipients we are sometimes struck by the speaker's lack of awareness of or sensitivity to what the questions or statements represent, and occasionally we are unsure as to how to respond. We know that in responding we might be legitimizing the questions and statements that construct some of us as outsiders and others as "real" Canadians. Sometimes we even voice these same questions and comments, expecting recipients to understand that we "are not like the others" who ask such questions or make such comments. We expect that individuals recognize us as being genuinely interested in "knowing" them and in wanting to engage in meaningful conversation.

The motivation for this collection of articles comes partly out of this dual phenomenon: of being recipients as well as initiators of some of these questions and comments, and being uncertain about how best to ask the questions or respond to them. As the stories of the contributors demonstrate, they too have often had to grapple with similar questions and comments, particularly as they confront their own and/or other people's essentialist views and construction of them as "different." Our aim, then, is to offer, through these contributions, a study of how personal exchanges and interactions — that is to say, *our encounters* — inform our understandings of the complex ways in which race, ethnic, and language identities find expression in daily lives. It is not our intent to nullify or minimize the complexity of such matters. Indeed, over and over again the contributors demonstrate these complexities and dynamism in their stories. Rather, we want to make explicit how identities related to race, ethnicity, and language influence and inform individuals' life experiences and relationships.

Obviously, race, ethnic, and language identities intersect with social class, gender, sexuality, dis/ability, age, and other demographic characteristics to form the complex, multiple, dynamic, and contingent identities that we all have. As Stuart Hall (1990: 222) writes, "Identity is not as transparent or unproblematic as we think. Perhaps instead of thinking of identity as an already accomplished fact, which the new cultural practices then represent, we should think instead of identity as a 'production,' which is never complete, always in process and always constituted within, not outside representation." Clearly, then, the contributors' accounts of their experiences can alert us to the contextual and relational nature of identities, and to the various players and events that contribute to their process of becoming as well as to them being who they are, and their negotiation of identities

2

within situational and historical constraints and contexts (see Hall 1990; James 1999; Spence 1999; Yon 1995).

Insofar as race is socially constructed and a set of social relations (Omi and Winant 1993), then racial identity, as Michael Apple (1993: vii) points out, "is not a stable, permanent, united center that gives consistent meaning to our lives. It too is socially and historically constructed, and subject to political tensions and contradictions." The same can be said for ethnicity, a term that is often linked with race and often used in place of race. But, however used, both terms relate to individuals' positionality with regard to social, cultural, and political location within our society. And as the contributors demonstrate, race, ethnicity, and, correspondingly, language are part of the subjective ways in which we and others make sense of who we are, the places from which we speak, our encounters with others, the relationships we establish, and the experiences we have. Whatever the case, the "memory-work" (Norquay 1993)[1] from which our stories emerge reflects our generated memories of the past, our perceptions and analyses of the social contexts we traverse, and our understandings of our positions with these contexts (see Fentress and Wickham 1992: 126 on the notion of "re-telling of the past"; and Errante 2000 on "ways of remembering and telling").

We expect that as you read the various articles/stories/poems here, you will identify some of your own experiences or find your own perspectives reflected in the interpretations of issues with which you too grapple. In this regard, perhaps, the readings will serve as a source of empowerment. We also expect that you will compare your experiences with those of the authors and recognize similarities or commonalities, and of course differences. We trust that in recognizing the commonalities between us, even as they co-exist with our differences (James 2000), that the many dimensions of our lives will be revealed and we will learn to be more respectful of each other.

We also hope that this collection will add to the discussions of identities and the debate on equity, diversity, and multiculturalism in Canada, and that in doing this it will contribute as well to social action and change. After all, social action results not only from policy reform and government enactments but also from an awareness of others' experiences and from confronting our very own ideologies, attitudes, and feelings. That we have placed experiences at the centre of this discourse on social action and change does not mean that we want to limit analysis of the issues to individual experience. Rather, it means that we intend to illustrate how, through the understanding of individual experiences, we gain insight into the ways in which the   3 social structure shapes and mediates identities, experiences, and interactions: how it excludes some people and prevents many of us from truly knowing about each other; and how through our attitudes and actions within that structure we reinscribe difference and maintain inequity. Changes on the individual level brought about through increased knowledge of others can lead to changes in social structure.

It is precisely because of how the social structure operates that we remain misinformed, ignorant, and thus separate from each other. In his book *Inside Separate Worlds*, David Schoem (1991: 4) comments, "The effort it takes for us to know so little about one another across racial and ethnic groups is truly remarkable." It is remarkable, because we live in the same country, are educated together, and work together. Despite all this — despite our lives being intertwined socially, culturally, economically, and politically — we still manage to be ignorant of each other. Consequently, what little we know about the world around us is shaped by stereotypes, gossip, rumours, and fear. (We will save discussion of the media's role in this for another book.) This collection, therefore, is an effort to challenge, or confront, the ignorance, stereotypes, and fears that are all part of a prevailing system of racism, ethnicism, ethnocentrism, xenophobia, and discrimination.

In *Talking about Identity* the contributors share their unique histories and perspectives, providing a glimpse into their respective worlds and alerting us to the relevance of spaces for voices to articulate individual experiences and interpretations. In some cases, the authors provide information that has remained, until now, the domain of private thoughts and stories. Nevertheless, in sharing some of these private thoughts and stories, we understand that we must take risks if we are to contribute to social action and change.

Often, when another person's ideas or information make us uncomfortable because they seem "unreal" and/or challenge our "truths" and/or "facts," we find reason to question their validity. A common response is to reject these ideas as unfounded or "biased" — while failing at the same time to consider the ever-present "biases" that result from our own vantage points or world views. This tendency must be confronted if we are to hear each other and build an inclusive and equitable society. In making an attempt to understand the contributors in terms of how we describe our realities, construct our identities, conduct our lives, and interpret our experiences, we are, in a way, acknowledging and accepting who we are and our differences — a process that is absolutely critical in fostering healthy and harmonious relations.

The different styles and genres here are indicative of the various voices that need to be heard if we are to understand and appreciate our complex realities (Schucter and van Pelt 1992). These layered complexities are communicated through personal narratives, "academic" essays, short stories, letters, poems, journalistic articles, and comic illustration. Many of the pieces are controversial, and liable to provoke argument and debate. We do not see this as a negative, for it is our belief that discussion and debate concerning questions of identity, equity, and inclusion in a changing society must necessarily include many voices and diverse perspectives.

The book's five sections represent various areas of discussion around questions of identity in today's Canada (although there is considerable overlap between sections, and grouping contributions based on people's personal experiences around themes is always limiting and problematic). The question raised in Part I — "Who's Canadian, Anyway?" — is a key to the themes of identity raised throughout the book, particularly when people continue to be asked "Where are you from?" or be grilled about their "accents," skin colours, languages, names, or ethnic origins. Inherent in the questioning is the view that such people are not "Canadians." The experiences detailed here challenge us to think of Canadians as having different colours and accents, and as speaking different languages. No one individual, then, is more "Canadian" than another. On the contrary, some individuals may be more consciously Canadian because they have made a deliberate choice to live in this country; so for them being Canadian is not simply a matter of an accident of birth.

The articles and the comic illustration in Part II address, among other things, the issues related to, and the problems of, people growing up in Canada as members of racial and ethnic minority groups. Growing up is an especially precarious time, when being seen as "different" or, worse still, viewing oneself as "different" can be quite traumatic. Most children or young people just want to fit in and be like everyone else, and those who are racially and/or ethnically different face a particularly painful time.

Given their predominant themes, many of the pieces throughout the book could fit into Part III, "Roots of Identity, Routes to Knowing." Nevertheless, the articles in that section focus attention on how identities are contextualized and constructed in relation to "roots and routes" (see Spence 1999) pertaining to race, ethnicity, language, colour, gender, sexuality, and citizenship. Notwithstanding the multiple, fragmented, shifting, incomplete, and sometimes contradictory notions of racial and ethnic identities, the authors demonstrate how

5

their identities are a product of the ways in which they view themselves, as well as of how others view and interact with them on the basis of race, ethnicity, gender, language, colour, immigrant status, and name.

In Part IV, "Race, Privilege, and Challenges," the authors explore how privilege and challenges are both very much a part of their experiences as members of particular racial and ethnic groups holding middle-class professions and positions in society. What becomes clear is the extent to which experiences with privilege and disadvantage (or challenges) that are linked to race and ethnicity are relational and can best be understood by placing them in context, including the biographies of the interacting individuals. In this section, contributors critically examine whiteness; and we get glimpses into the contradictions of being racial and ethnic minorities in the traditionally "white, middle-class" academe.

It is often said that "everyone stereotypes" because it helps us to categorize a vast amount of received information about others. However, stereotyping, and in effect essentializing individuals' identities, often lead to blatant misrepresentations, which can have serious, negative consequences for individuals or groups. In Part V, "Confronting Stereotypes and Racism," the authors expose the pitfalls of stereotyping, noting that seemingly innocent statements rooted in Canada's social, cultural, political, and economic structures sometimes have racist and discriminatory implications. In addition, the authors reveal some of the ways in which they and others have dealt with racism and stereotyping in public and private encounters. Their contributions indicate a critical analysis, if not consciousness, of Canada's "Anglo-Celtic ethnocentrism" and "smiling racism," which are rooted in Canada's social, cultural, political, and economic structures, and which mask the intolerance — more precisely, the non-acceptance — of our differences (James 2000).

In the end we hope that the various stories told, analyses presented, and perspectives advanced will stimulate and encourage a re-examination of existing ways in which we view and think about others and about identities. This project requires us to transform not only how we interact with people who are different from us, but also the language we use to describe and define them. But language is problematic; it is not neutral. The words and terms we use reflect particular, and often comfortable, perspectives or frames of reference. We need to be aware, for example, that the terms "racial minority" and "ethnic minority" — used routinely by social scientists — can serve to marginalize groups identified as being outside the mainstream or majority (white Anglo-Celtic) culture. The term "non-white" is objectionable because it defines people by a negative — it makes "white" the norm against which all other groups are measured. For our purposes here we use the terms racial minority and ethnic minority to indicate power relationships inherent in our society: "majority" represents not simply numbers, but the cultural group with political and economic power, as compared to the "minority," which does not have access to that power. As Arun Mukherjee points out in her article here, "I use the term 'non-white' in order to talk about the binary relationship of power where 'white' is the dominant term because there is no denying that we live in a racist world order." On the other hand, the term "people of colour" is used to apply to all people(s) who are not white. "This term has gained credence and is widely used," one "person of colour" says. "Personally, I think it's a way the dominant culture lumps the 'rest of them' together. For me it is the acceptance of the dominant view (as espoused by the dominant culture — white) that everyone else is 'people of colour.' I guess white isn't a colour" (quoted in Arnold et al. 1991: 7).

Clearly, whatever words we use will have limitations in that they are products of particular political and cultural arrangements rooted in classism, sexism, racism, and heterosexism. When we talk about our personal experiences, we employ terms that best communicate our unique situations and political perspectives. Therefore, readers will not find a uniformity of terminology in the various contributions here. As editors, we did not feel that we should change the writers' terminology, for the use of language is a problem we do not know how to solve. We trust, however, that readers will bear in mind the significance and limitations of words as you follow the contributors' efforts to employ more inclusive and non-discriminatory language. Ultimately, we hope that this consciousness of the influence of language on our encounters and perceptions will mean that we endeavour to use words and terms that are inclusive and positive rather than those that are exclusive and reflect and perpetuate negative stereotypes and attitudes.

Note

1 Norquay (1993: 243) refers to memory as a process of remembering that involves new reconstructions, interrogation of what is remembered, and "the harder, more painful work around what is forgotten." See also Norquay 1998.

PART 1

WHO'S CANADIAN, ANYWAY?

"Where Are You Really From?" Notes of an "Immigrant" from North Buxton, Ontario

••••••••••••••••••••••••••

Adrienne Shadd

When the nineteenth-century Quebec historian François Garneau decided to write his Histoire du Canada (1846), he deliberately suppressed information about the existence of slavery in New France, leading the public to believe that the "peculiar institution" had never tainted our soil. Even though the fourth edition of his work in 1882 attempted to make up for this omission, the misinformation of a generation had effectively taken place, with a lasting impact to this day.

Until recently, tourist brochures and advertising outside Canada had never reflected the diverse makeup of this country. That is why tourists travelling to Nova Scotia, for example, always express surprise at the existence of a large and distinct Black community there. That is also why filmmaker Sylvia Hamilton's documentary Speak It! From the Heart of Black Nova Scotia includes a scene of the young narrator on a Halifax wharf while the famous Bluenose sails serenely behind him in the harbour. With this one brief image, Hamilton symbolically counteracts centuries of erasure of people of colour from Canadian media.

A few years ago my cousin Dolores Harold, who lives in Detroit, Michigan, was upset because a reunion booklet of the Chatham high school that she attended seemed to have omitted all of the Black students in its depictions of former students and their exploits. Given the artistic, scholastic, and sports achievements of her friends and relatives at the school, it seemed so unfair that none of them was represented in the booklet.

As a researcher in African Canadian history, I am constantly reminded that the four-hundred-year presence of Blacks has been written out of our history and obliterated from the Canadian psyche in general. First brought as slaves in the seventeenth century, later arriving as refugees or fugitives from U.S. slavery (late eighteenth to the mid-nineteenth century), and emigrating in the twentieth century from the Caribbean, Africa, and elsewhere, people of African origin and descent have been on the scene for centuries. Yet the very concept of a "Black Canadian" or "African Canadian" is — in the public perception — a contradiction in terms. The opening examples serve to illustrate just some of the ways in which this contradiction has been reinforced and perpetuated over time.

What is the impact of this kind of invisibility (note the irony here!), of being a nonentity in your own country? I will refer to my own experiences to illustrate how the denial and omission of the Black presence affects interpersonal interaction. I want to illustrate just how psychologically taxing it can be to be "Black" and "Canadian" in typical everyday encounters. For those of us living in large urban centres, there are constant reminders that we are not regarded as truly "Canadian."

In my case, I am a fifth-generation Canadian whose ancestors came here from the United States during the fugitive slave era, as abolitionists and free Blacks trying to escape racial oppression in their homeland. Yet, routinely, I am asked, "Where are you from?" or "What nationality are you?" as if to be Black, you have to come from somewhere else.

I respond that I'm "Canadian." Although light-skinned, I sport some form of "natural" hairdo, and therefore assume that my "African-ness" is apparent. This in itself is a gamble when speaking to most non-Black immigrants, because they perceive only the most "visible" African people (that is, dark skin, thick lips, broad nose, very kinky hair, for instance) as being Black. I nevertheless play along. The scenario usually unfolds as follows:

"But where are you *originally* from?"

11

"Canada."

"Oh, *you* were born here. But where are your parents from?"

"Canada."

"But what about your grandparents?"

"They're Canadian."

As individuals delve further into my genealogy to find out where I'm "really" from, their frustration levels rise.

"No, uh [confused, bewildered] I mean . . . your *people*. Where do your *people* come from?"

"The United States."

At this point, questioners are totally annoyed and/or frustrated. After all, Black people in Canada are supposed to come from "the islands," aren't they? At least, that is the stereotype. One woman was quite indignant upon my telling her this, as her sneer seemed to imply that I had a lot of nerve not matching her preconceived image of whom and what I was.

Of course, there are variations on this theme, like the people who respond to my answer "Canadian" by hastening to point out to me that I couldn't be. As one South Asian man asked me after I told him I was Canadian, "But what about your hair?" "I didn't tell you I was a white Canadian!" I responded.

If I factor in race and ethnicity, whether one is Canadian-born or foreign-born, recentness of arrival in Canada, and so forth, the variations have a certain predictability: (white) English Canadians, when I respond "Canadian," rarely delve further into my background, and, I presume, take my response at face value. Perhaps they consider it impolite to ask the hard questions.

Among Blacks, it is the East Africans — the most recent immigrants — who most closely follow the above sample dialogue. This is because this image of Canada as a "white country" is so very pervasive. It is as prevalent in information disseminated about this country around the world as it is in our schools here in Canada. Long-settled Blacks from the Caribbean or West Africa are aware enough to know what I mean when I say that I'm Canadian, although some still believe that it must mean I'm a "Nova Scotian." (Because Nova Scotia has the largest Black population in Canada per capita, and the largest indigenous Black population, some believe that all native Black Canadians come from there.) Clearly, foreign-born non-Blacks remain the most intransigent on the issue of my origins; the more recently arrived they are, the more consistent with the above scenario.

These situations are usually very frustrating for me because, as the conversation develops, I realize that the individuals have not grasped the very concept of what I represent, even when I go to the trouble of explaining it to them. Apparently, it is just too baffling to comprehend. And what about my reaction? Should I get angry and say something rude? Should I ignore their ignorant comments? Or should I give them a short history lesson?

I suppose humour is the best policy. I know people from Toronto who, when asked which one of the "islands" they come from, respond "Centre" or "Toronto." Based on my own experience, this would sail over most people's heads. I have tried becoming indignant. On some occasions, I have provided information on the history of Blacks in Canada. On other occasions, I have provided no information apart from responding "Canadian" to their questions. Yet for some, no answer I supply satisfies them. One dimwit even came back a few weeks later to grill me on this very same point.

Yes, I am Black, I am Canadian, and I grew up in North Buxton, Ontario. This rural Black community near Chatham was once a famous settlement of ex-slaves who escaped on the Underground Railroad. When I was a little girl growing up in North Buxton, I was very much situated in a particular family and community. We were part of the landscape of southwestern Ontario. Everyone knew the family name, and it was, and is, well-respected. In retrospect, it felt good to belong and not have to explain to anyone whom I was and where I came from. Even though racism was a fact of life, and we lived a quasi-segregated existence, I had a sense of being part of the fabric of the society. No one questioned our right to be there — at least not in that stretch of land we had staked out and claimed as our own.

Of course, whites, not knowing the history or significance of Buxton, believed it was the other side of the tracks, a rural Black enclave of "poor" or "underprivileged" people. This was brought home to me at a party a few years ago when a man, after asking where I was from and hearing me respond "North Buxton," excitedly informed me that he too was from the "wrong side of the tracks." I guess the poor fellow was trying his darndest to establish a rapport, but in his zeal he hadn't considered he might be insulting me.

No, it would be wrong to assume that Buxton was the "wrong side of the tracks." Not that Buxton didn't have its share of poorer individuals. It certainly had more than its share of town drunks! But it also held a middle-class rural gentry of farm owners/operators and their families; people who sent their children to university; people who were active in the church and community, CGIT (Canadian Girls In Training), baseball, Home and School, the North Buxton Maple Leaf Band, community dances, Christmas pageants, and many other

13

activities. The sons and daughters of Buxton have gone on to become teachers, doctors, nurses, school principals, labour leaders, artists, writers, and composers, to name a few. Many successful people have come out of this tiny community, even though historically many of these individuals had to go to the United States to be educated at segregated Black colleges and were obliged to practise their professions in the much larger African-American community. There were numerous positive role models and institutions that we established and ran. In the minds of that man at the party and many others, however, the terms "Buxton" and "successful people" are antithetical.

I suppose that this is a perfect example of what happens when an entire racial group is oppressed and held at the lowest rungs of society, when caste and class almost completely overlap. By virtue of membership in the lower-caste group, everyone is stamped with the badge of inferiority. Even those who have been upwardly mobile are "tainted" by the negative perceptions and stereotypes associated with group membership. This is precisely what is meant when Blacks tell the joke: "What do you call a Black doctor?" Answer: "A nigger!"

Yet, I dwell on this question of where I'm "really" from because North Buxton has even deeper, almost spiritual, meaning for me. It has come to represent a strong and visible symbol of our long and rich presence in this land. As one of the few remaining indigenous Black communities in the province, North Buxton has a history and culture that emanate from its unique vantage point as an "African" enclave in a sea of British culture and tradition. It is all the more important since this "other" aspect of Canada has been deliberately buried. Blacks (and many others) from across Canada and the world have flocked there to see for themselves this famous community that was the first to exercise Black power at the voting booth. Canadian-, American-, and Caribbean-born alike are rallying around this symbol of Black Canadian tradition and culture that is uniquely ours. And the annual Labour Day Homecoming weekend, now a seventy-year-old tradition, is increasingly becoming a celebration that attracts more than just former residents and relatives. For Black people regardless of origin, it has become a celebration of our African Canadian roots in this country.

Perhaps the greatest significance of North Buxton, however, is more personal still, appreciated most by those who grew up there or in similar situations. In an essay entitled "Revolutionary Black Women," from her book *Black Looks: Race and Representation*, feminist theorist and cultural critic bell hooks describes growing up in a segregated rural Black community that was very supportive:

Our segregated church and schools were places where we were affirmed. I was continually told that I was "special" in those settings, that I would be "somebody" someday and do important work to "uplift" the race. I felt loved and cared about in the segregated black community of my growing up. It gave me the grounding in a positive experience of "blackness" that sustained me when I left that community to enter racially integrated settings, where racism informed most social interactions.

Yes, this is Buxton's greatest legacy for me. It is the place where my positive sense of self was first developed. It is the place that encouraged and reinforced academic excellence, and where it was assumed that I was intelligent and an achiever. It was not the place where these characteristics were snuffed out because of the colour of my skin. Relatives who received all of their education in Toronto have not fared as well in the educational system, leading me to believe that my early "segregated" educational experience was crucial. Many Black educators both here and in the United States are coming to the realization that chasing after the "integrationist" dream was a dismal failure. This is why Black-focused schools have been proposed in Toronto, to great public outcry as a form of reverse racism. However, these educators are trying to address the tragedy of high dropout rates and streaming in creative ways that speak to the positive aspects of segregated Black schooling.

Buxton provided an excellent grounding for me in that it was there that I learned that somehow, some day, I would make an important contribution and make my community proud. Without it, I have to wonder how my life might have been different. It most certainly has been instrumental in the strong, positive racial identity that I have carried throughout my life, even in the days when the question of an African Canadian "experience" was unheard of, much less taken seriously by most Canadians. Ultimately, it has enabled me to come to terms with my racial being in a racist context in a far more effective way than if I had grown up in denial of whom I really was, something all too common for people growing up in predominantly white settings.

So you see why a seemingly innocent question like "Where are you *really* from?" evokes a very strong response in me. By asking it, you are unintentionally denying me what is rightfully mine — my birthright, my heritage, and my long-standing place in the Canadian mosaic. If nothing else, I hope that you have gone away with at least one message: if you see a Black person on the street, or if you are meeting someone for the first time, don't assume that he or she

15

comes from some other country. They might just be someone like me, who is sick and tired of being assumed to be an immigrant. If you are bold and brazen enough to ask the impolitic question, and they tell you they're Canadian, trust that they know their own background better than you, a perfect stranger. Even those who have come from other countries get tired of being constantly asked the question, as if they have just stepped "off the boat." The president of the Canadian Advisory Council on the Status of Women, Jamaican-born Dr. Glenda Simms, remarked in a speech at a women's forum that she too was tired of this "immigrant" label that people want to slap on her at all costs. "We have to deconstruct these labels, stop hanging on to being 'immigrant women,' stop buying into the hierarchy of the oppressed and be proud Canadian citizens," she boldly told her audience.

In one of the many encounters around my origins, I had an exchange with a Guatemalan Canadian who had asked me "the question" at a streetcar stop one evening. On that occasion, I argued with him because of his insistence that I could not be a Canadian. In the end, however, he had the last word on the matter. "Except for the Native people," he stated, "the rest of us are just immigrants anyway." I couldn't argue with that.

WHAT'S YOUR BACKGROUND?

•••••••••••••••

KAI JAMES

My name is Kai, and I'm Canadian. However, I am unlike many other Black youth in Canada whose parents emigrated from the Caribbean in that I identify as a Canadian. Yes, I was born here and I'm one hundred per cent Canadian. Whether they like it or not, even the majority of those youth born in the Caribbean but raised in Canada are Canadians. They are as Canadian as our first prime minister, Sir John A. Macdonald, who was not born in Canada but in Scotland.

What makes Sir John A. and millions of other citizens who have immigrated to this country Canadian is very simple. All have contributed to Canadian society to some extent, big or small, culturally, economically, and politically. And they continue to constantly reshape and redefine what we know as "Canadian," a notion that changes every day. So why do some Black youth constantly deny their Canadian identity even when they were born in Canada?

There are many reasons for this, and perhaps the biggest of them all is how we perceive the image of a Canadian. A contributor to this image is the school curriculum. Throughout my years in elementary and high school, African Canadians were rarely included in the curriculum. We learned about a few African Americans, such as Harriet Tubman and Martin Luther King Jr., but mostly we learned about William Lyon Mackenzie, Wilfrid Laurier, Marie and Pierre Curie, and other European Canadian politicians, scientists, and authors. These images contrast greatly with those of the musicians and sports stars idolized by Canada's young Black people. Therefore, considering that our notion of a Canadian has been distorted from a very young age, it is no wonder that the people we most admire and emulate come almost entirely from the United States or the Caribbean.

This brings us to reason number two. The urban youth culture (a term now often used to denote all contemporary cultures pioneered largely by Blacks) practised by Black youth in Canada, inner city and suburbs alike, is often defined by its music. Among the Black youth I'm speaking about, many of whom I've met in school, at jams, or in other social forums, the main genres of choice are hip hop, R&B, reggae, and soca. The music is most powerful when presented to us in video format, formerly brought to us by MuchMusic, a Canadian music station, which has now lost most of its Black audience to B.E.T. (Black Entertainment Television), based in Washington, D.C. The Canadian station is the only source of Canadian urban music on television but cannot compete with the U.S. station, which plays R&B, hip hop, reggae, and soca twenty-four-seven as opposed to MuchMusic's ten or so hours per week. This is another way in which we are influenced by American cultural forms.

Many Canadian cities have a hip hop community. Toronto actually has large hip hop, dance hall, and soca communities, each with talented artists. However, with the exception of a few innovators, most acts are attempted replicas of styles honed in the United States or the Caribbean. Through our style of dress, our vocabulary, our goals, and our own artistic expressions, we tend to identify with some of the most commercially successful artists of these types of music — artists like Jay-Z, Snoop Dogg, Sporty Thievz, The Hot Boyz, Destiny's Child, Bounti Killa, and Machel Motano. This is another reflection of how we see ourselves as Black youth in Canada.

For me this mistaken identity becomes most apparent during conversations with young women, specifically those I'm meeting for the first time. A common question used to break the ice is "What's your background?" which, in this context, really means, "What is the nationality of your parents?" And it is generally assumed that if you are Black your parents are probably from the Caribbean. Most young women reply, "I'm Jamaican," or "I'm Guyanese," or "I'm Trini," even if they were born right here in Canada. But those who were born in the Caribbean enjoy a type of prestige that comes with being a bona fide Trini, or a bona fide Jamaican, sometimes called "freshies." They are part of a culture that those born in Canada can only imitate. Some people born in Canada will go so far as to lie in order to achieve that persona. During a conversation between two young Canadians one may also hear an exaggerated Jamaican, Trinidadian, or New York City accent. I think that traces of all of those accents exist in the speech of many Black youth born in Canada.

So I ask myself, are we any different from any other ethnic group in Canada in our attempt to hold on to the only roots we know? Can we use the nationalities and cultures of our parents to create a sort of individuality or a detached form of nationalism in this cosmopolitan mosaic we call Canada? Are we as Canadians destined to be a mere extension of American society, both in its mainstream and more marginalized cultures?

Only one thing is for certain. The current generation of Canadian Black youth is clearly Canadian. We have been educated in the Canadian school system. We've been immersed in Canadian institutions, the Canadian political climate, and the Canadian geographic environment. A great number of us have grown up playing and sometimes living a sport invented by a Canadian and developed in North America. At the same time, aspects of Caribbean culture are present in our style, slang, and values. Black youth in Canada have created a cultural blend that is truly unique and truly Canadian.

For example, a greeting in Jamaica is "Wha'ah gwaan?" while a Canadian greeting might be, "What's going on?" Canadian youth have blended the two to say, "What's gwawning?" You can hear that greeting when you walk through the halls of many high schools in and around Toronto, and it is used by students of all ethnic backgrounds. We are Canada and Canada is us. So what else could we be but Canadians?

Jewish, Canadian, or Québécois? Notes on a Diasporic Identity

••••••••••••••••••••••••••••

Susan Judith Ship

I must confess that when I was first invited to write about Jewish identity and experience in Canada and more specifically in Quebec, I only reluctantly agreed. My immediate reaction was one of profound discomfort. Perhaps more curious is why I felt so ill at ease. After all, it should be relatively easy for a Jewish woman to write about Jewish identity and experience in the country where she was born. My starting point, then, became the need to interrogate more closely the sources of my discomfort in writing about these issues.

Part of the difficulty in defining my own sense of Jewish identity and Jews is that as a social collectivity with a unique history, we defy the neat categories of sociological and political analysis. Do Jews constitute a people, a nation, a religious group, an ethnic group, or a cultural group? Is Jewish identity a religious, cultural, ethnic, or political identity, or simply a matter of ancestry? In the end it proved much easier to speak about the identity of Jews as "outsiders" in Quebec and in the rest of Canada than about my own sense of Jewish identity. The complexities of identity at the individual level of consciousness and lived experience stand in stark contrast to the social construction of Jews as a simple category of "otherness."

Despite the historically changing definitions of Jews, as a "race," as a people, as a nation, and as an ethnic minority, cultural minority, and/or religious minority, what has remained constant in our diasporic experience and identity in Quebec and Canada, as in Europe or elsewhere, is the construction of Jews as a social category of "otherness" on the basis of religion, culture, and/or physical appearance and the persistence of anti-Semitism in its various, changing forms and faces. This pervasive tendency to view identity — ethnic, "racial," religious, class, or gender, for that matter — in singular, homogenizing, static, and totalizing terms is, in part, the legacy of outmoded categories and ways of classifying peoples that inhere from a historically specific Eurocentric perspective and experience whereby a single social signifier becomes the indelible mark of "otherness," of difference if not inferiority.

At the same time, diasporic identities are themselves always complex, multiple, shifting, fragmented, and relational: historically and socially constructed from within and from without. Defining Jewish identity in singular, monolithic, and homogenizing terms as either a religious, cultural, ethnic, or political identity, or even as a matter of socialization, is inadequate for capturing the complexity of lived experience and consciousness of individuals and collectivities. Identities themselves change over time. At various moments in my life I have defined my identity as a Jew on the basis of ancestry or birthright alone, on religion and ritual, on the intellectual and left-wing political traditions of East European Jews, and on ancient roots in the Middle East.

Alternatively, part of the discomfort that I felt in writing this article is intimately related to the politics of representation that in its current form now dominates much of the academic scholarship on identity politics and minorities, whether it is ethnic minorities, people of colour, First Nations, women, or gay people. The explicit assumption is that the authenticity of experience is a sufficient criterion for truth and representativeness. While this is a welcome corrective to the authenticity of neutrality that previously dominated so much of social science research and writing on minorities — work in which so-called neutral, outside observers speak about and too often for minority communities — the recourse to personal knowledge does not itself resolve the problem of objectivity. I have to ask myself, as an insider, how do I maintain enough emotional distance to objectively represent the thoughts, feelings, and experiences of the broader Jewish community in Quebec or Canada? In what ways can my singular and particular experience of being Jewish and the meaning I give to Jewish identity be said to constitute an objective and representative statement on diasporic Jewish identity and experience? Suffice to say, these questions have no easy answers. While I can only speak for myself, some of what I am about to say will no doubt resonate with "truth."

The dispersion of Jews around the globe has produced a Diaspora of people whose cultures, mother tongues, skin colours, and historical trajectories reflect the rainbow of humanity in all its wondrous diversity. I had to ask myself, what do the diasporic experience and Jewish identity mean to Sephardic Jews born in Morocco who immigrated to Israel and then to Montreal? To Russian and Polish Jews born in South Africa, now living in Toronto? To East Indian and Ethiopian Jews living in Canada? Or to first-, second-, third-, or fourth-generation Ashkenazi Jews living in Winnipeg, St. John's, Vancouver, Montreal, or Toronto? I have to ask, "Who can speak for whom?"

The issue of who is a Jew is no less complex. My ancestry and birthright as a Jew are clear-cut, at least according to ancient religious law. To be Jewish one simply has to be born to a Jewish mother (or, alternatively, to convert). But the issue of who is a Jew in Israel with rights to automatic citizenship is both contentious and controversial. Judaism itself means different things to different people. Some emphasize nationhood or peoplehood. Some emphasize religion, while others stress culture. For some people it is all three elements, while for others being a Jew is simply a matter of birthright.

What, for example, is Jewish cultural identity? As a second-generation Jew born in Montreal, I have had to confront, negotiate, and come to terms with complex cultural heritages that are intimately bound up with and shape my own sense of Jewish culture and identity: the East European (Russian and Polish) cultures of my parents; cultural roots, however tenuous, that stretch back to antiquity to the deserts of the Middle East; the Anglo-American culture of Canada; the French Québécois culture of Quebec; and the distinct cosmopolitan multiculture of Montreal.

At the same time I have always thought of diasporic Jewish experience and identity as being at the interstice of "Western modernity" and "antiquity." No matter how cosmopolitan and internationalist, as Jews we carry with us the ancient traditions of non-European civilizations of the Middle East, Africa, and Persia (not to be confused with primitive, backward, or inferior), which always raises the problematic issue of "roots" and "race." I have always had an ambiguous relation-

22

ship to "whiteness," and I do not define myself as "white." Despite
my Ashkenazi (European) ancestry, I am often mistaken for one of my
Semitic North African or Arab sisters. Irrespective of our European
ancestry and our contributions to European civilizations, white Christian Europeans have long considered Ashkenazi Jews as Europe's primary internal "other" — a dubious distinction we shared with the
Gypsies — and alternately as "Oriental" or "Black" — a pariah status
that we have historically shared with other "non-whites" despite our
very different historical trajectories. To the extent that Jews are now
considered to be "white" in Europe and in the Americas, we are
viewed as "honorary whites" rather than as "authentically white."
Even this is a relatively recent phenomenon.

It was not that long ago, in the racialized mind of Europeans, as
Sander Gilman (1994: 45) points out, that "the icon of Jewish physical difference in the Diaspora" was viewed as "the result of the Jew's
close racial relationship to or intermixing with Blacks." Our so-called
racial distinctness from "Aryans" and imputed inferiority provided the
justification for the extermination of the whole of European Jewry —
irrespective of self-identification. Conscious of the long intellectual
and political history of anti-Semitism in Europe and the ritual persecution of Jews all over Europe, I find it difficult to identify myself as
"white" or "European." My sense of self as a Semite and my link with
my ancient roots provide a more positive sense of my self-identification as a Jew.

For religious and observant Jews, such as my Hasidic neighbours,
self-identity as a Jew is straightforward, but for secular Jews such as
myself it remains an inescapable dilemma; the price to be paid for
assimilation. For secular Jews, it has been argued that self-identity
represents "an ambiguous stance and affiliation vaguely associated
with culture, religion, history and politics" (Azoulay 1997: 120). As a
woman and a feminist, I have had to confront and come to terms
with the patriarchal foundations and dictates of Orthodox Jewish tradition (most pronounced amongst Ultra Orthodox adherents), within
which I was raised. The education of boys and girls is different and
intimately related to their separate spheres of influence. Girls and
women historically were excluded from certain forms of higher religious learning and from Jewish mysticism. The Yeshiva is, after all,
for men. I chose to reject Judaism as a religion wholesale rather than
struggle within it, as some women and feminists have chosen to do,
or to simply accept the traditional female roles, as yet many others
have done.

Montreal's Jewish community has been described as an "island of   23 old world observance and tradition, of continuity and confident Jewish identity" (Cherney 1998: B2). I must confess. I do not conform. I usually place little significance on "being Jewish." I am not observant (religious). I do not actively celebrate my Jewish culture or heritage. I am not a Zionist. Yet there are significant moments when "being Jewish" evidences an identity I can neither erase nor deny.

The singular and most important moment comes on Yom Hashoa — Holocaust Memorial Day — when my "being Jewish" becomes both an undeniable fact and an omnipresent reality. The haunting image of Auschwitz stands as the stark reminder of Jewish experience and identity in the Diaspora. It is the moment when Jewish identity ceases to be a dilemma, a crisis, a quest, a project of becoming, a dialogue, or a discursive representation. It is the precise moment when I experience being Jewish in a profoundly deep and visceral way, in all its complexities and contradictions. It is the exact moment when I experience the pain, the horror, the anguish, the torment, and the grief of generations in the very core of my being, for all who were hunted down and exterminated precisely because they were Jewish, whether they identified themselves as such or not. It is the precise moment when I am overwhelmed with the guilt that all survivors — immediate or not — carry with them and, alternately, the intense relief, "There but for the grace of God go I" — an odd statement for an atheist.

Yom Hashoa is the precise moment when I am confronted with the indelible reminder of religious, racial, and cultural "otherness" of what it means to be a Jew in the Diaspora. It is the very moment when I am made to feel the extreme fragility and vulnerability of our position as "honorary whites" within dominant white European Christian societies — whether in Canada, the United States, or Europe. It is as always the stark reminder of the limits of "passing" as a non-Jew and of the extent to which we can and do integrate, let alone assimilate, into dominant white European Christian collectivities and the extent to which we shed our "racial identity" as Jews.

It is the precise moment when I, as a Jew, am confronted with the burden of Jewish survival as a duty. I understand this not as my parents might have understood this — as a renewal of faith, as a more intense adherence to cultural and religious traditions, or as a profound engagement with Zionism, but as a commitment to struggles for social justice and the elimination of all forms of oppression, not simply for Jews but for all peoples. This is for me the real lesson to be learned from the Holocaust.

I am reminded of "being Jewish" in the more mundane settings of everyday experience in post-Holocaust multicultural Canada and Quebec whereby "otherness," difference, and anti-Semitism continue to form not only the backdrop of Jewish experience in the Diaspora but also a negative sense of Jewish identity. To be fair, gone are the days of discriminatory laws, quota systems, and restrictive immigration policies designed to limit the Jewish presence and our full integration into Canadian and Québécois society and economy. But anti-Semitism has not disappeared from the landscape.

In many situations I am still reluctant to identify myself immediately as Jewish, always wondering who is going to make an anti-Semitic joke or comment, or wondering who is going to dredge up the usual stereotypes: "You are not like the rest of them," "You are just like us," "All Jews are cheap," "All Jews are smart," "All Jews are rich," or "Jews have too much power." More disturbing still are the occasional, recurrent public manifestations of anti-Semitism, whether the desecration of Jewish cemeteries and synagogues or comments such as the one made by the late prominent businessman Pierre Peladeau only a few years ago: "Jews take up too much space in Quebec." No less disturbing is the persistent presence of the Jim Keegstras and Ernest Zundels, anti-Semitism on the Internet, and the growth of white supremacist neo-Nazi groups in Canada.

The relative homogeneity and dominance of Anglo/French culture in most of Canada and Quebec still make me ill at ease even though I was born here. Too many people, particularly in Quebec, still ask me where I was born, what my nationality is (I thought I was Canadian), where my parents were born, and what languages I speak. Although some people, perhaps most, are genuinely curious, I am, however, reminded of my status as "other" and somehow obviously "different." But then I understand. I speak French with a funny accent. I don't have blond hair or blue eyes. I don't look Nordic or Norman. I don't belong to either of the "two founding nations." Therefore I must be in that "other" category — the eternal immigrant.

The reaffirmation of "otherness" is also conveyed in everyday experience and in the language of exclusion embodied in the collective representations of "us" and "them" that underpin the politics of national identity in Quebec. I was enrolled as a student in the political science department at the Université du Québec à Montréal in the early 1980s, and I can recall a heated discussion on the topic of immigrants and French-language usage in one of my classes. The professor, a sympathetic and open person, did her best to explain the complexities and difficulties of integration faced by newcomers to Quebec. I cannot fault her. However, in typically Québécois fashion, 25 the terms "us" and "them" — *"nous et les autres"* — were bandied about. I suddenly wondered, as an anglophone Jew born in Quebec: where am I in all of this?

That question was soon to be answered for me. When I was taking a course on Quebec-Canada relations, Louise Harel, the Parti Québécois MNA and long-time ardent *indépendantiste*, came to our class to speak about the strategy of creating a federal wing of the Parti Québécois. While listening to her speak, I began to notice that she was directing most of her comments to the right side of the lecture hall and rarely to the side where I was sitting. I wondered why she was ignoring our section of the room. When I looked around, I saw that all the students of African, Haitian, and North African origins were sitting together — with me — to her left. The message from her non-verbal behaviour and body language reinforced the growing discomfort I already felt. I understood. We were not "Québécois" but *"les autres"* — *les Noirs, les Arabes, les Juifs, et les Anglais* — and we weren't really a part of their political project anyway, as Jacques Parizeau was to remind us years later on the night of the Quebec referendum on sovereignty in October 1995, when he said that the defeat of the independence option was the result of "money and the ethnic vote."

The reaffirmation of "otherness" and "difference" was no less evident in the 1996 Canadian census. I found the census form profoundly disturbing. On a rational level I understand the desire to collect data on the religious, ethnic, and "racial" backgrounds of Canadians for purposes of improving employment equity and specialized services to specific minority communities. Nevertheless, on a deeper level I was reluctant to officially identify myself as Jewish. I felt uneasy about "Jewish" being the most salient aspect of my identity. I understand my hesitancy. It harks back to an older and darker period of Canadian history when only Jews and Blacks were identified as distinct categories of "otherness" in government documents (see the Canadian immigration statistics prior to 1967; these two distinct categories reappeared in the 1996 census). While the context in Canada is now different, more so for the Jewish community than for people of African descent, both social collectivities remain identified as the two primary and distinct categories of "otherness" — the former by religion and culture and the latter by reference to skin colour or "race." Old ways of thinking and seeing die hard. Despite the profoundly multicultural, multireligious, multi-"racial," and multilinguistic character of Canada, the dominant collective representation remains that of a country that is white and Christian, of predominantly British Isles or French ancestry.

Recently *La Presse* ran a series of articles on the evolution of the Jewish community in Quebec. The articles were informative, well-documented, and positive in perspective. They bore none of the traces of the anti-Semitism of Lionel Groulx's Quebec, but rather revealed the significant changes that have taken place in the status of the Jewish community and its relations with the larger francophone society. Yet I still found myself disturbed by these articles. The Jewish presence in Quebec dates back to 1738, and the oldest synagogue in North America is in Montreal, yet they still speak of *"les Québécois et les Juifs."* At what point do we cease to be outsiders in the country where we were born or choose to live?

Everyday terms to distinguish Quebeckers, such as *"Québécois pure laine"* or *"Québécois de vielle souche"* on the one hand and *"Québécois de nouvelle souche," "Néo-Québécois,"* Jews, or Blacks on the other hand, serve as continual reminders to those of us who are not of French or British Isles origins of our status as "outsiders." The language of exclusion and inclusion is deeply embedded not only in everyday speech and popular culture but also in the formal, legal-political discourse.

Identifying social collectivities in the Canadian context in terms of "nations" and "ethnic minorities or "cultural communities," as we are called in Quebec (or visible minorities, for that matter), is not simply about preserving cultural heritages, the affirmation of the right to be different, or the demarcation of socio-cultural boundaries between social groups. It is also a means of structuring and legitimating unequal power relations between social collectivities, of creating and maintaining an operative ethnic and "racial" hierarchy. Formal political labels, developed by academics and government bureaucrats and enshrined in policy, and which distinguish social categories of citizens, carry with them attendant rights and privileges. They establish a hierarchy of belonging.

I was born here and I do have roots here. I am tired of being referred to as an ethnic minority. I am tired of being referred to as a cultural community. I do not want to be integrated as a member of a minority whose rights need to be protected. When do I cease to be a member of an ethnic minority in Canada or a cultural minority in Quebec? When do I cease to be a Jew and become Québécoise? When do I cease to be a Jew and become Canadian?

Québécitude
An Ambiguous Identity

••••••••••••••••••••

Guy Bédard

Accepter de réflichir sur les ressorts qui sont à l'origine de notre iden-
tité, c'est déjà un peu admettre que celle-ci est une construction de
l'esprit. À tout le moins, c'est reconnaître que ce qui va de soi, ce qui
semble appartenir à l'éternité, être déterminé par les conditions objec-
tives d'existence des individus ou à l'évolution historique des collec-
tivités, a encore besoin de l'apport de la raison pour voir clairment le
jour. C'est aussi une manière d'échapper aux idées qui façonnent
notre être, s'expatrier de soi-même.

All identities are a construction of mind. The emergence of the
Québécois identity is a perfect example. Even though I readily subscribe to this identity, I must admit that, on a philosophical level, I still
have difficulty grasping the concept of Québécois identity and how it is
constructed. Through my life history and experiences, therefore, I want
to explore this identity and how, at this stage in Quebec's history, it
has become increasingly inconsistent and contradictory for me.

For as long as I can remember, I have never identified myself as
other than Québécois. And yet it is only recently that the term has
even appeared in the dictionary. Prior to the 1960s, I would have said
that I was French Canadian. In so doing, I would be defining myself
first and foremost as a French-speaking Catholic, and therefore as a
member of a community whose demographic boundaries extend

beyond the borders of the province of Quebec. My reading of Quebec history also tells me that in another era I would have called myself *Canadien*, but in a particular way that most Canadians today would be completely unable to imagine. Up until the middle of the nineteenth century, the term "Canadian" referred almost exclusively to the descendants of the French colonists. (Jacques Cartier used the word "Kanada" to identify the Aboriginal peoples who lived in the St. Lawrence Valley. Shortly thereafter, it came to signify the inhabitants of French origin born in the colony.) Others preferred to call themselves British subjects: Irish, Welsh, Scottish, and English. So how did the term "Québécois" come about? And why do I feel that I must now identify myself as a Québécois? No book has ever explained this to me.

To be honest, there was a time when I would never have called myself Québécois. This was during my childhood, when the boundaries of my universe did not extend beyond family, the part of the street where we lived, the route I took to school, and the friends I made. After this early period, everything turned upside down.

Three incidents stand out in my mind: the parade down chemin du Roy when Charles de Gaulle travelled the historic route down the St. Lawrence River linking Montreal and Quebec in the days of New France (this happened prior to the now-famous *Vive le Québec libre!* speech), a visit to Expo '67, and reading *White Niggers of America* by Pierre Vallières.

I was nine years old at the time of the first two events. I barely remember de Gaulle's visit. However, I do remember that my parents were very proud to have been there when de Gaulle passed through Quebec City. This feeling, and perhaps the crowd's enthusiasm, as well as the obvious interest of my parents in all that spoke of our heritage, contributed to shaping a constant, but not well-defined, identity: an attachment to my roots, to my origins, and to my ancestors.

The second event is much fresher in my memory; it also reveals the ambiguous character of my early identity. Leaving Quebec City to visit Expo '67 in Montreal, I was to discover another country, a foreign land that allowed me to recognize my own. This was not China, or the USSR or Great Britain, or any of the countries that had built pavilions on Île Sainte-Hélène, where the international exposition took place. This was simply Montreal, the metropolitan centre. At nine years old, I had a sense of geography and space that was still quite limited. The never-ending voyage and the turbulence and feverishness of a big city were impressive. At the very least, the distance that separated the two cities, as much a function of their differing lifestyles as the number of kilometres one had to travel between them, was enough to impress upon me the idea of difference. There existed a country called Québec (without a doubt, to avoid confusion, others called it Quebec City) to which I identified and belonged. I became Québécois in the sense that I certainly was not Montréalais.

In retrospect, this anecdote might seem rather insignificant, the simple manifestation of the fertile imagination of a nine-year-old and his ignorance of the basics of geography. However, on further reflection, it brings out the ambiguous and changing character of Québécois identity. The increasing uneasiness that I feel each time I hear nationalists say *Le Québec aux Québécois* illustrates this in yet another way. In adhering to this battle-cry, some *indépendantistes* are necessarily forced to admit that there are certain individuals whose status as residents of Quebec is not enough to qualify them as Québécois. Therefore, they adopt a logic of exclusion. But this is not what bothers me most. Is there an identity or a way of thinking that is not ultimately exclusionary? After all, those who call themselves Canadian do not treat other peoples of the world any differently. No! What profoundly embarrasses me about this slogan *Québec aux Québécois* is that it forces me to choose between a territorial concept of Québécois citizenship — a perspective that, let us remember, is defended by a good number of *indépendantistes* — and an ethnic definition of Québécitude based on race, culture, and language: social markers for exclusion.

Somehow, I know that to say Québécois presupposes race, culture, and language, or at least one of these elements. It implies that we need to find affinities with a group, a community. There would not be so much commotion about Québécois identity if we were living, as some *indépendantistes* insist, in a "normal country" — that is, an independent state. In other words, there would not be this dichotomy if Quebec were independent. At least, the racism or xenophobia of this ethnic definition of Québécois identity would be completely clear. The problem is that, as things stand, there is a lot of confusion in this respect: it is often difficult to distinguish between the simple act of self-affirmation and racism.

Nor is the territorial criterion of Québécitude sufficient for me. After we agree on the boundaries of the territory concerned, we must then establish a full and complete definition of Québécois citizenship. Using ethnicity as a basis for identifying oneself as Québécois is too dependent on how each one of us envisages the criteria, and on our individual life histories and experiences. Imagine for a moment if I had kept the vision of Quebec that I had when I was nine years old, and you get a sense of the breadth of perspectives on this issue.

For me, the real *prise de conscience* came when I was twelve. During his stay in prison, Pierre Vallières, the presumed head of the *Front de Liberation du Québec (FLQ)*, wrote a book about his childhood and adolescence, *White Niggers of America*. Vallières made me aware of a whole world of oppression, of the *porteurs d'eau*, the francophone proletarians of Montreal subjected to the "Speak White" dictates of the anglophone bourgeoisie. For the first time I realized that this city, Montreal, was also mine, was in some small way my home too. Oh! To be sure, there were enormous differences with Quebec City: 95 per cent of the population in Quebec City is francophone; the English presence is insignificant. But what Vallières described closely resembled my father's life. He had to quit school at the age of ten. He sweated for English bosses who couldn't be bothered to communicate with him in French. I couldn't help but notice that in one of the factories where my father worked for several years and where the overwhelming majority of employees spoke only French, signs were exclusively in English.

I do not know if this vision of my father's lived experiences is totally accurate; it may have been distorted and exaggerated by the eyes of the child that I was. However, it was enough for me to accept Vallières' vision of the world: *Vive le Québec libre!* and socialist to boot. The history books took care of the rest. They recounted a long series of events that marked the relations between the francophone and anglophone communities of Canada: the deportation of the Acadians, the English Conquest, the hanging of Louis Riel and the crushing of the francophone Métis rebellion in western Canada, the implementation of laws at the turn of the twentieth century prohibiting the teaching of French in schools in the other Canadian provinces, and so forth.

I felt that I belonged to an oppressed and persecuted people. I had the impression that the others, the anglophones with whom I had no contact other than what I read in books, were constantly seeking to annihilate the group to which I identified and belonged. The demographic decline of francophone communities outside Quebec was ample proof.

And yet these beliefs never fully rang true for me. To hold onto this perception of being an oppressed and persecuted minority, I had to appeal to experiences that frankly were foreign to me, that came from a history I had never personally experienced. I was a child of the Quiet Revolution; I lived in an era when the use of French was more prevalent than at any time since the Conquest. From this point of view, outside of Montreal, you could say that Quebec has been reconquered. Since moving to the metropolitan centre of Quebec —

Montreal — I can see that French is well-entrenched here, too. The threat of assimilation has been reduced to the point where it is no longer feared. And if there is still oppression, it certainly does not manifest itself in the same way. Through the years, the Quebec state has encouraged the emergence of a francophone bourgeoisie that knows how to exploit the country's natural resources as well as anyone. So why do I still have the desire to call myself Québécois?

It is perhaps the force of collective habit and the pressure of institutions. In thirty years, the term "Québécois" has become common usage. First affirmed by the poets, novelists, playwrights, and *chansonniers*, the term is today used by virtually everyone. The media are its foremost proponents, where even the news coverage is influenced by its implications (everything that happens outside Quebec gives the appearance of being somewhat foreign). Governments have also adopted it. I cannot think of a single politician who would dare not use the term. Even the members of the communities called anglophone and allophone now demand to be included in that so-named collectivity. The term is celebrated, emphasized, displayed, and asserted.

However, this is not the only vision or perspective of the world here. As in all Western societies, identity has become considerably more complex and dynamic, crossing many boundaries. Certainly, the rise of advanced communication and technology has given birth to the concept of a global village. Moreover, I frequently have the impression that I have more in common with intellectuals in London, New York, or Bangkok than with Quebec workers or the convenience store owner in my own neighbourhood. To invoke the weight of habit or the power of institutions to explain why I identify myself as Québécois seems unsatisfying. It is to forget that this identity is in competition with other identities.

I do not know precisely what it is that makes me Québécois. All I know is that occasionally I feel as foreign in Paris or Toronto as I do in Amman when the chanting from the mosques fills the small hours of the morning. It is difficult to understand. However, a number of events in the history of the Québécois community resulted in the construction of a "collective imagination" that distinguishes this community from others, defining it vis-à-vis the rest of the world, whereby my diverse personal experiences have imprinted this "imagination" in my mind. In short, apart from the historical and cultural specificities, the process by which a Québécois identity was born is not much different from the formation of other community identities around the globe.

I Want to Call Myself Canadian

••••••••••••••••••••••••••

Katalin Szepesi

I want to call myself Canadian, but I'm not allowed. My name is Hungarian by origin, so therefore I am Hungarian. It doesn't matter that on my mother's side I'm seventh-generation Canadian and before that our family came from Great Britain. It doesn't matter that I can't speak Hungarian and have only a marginal understanding of the culture. It doesn't matter that I was born and raised in Canada. It doesn't even matter that I'm white. Katalin Szepesi is not a Canadian name, so Katalin Szepesi will never be a Canadian.

My cousins on my mother's side are Canadian. They have last names like Moreton and Thompson. People can spell and pronounce their names on first hearing, unlike my foreign name. Sometimes they call me Cathy. If my name was Cathy I could be Canadian as long as I didn't tell anyone my last name. I would also have the hope of becoming a full-fledged Canadian if I married a white person with an Anglo-Saxon name. My husband could have been born and raised in another country, but if he had an Anglo name then I would get my status.

My brother's name is Stan and my sister's name is Esther. Most people don't bother learning their last name since it's too much of an unnecessary challenge. However, both of my names are Hungarian so I am forced to identify with my Hungarian heritage. My mannerisms have become more Hungarian than those of my brother or my sister. Others have made me who I am.

White adult immigrants will never be Canadian because they will retain their accents. Accents are frowned upon in Canada unless they are British or Australian — then they are considered sexy.

However, if immigrant parents are white, they will still need to change their names if they want their kids to inherit the title of Canadian. As long as "ski" is at the end of a name, that person will always be considered Polish.

Native peoples don't want the title Canadian. Blacks and Asians will never achieve it. If being a true Canadian is being British and bigoted, then I'm glad that true Canadians are becoming a minority in this multicultural society.

Hello . . . My Name Is . . .

Katalin Szepesi

Longing for it
not to happen
ONE MORE TIME.
And what's your name?
Wrinkled nose, puzzled eyes.
I must repeat.
Spelling not helpful.
Nationality then requested
to excuse the unintended butchery.
Comparing my identity
to objects and places
for the sake of memory.
Next, considered *interesting, different*
and sometimes *pretty*.
Last name not attempted.
Too difficult, not necessary.

PART II

GROWING UP "DIFFERENT"

My Mother Used to Dance

Valerie Bedassigae Pheasant

She was graceful and light. Her movements made the room disappear. There was only her. Every shift and swirl of her warp caused the air to move so that I could see the patterns in the air. I looked at her face. It was my mother's face, but it was possessed by a spirit that I had not seen before. She kept moving, without touching the floor. She smiled and danced. Her face radiated — my mother was free.

I sat on the banister railing for what felt like an eternity watching my mother. As silently as I crept to watch, I left. I wondered why she did not dance for us. That was the first and only time I saw my mother dance with abandon. What I did see was a gradual freezing of her emotions and a treacherous walk with silence. Her metamorphosis had happened before our eyes and we were unable to stop it. Why didn't she yell at them? Why didn't she tell them — no? Where did the fire go? When was it that the dancing stopped?

The cocoon that encased my mother was woven by inside thoughts that constricted her more strongly than anything tangible in the human world. Inside thoughts reacting to outside action generated towards our family's Nativeness. Blatant racist remarks and statements by women who did not care to know us. Each word, each comment diminished her capacity to speak — she moved slower and slower.

I went with her to different places. What I saw fuelled my anger.

My anger was directed towards my mother in the beginning, because I could not measure her resistance. It was a strange relationship. We walked together, each of us trying to recognize and locate our safe space. There was none. Not there.

My mother liked to play Bingo at the church hall occasionally. I went with her. She paid our admission, and sometimes she bought us pop and chips. All expensive. On occasion we won. It was nearing Christmas and our hopes were high. It was hard to find seats. We found some. We looked around at the other women at the table. Nobody said hello. They looked and I looked back. My mother sat down and arranged the cards. We sat and waited. The other women talked amongst themselves in what resembled a huddle. They glanced furtively in our direction. We sat and waited — I watched. Whispers. Whispers coming from the huddle. Whispers that called out, too loud, clanging around in my ears, "Smells like Indians!" Instinctively, I breathed in deeply. Did they mean us? I could see them staring at us. My mother's head was down. Tears? I looked back at them. I knew it was us. We moved to another table. We do not speak about what was said about us. We do not recognize them. We cannot give them more power. My anger grows. My mother's spirit staggers.

My education began years before and was not always confined to the classroom. The real lessons took place outside the classroom — in this case, right outside its door. I have to accompany my mother to the school for parent-teacher interviews. We go from teacher to teacher. My mother glances at the report cards and listens to the teacher pass information to her about her children. Each in succession. We are almost finished. It is time for her to see the grade three teacher. I am instructed to wait outside the door. My mother is alone. In the stillness I can hear everything that my mother hears. I am afraid to move. The voice grows loud in my ears, telling her that her son doesn't know what to do. How can he pass? He has trouble reading. The voice grows louder, trying to convince her. I hear no response. Pages are being torn out of a workbook. The voice burns in our ears . . . "He cheated. He could not have done this. This work will not count!" More pages being ripped. I feel the shame and the guilt. It grows quiet. A chair moves. The door opens. My mother walks out. I am waiting. I see the humiliation and the pain. My anger ignites, recedes, and begins to smoulder. My mother is exhausted. We go to the next teacher.

More pressure is put on the older children to help the younger ones with their homework. We do it because we cannot allow people to think that we are "stupid Indians." I detest these people I do not

39

know. How can they make a judgement about Native people without knowing or caring to know about us? — judgements made in ignorance. I decided that someday I would tell them about things they did not want to hear, about things they were afraid to ask. I decided to talk back. There was nothing to lose. People hated us anyway.

We went on in a continuing fashion. My mother's walk slowed down. She stopped going out. When she did, it was with reluctance. I was cautioned to be quiet. I could, I might, get hurt. What did it matter? The hurt was not going to stop by itself. The hurt fuelled my anger. It grew inside me. I liked how it felt — powerful — but it was a power I instinctively knew would eat my spirit and leave me empty. My mother knew it too. We did not speak about it. I went out and she stayed inside.

I played with the idea of dropping out of school, but I wanted a good job. I wanted to have money. I wanted to have purchasing power. I was tired of watching my mother eat last. I stayed in school. My education continued. All the while I dreamed of leaving the small, ugly mining town that was teaching me. It taught me that if your father did not work for the single industry with the corporate monopoly, you were excluded from certain places. The income of your family categorized you as "rich," "not-poor," or "poor." If you excelled at something — anything — then others would make sure that it did not happen again. And I was also taught that girls were liked better when "they put out."

We were all working-class kids in a working-class high school. All subject to the rules, but for a few of us there were more rules with unrealistic demands. I hated the rules and hated the kids that exalted "the mine." They fantasized about the money, the women, the cars, the notoriety, the shift work, the money, the holidays, the wife, the husband, the house, the kids, the, the, the, the. I hated the fatalism. Didn't they know there was more than the "mine," more to live for? Didn't they want to be free to see new places, meet new people? I hated them. I saw the trap. My fire raged.

My journey began to be a lonely one. I went on, unsure of my destination but knowing that my spirit was strong, that it would lead me. Without being given specific instruction, I had to walk through that raging fire. How? With what? I was afraid. I was unsure of when. It was foolish of me to worry. I had to keep on. As children we are taught that "You will know when it is time. Make sure you are ready." I was confused about how to get ready, but my spirit would be guided. The nurturing of my spirit began when I was born. In subtle, sure, and gentle ways, my family — mother, father, grandmother, grandfathers, aunties, brothers, sisters, and cousins — gave. As my journey took me out of immediate contact with them, we met through other people we knew. I was still getting ready. You cannot measure time when "getting ready" is taking place. (Do not confuse this with preparation, which is structure.)

I went along. Times were becoming more confusing. Instructors of psychology and English wanted to know about my "fixation" with my mother. Why, they inquired, did I feel so loyal to her? Why couldn't I let go? Why did I feel obligated to her? Confusion. Static in my brain. Did I know I looked Oriental — not (gasp) Indian. Oh, your father is only half . . . (relief). But you read that aloud so well. So what do Indians do at home? Was your mom born in the bush? Bingo players — all of them. I watched and listened. These comments were petty and stupid. I would not waste my talk on them. Fuel for the fire or energy for my spirit, I did not know which.

I continued in formal education. A change would occur in desks only, from the student's desk to the teacher's desk. I was still learning. Teachers' College reinforced the knowledge that the classroom did not reflect society; did not reflect the values of all families; did not utilize stories of women and stories of non-white people; evaluated from one perspective only; did not justify our existence; perfected exclusion. I was inside, but inside what? Why was I here? Who was I walking with and where were we going? I allowed myself to be led. I questioned without articulating the words. I slowed down but did not stop. The assault on my spirit continued. Words. Words that burned me. Words that festered and left wide scars. From the Masters, more words. . . . Did I really think that I belonged at Teachers' College? Did I really think that I would pass? Did I really think that practice teaching in a Native school was a good idea? Did I really think I would get a job? I could feel my anger blazing, almost out of control. I was choking.

My mother telephoned the week before exams and asked when I was coming home. I went home for the weekend. After that I decided that I would hitchhike to the college and stay in Sudbury with a friend. The week's tests that followed were not in the written examinations, but in me. Each day I ventured out. Each day I wrote my examinations. Each day I was tempted to quit.

On the day after examinations, I caught a ride with a man travelling out West. It was a hot, clear day. He tried to make conversation. I was too tired to speak. We travelled along in silence. The car moved. It seemed like the wheels were not on the ground. We were skimming along. The driver kept glancing at me. I moved close to the door and found the handle — looked directly at him. He watched the highway. My head began to dip and my eyes closed, but I was awake. I checked around the car. My eyes opened and I began to hear my name being called. I looked towards the driver. He was quiet, still looking awkwardly in my direction. No words were exchanged. I saw fear in his eyes. He looked back at the highway. We drove on in silence. The voice was calling. It was clear now. I wanted to sleep. If only I could close my eyes. "VALERIE! . . . VALERIE! STAY AWAKE. . . . LISTEN TO ME!" the voice demanded. I looked out the window. Something was outside, moving alongside us. I could sense its power. It was connected to me. The voice called me again. It was talking, soothing me, guiding me, warning me, containing me. From the other side of the car, the man was asking, "Are you alright? Do you want me to stop?" I could smell his sweat and hear the fear in his voice. I looked in his direction, my flames reached out to touch him. He became quiet and drove on, careful not to excite the flame with his breath. Outside the car, still beside us, the woman's voice familiar from the womb was again speaking to me. I talked back without words. My mother told me not to be afraid. I passed through the fire.

Parent-teacher interviews for my daughter. I go alone. I am afraid. Each time, I am afraid. I recognize the fear — we have met before. Now I am the mother. There is no child outside the door. I will not let her come along. The meeting is between adults — both trained in the same Bingo Palace. Only this time one of us refuses to be a player.

We meet. Cordial greeting. Forced pleasantries. I am asked what the problem is. Why is it that your daughter will not participate? Why does she think she can get away with this? How come she didn't finish her project on the family unit? I cut in. I willed my voice to an even tone. There are explosions in my brain. I refuse to have this woman speak to me in a condescending fashion. I inquire about my daughter's lack of participation; about the model of family structure that is being recognized and rewarded in class. Ours does not fit the mould. I explain. My words are vaporized. I ask about forms of resistance being demonstrated by other girls. None. I ask about the manner in which questions are directed at my daughter. The teacher's voice rises by several decibels. She yells, "I am sick and tired of hearing Athena this and Athena that. She is not that special. What's all the fuss about?"

I breathe in. I stare in disbelief. I refuse to accept the blame, and feel the guilt and shame this woman, this teacher, is trying to place on me. Sparks are flying. I must remain in control. I refuse to speak. I can only stare. She stops to catch her breath. She demands to show me her proof. I move the chair and stand up. She steps back. I look at her with disgust. I start towards the door. She yells out at me, "I am not finished yet!" I am overwhelmed by her bile. I begin to smile, the images of long ago play themselves out, and the anger subsides. The spectre of my younger self shadowed in the doorway looks on, lips upturned and eyes strong and steady. I turn and distinctly reply, "Yes, but I am." My smile grows. I walk out on shaky legs. Somewhere music — and my spirit starts to dance.

Tears? Yes, there are tears. I cry for my mother, myself, and my daughter. I cry because our children's spirits are still being assaulted — not educated. My tears (I am reminded) are good. They help us to heal. They return to Mother Earth. They cleanse us, help us grow.

My anger is still in me. It is mine. I earned it. I share it. It belongs to all of us, collectively. The forces of religion, education, society, the judiciary, the media, make it a real, everyday occurrence. At times I do not realize there is a difference between being happy, being angry, and being alive. I have had to make friends with anger. We are together when people continue to say — you sound so angry when you speak about the education system. Yes I am, because it continues to perpetuate inaccuracies. I am angry when Aboriginal peoples are labelled "Indians." I am angry when a person is devalued by the colour of their skin. Yes I am, when children are victimized. Yes I am, when I am patronized. Yes I am, when teachers continue to tell us that we were discovered out of our own savage chasm of non-sentience. Yes, I am angry when people are silenced. Yes I am, when people try to use me to justify their theories. Yes, I am angry.

Who says we can't dance? "Whoever pays the piper, calls the tune" — well, we've paid the piper for half a millennium. It's time to call the tune. It's time to dance.

Zebra:
Growing up Black and White in Canada

•••••••••••••••••••••••••

Lawrence Hill

> Eenie meenie minie moe
> Catch a nigger by the toe
> If he hollers let him go
> Eenie meenie minie moe
>> — schoolyard rhyme

The white, churchgoing people of my neighbourhood may have supposed that I, having atheists for parents, revelled in freedom from the burden of Commandments. Not so. We had two.

Under the roof of my parents, the Penultimate Commandment posed no constraints on my life. I had no reason to violate it. It was: *Thou shalt not utter the word nigger.* The Ultimate Commandment, however, caused me great anxiety over the years. It was: *Thou shalt not fail to rain the fury of hell upon anyone uttering the said word.*

As the light-skinned son of a Black man and a white woman, I felt safe from the word *nigger* during my boyhood. Nobody aimed it at me, in my first ten years. And when I did hear it used generally, I did not feel singled out. Somehow, it didn't apply to me. I recognized it as an attack on a whole race of people — including my father, his parents, and their ancestors. But years would pass before I saw myself as belonging to that race.

Nevertheless, I understood the Ultimate Commandment at an early age. I remember standing nervously in a schoolyard during the spring of my second grade, while classmates were about to determine who would be "it" to start a tag game.

I knew how their rhyme went. I knew it couldn't go unchallenged. But the prospect of losing new friends terrified me. So I jumped in to recite it myself, changing one key word as my parents had suggested:

Eenie meenie minie moe
Catch a tiger by the toe
If he hollers let him go
Eenie meenie minie moe

before the offending word could be spoken, secretly grateful for the chance to avoid confrontation.

People rarely called me *nigger*. But the word had a way of vaulting into conversation at times when nobody — not even I — was conscious of the racial difference between my white friends and me. I would object to the word, but that drew attention to my own racial identity — something I would take years to define.

In the 1920s, Langston Hughes wrote "Cross." It began:

My old man's a white old man,
And my old mother's black . . .

and ended:

My old man died in a fine big house,
My ma died in a shack.
I wonder where I'm gonna die,
Being neither white nor black.

I first read "Cross" as a young teenager, and identified with the lament of the young man with no clear fix on who he was. I still love the poem. But now I see in it an irony that Hughes must have recognized: although the narrator didn't know where he would die, he couldn't have had any doubt where he would be buried — in a cemetery for Blacks.

In the United States — the country of my paternal great-great-grandfather, who was born a slave — anyone known to have any African ancestry has been defined as Black. In the past, that definition stuck for the purposes of slavery and segregation. Today, it still holds true for more subtle forms of discrimination. Where many of my relatives live — New York City, Washington, D.C., Baltimore, and North Carolina — Americans are accustomed to noting slight traces of African heritage. People as light-skinned as I am are frequently identified as Blacks.

Not so in Canada. Certainly not in Don Mills, Ontario, where I grew up from 1960 to 1975. Most people assumed I was white. Some Blacks thought so too. In 1975, for example, I had a summer job washing floors at Sunnybrook Hospital in North York. Most of my co-workers were Caribbean immigrants. One day, in the locker room, I told one of them that my father was Black. He said I was lying. I showed him a photograph. By the next shift, every West Indian in the hospital knew who I was.

"My father is Black." That's quite different from saying, "I am Black." I thought of myself as Black at the hospital. I usually thought of myself that way in the company of Blacks. But in the locker room of the hospital, surrounded by dark-skinned West Indians, I didn't say it outright. Imagine the laughter. *Hey, George, do you hear what this man's saying?* So I eased in the back door. By saying "My father is Black," I was saying "Decide for yourself what that makes me."

Why did I lack the confidence to call myself Black?

Part of it had to do with growing up in neighbourhoods, attending schools, and competing on sports teams in which I was usually the only person of colour — and my colour, such as it was, generally went unremarked. On the whole, white people paid little attention to my racial background, and I tended not to think about it as I played and studied. I saw myself as being the same as the white people who surrounded me.

On the other hand, sometimes I was proud of my Black ancestry. Such moments came when my parents drove us to visit relatives in Washington, D.C. I'll never forget playing tag in a park off Chain Bridge Road, wondering whether my cousins would accept me. Some of them were also light-skinned. That made me feel better. It gave me hope that they would see me as one of them. I remember noting that my mother seemed whiter than ever before. Still, she mingled easily with my Black relatives. They accepted her! Surely, I reasoned, they accepted me too!

Other moments of strong racial identification came in the intimacy of our house. Hearing about Muhammed Ali and Martin Luther King, Jr. had something to do with that. So did welcoming Black friends of my parents. But the most powerful influence came from my father.

He pointed out Blacks wherever he saw them ("Larry! Did you see that Negro doctor?" or "Hey! A coloured bus driver!"). He had many contacts with Toronto's Black community.

My father never sat me down and said, "You are a Negro." He didn't tell me, or my brother or sister, what we were. He let us work it out for ourselves. He made only one type of reference to my race, and it was in jest. Occasionally he called me a zebra, which I thought quite funny. Within our family, it became a private expression for people of mixed race.

Living among and accepted by whites, I often spent weeks at a time without thinking of myself as different or thinking at all about my own race. Yet when those moments of introspection took place, I thought of myself as Black — but only timidly. It was hard to see myself as Black when nobody else did.

At the age of fourteen, I entered a private high school so exclusively white that it made me more conscious — and proud — of my own background.

I joined a music class and decided to play the saxophone. But the teacher told me that Negroes lacked the correct facial structure to play the instrument properly. My first thought was, "I can't tell my dad about this because he'll storm into the headmaster's office and demand that the teacher be disciplined. Everybody will hear about it and I'll never live it down." I kept the incident to myself. I knew the teacher was an idiot, but he was my teacher, and it was my first week in school, and I didn't have the courage to argue with him or to tell him that I had grown up listening to Black saxophonists such as Illinois Jacquet and Coleman Hawkins.

I merely insisted on taking up the saxophone. Unfortunately, though, I had puny lungs. No rhythm. And when I fought to hold long notes, my cheeks felt like they were stuffed full of gum. But I stuck with the instrument. I held on for a year, signing the sax out after school and dragging it home on the bus. I practised and practised to prove my teacher wrong. He gave me an average mark at the end of the year. I felt relieved to pass the course, and I never studied music again.

I began thinking much more about race. I wrote a short story, my first, about a Black youth who runs away from a bigoted North Carolina town with his white girlfriend. I wrote an essay about Langston Hughes. I began reading other Black literature — and it troubled me.

Soul on Ice, by Eldridge Cleaver, suggested that Black men sought white women only because they were forbidden fruit. Cleaver wrote powerfully. But he was unable to convince me that interracial relationships were inherently flawed. He couldn't rebut the protest rooted in my own upbringing — a protest that sprang to mind as I read his book: "But what if they LOVE each other?" *The Autobiography of Malcolm X* also fascinated and upset me. During his most militant phase, Malcolm X insisted that white people were devils. I rejected

47

the idea outright. "How can he say that? My mother is white! She's no devil!"

In the summer of 1974, when I was seventeen, I travelled in Europe. In Belgium I saw signs posted outside nightclubs saying "No Blacks" or "No North Africans" or "North Africans Must Be Accompanied By Women." The signs horrified me. But even more repugnant was the reaction of Belgian acquaintances, who defended the rules as necessary to prevent Blacks from acting up.

That same year, I took my mop of tangled curls to a Black hair stylist. I had worried about it for weeks in advance, uneasy about how the hair stylist would see me. Definitely not, I hoped, as some curly-haired white kid who thought an afro would look cool! Cliff, the stylist, was too professional to make me uncomfortable. He merely grumbled about the hour it took to untangle my mop, sold me a pick, and sent me out with a modest afro.

At school, most people looked but said nothing. A few teachers said kind words about the new look. Only one student, whose name was David, gave me a hard time about it.

"Jesus, Larry, you look like a French poodle!"

"It's an afro. It's common among Blacks."

"Black! How can you say you're Black? You're not Black! You're barely darker than me!"

My mouth dropped, but I said nothing. The words made me burn with anger. They rang in my ears for weeks to come. I wanted to wrench out David's hair and yell: "Yes I am! Yes I am Black!" I wanted to scream that Blacks had been defined for centuries on the basis of their racial origin — something not necessarily emphasized by skin colour. I never did speak to David about it. But by challenging my racial identity, he helped drive me to a more insistent self-image. Periods of time still passed during which I gave no thought to race. But when I did, my thoughts turned to my own sense of Blackness.

In Canada or Europe, racism — even when directed at other people — reminded me that I was Black. Something else did that too. After I left home to study and work in other cities, people began asking, "What *are* you, anyway?"

In English Canada I heard this question only occasionally. But from 1978-80, when I studied in Quebec City, people asked me every week about my "national origin."

In the winter of my first year there, transit workers went on strike. I began hitchhiking daily from my bachelor suite on Cartier Avenue to Laval University. I found that Quebeckers readily picked up hitchhikers. I also discovered that they felt no compunction about grilling me about my racial origin. I must have had this exchange thirty times:

"Where are you from?"

"Toronto."

"You don't look like someone from Toronto."

"Well, I am."

"But what is your nationality?"

"Canadian."

"But where were you born?"

"Just outside Toronto."

"And your parents?"

"The United States."

"Ahh, the United States."

But still, they weren't satisfied, and wouldn't be unless I described my racial makeup, which I usually refused to do — not because I was ashamed of it, but because I resented that it was demanded of me.

In the summer of 1979, at the age of twenty-two, I spent two months in the West African country of Niger. I travelled with a group of six Quebeckers, as part of a cultural exchange that involved living with young people from Niger. Together, we planted trees to help protect fertile lands from the expanding Sahara Desert.

I liked my fellow travellers. Today, twelve years later, three of them are still among my closest friends. But there was a time, shortly after my arrival in Niger, when I wanted nothing to do with them. Their presence made me feel white. And that summer, with an intensity that I had never anticipated, I wanted to be Black. Welcomed and loved as a brother.

I dove headlong into learning to speak Djerma. I ate and drank whatever was offered me. I held hands with African men, as is the custom there between male friends. Most people of Niger offered me great hospitality, but they appeared to see me as white. Before I could summon the nerve to tell people that I was one of them, I became sick. I was overtaken by vomiting, diarrhea, and a fever that climbed out of sight. Hospitalization followed, and a blood transfusion, and days of intravenous feedings. I lost twenty pounds in a week.

My friends from Quebec slept on the floor by my hospital bed, carried me to the toilet, and fed me when I could eat again. They never left my side. I loved them and left the hospital a changed man.

I discovered that bringing my white friends into conversation with Africans was more rewarding than hoarding new friendships to the exclusion of the Quebeckers. I knew what I was, and I felt it tranquilly. I was both Black and white, and this was irrevocable, whether other people noticed my colours or not.

Years have since passed, but I still feel that way. I'm a man of two races.

"Zebra," of course, sounds faintly ridiculous. I wouldn't use the word in a serious conversation, but I do prefer it to "mulatto." Indeed, "mulatto" offends me more than "nigger." To say "nigger" is to say, "I hate you because you're Black." At least I know where I stand. But "mulatto" reduces me to half-status — neither Black nor white.

Even as a boy, I sensed that terms such as "mulatto," "half-Black," and "part Black" denied my fullness as a person. I recognized the absurdity of calling somebody "one-half" or "one-quarter" or "one-eighth" Black. Ancestral identity, I knew, couldn't be apportioned mathematically. One couldn't assign this colour to the heart and that to the liver. And at the same time, a person like me couldn't be all white and not Black, or all Black and not white, unless society imposed one colour on me.

I didn't grow up under apartheid, or slavery, or racial segregation. I grew up in a country in which I had a say in what I would be. That meant periods of ambiguity. It meant confusion. It meant anxiety. But it also meant the opportunity to come full circle and to decide, years after my father first poked me in the ribs and teasingly called me a zebra, that I truly was both Black and white.

Two years after my first trip to West Africa, I returned, this time to Cameroon. I met the French Canadian woman who is now my wife. We now have two young daughters. I hope to infect them with enthusiasm for the many wings of their family. I don't know how old they will be when they start asking questions about the meaning of Black and white, and about how they fit into the picture. I'll answer what I can, and share with them what I know. But I won't tell them how to think. When they are old enough to play with the big questions, they will be ready to start moulding their own answers.

"I Am Canadian but My Father Is German"

Lori Weber

•••••••••••••••••

Part German, part Irish/English mix, but Canadian. Is this the best place to start? Isn't the street that I grew up on more important? There, in the Park Extension area of Montreal, we were a patchwork quilt of origins: French, Irish, Greek, Italian, Swedish, Japanese, Chinese, Dutch. Each flat had its own particular flavour, its own particular smells. Our Japanese friends were looked after by their ancient grandmother, who was as shrivelled as an apple doll and who allowed us to do whatever we wanted. It was in their flat that all the kids gathered to colour on the walls. When they came out in the evening with bowls of noodles, we said, and we truly believed, that they were eating fried worms. In the corner of her eye the grandmother had a stye that looked like an upside-down volcano.

All these things somehow or other signified Japanese to me: the crayoned walls, the worm-noodles, and the stye. The Swedish girls across the street wore white starched shirts, even on weekends, and their blond hair was always neatly combed. They sang in a choir that had made a radio commercial that we all envied, yet they weren't allowed to slide down the two-storey bannister because it would stain their underwear. These characteristics I associated with being Swedish: neat, fastidious, stern.

★ ★ ★

In school all my friends are Greek: Rita, Roula, and Elli. They all have dark brown hair and eyes, but I am dirty-blond and my eyes are green. Their mothers make them do housework and they scream down to their children from galleries, unabashed, *"Ella tho, hligora."* Their grandmothers live with them and are always clad in black, their grey buns pulled tightly back. They sit statue-like on park benches, shoving over-ripe bananas into the mouths of their tiny grandchildren. Around their necks some wear bright blue evil eyes that dangle when the grandmothers bend over to pick dandelions in the fields beside L'Acadie. By the time I am ten I know more Greek than French. When we are just two we speak English, but when they outnumber me they switch to Greek.

In grade four a flood of tears overwhelms me, and my teacher, Miss Goldbaum, takes me outside. I confess the source of my misery: I can't always understand what my friends are saying. I feel small, defenceless, terribly hurt, and left out. She summons them and we hold a conference where she makes me tell each of them how their exclusion makes me feel. They are stunned, apologetic. They didn't realize. They assumed I understood. They promise not to do it again, but they do. Repeatedly, for years. The desire to speak their first language when they are together is too strong. To compensate, they make me an honorary Greek. They bring me braided cookies brushed with egg yolk, and when plans are being made for the Greek Easter parade they take me along for a costume fitting.

We are in the Edward VII schoolyard on Jeanne Mance. In one of the upper flats across the street my grandmother's two eccentric sisters live. One has a history of spontaneous nudity and the other plays the piano and was once engaged to an Indian from Caughnawaga (now Kahnawaké). I always pictured him in a skirt with a feather band around his head, carrying a tomahawk. The family, scandalized, broke up the liaison. These aunts are proof to me that not all English people are uptight and proper. They are aberrations, family sore spots. We do not visit them often.

We form a long line of girls, waiting to be measured. The sample costume hangs on the fence, which is made of thousands of wire diamonds linked together. It is lovely, a blue skirt and a white shirt, the colours of the Greek flag. I feel conspicuous, silly. But mostly I am envious of the connection that runs through the veins of the long line of girls, that seeps gracefully and historically into their tongues. The woman who measures me is compassionate. She switches to my tongue. She is amused. I know that she knows I am not one of them. I am an imposter, but she measures me anyway. I lift my arms and she wraps the tape around my flat chest. It is then that I start to cry. I cannot go through with it. Beyond the costume is the whole ritual I will have to partake in, the candlelight parade, the songs whose words I will not be able to sing. (The following year a Catholic friend takes me to her choir and I have the same reaction. The hymn rolls awkwardly over my tongue. I have to force it between my lips. It is as foreign to me as Greek.) I run from the schoolyard in tears and hop on the next 80 bus that will take me under the two tunnels home, deprived and solitary.

My parents seem to me to have no identifiable culture. They are atheists who listen to Bob Dylan, decorate the living-room wall with a poster of Che Guevara, and put up a plastic tree at Christmas. I know that my father was born in Germany, but this doesn't seem to make much difference to our family. He doesn't eat German food, or wear lederhosen, or even drink beer out of tall steins. In fact, I know very little about his German past. When anyone asks me what I am (which is a question everyone in Park Extension asks), I say, "Canadian, but my father is German." According to my father, Germans make the best immigrants because they blend in, assimilate. Later I come to think of it more as camouflage, a desire to remain incognito, to erase the past.

I don't know what being German means exactly, but I know from an early age that German is something to be ashamed of. ("You're Germish," the kids tease.) That is why it contains the word "germ." That is why Miss Goldbaum made me and Werner and Achim stand on our desks one day. She was teaching us about the war. She made us stand because she wanted everyone to know that just because we were German they shouldn't think we were in any way responsible for the horrors she was about to describe. We were innocent. We hadn't been born yet. Ironically, in that instant, something is born in me, an awareness that being German means something different from being Greek or Chinese or Swedish. It carries more weight, or at least the weight is different. It means being something that one has to apologize for, to be embarrassed of even. It's a lesson I will learn many more times. When I'm nineteen and applying to live in a house in Toronto, one of the tenants stamps out of the room and declares that if I am accepted he will be forced to take his showers at the U of T, given that the house has a gas stove in the kitchen. These words sting, as do the words, "Yuck, my least favourite people" (said with scrunched-up face) when I point out an available Master's student to a friend who is looking for love.

The worst part of these attacks is that there is no available defence. What do you say to the Jewish man who doesn't want to share his living space with a German? And what to retort to the friend who is repulsed by my suggestion, in particular once I'd learned that her own mother was a survivor of Auschwitz? This Germanness is a curse; it is a deep wart that no solvent can lift from the body. As an antidote, I think of the beauty of the country itself — the Alps, the Black Forest, Bavarian castles, the charming cobblestone towns — but I knew nothing of these as a child.

Later, as I grow, I will begin to cling to more solid knowledge, family facts that get divulged slowly, painfully. My father's father worked bringing relief to German families during the war, often travelling from town to town in the south. He wasn't sympathetic to the Nazi cause. My own father, always a rebel, once stole the German flag instead of the opposing team's during war games with the Hitler Youth that he was obliged to join. For this, his father was beaten. Then there is the arm, the severed arm of my grandfather, that somehow was taken as punishment for something. The how, why, and when of the episode have never been divulged, and probably never will be, but how my mind latches onto the image of this severed arm. It is proof that my father's family were not Nazi supporters. Supporters don't lose arms, they gain medals, favour. I believe that the arm allows me to, in part, share in the victim status, or at least lay claim to a minimal amount of victim status. The day I am refused tenancy in the house in Toronto I think that if only I had that arm I could hold it up like a trophy: V for victory and V for victim. This is why the defence of such attacks is so difficult. I am connected to the side that did the victimizing, and, as such, any defence of this side is unacceptable, unthinkable even.

Yes, that fated day in grade four Miss Goldbaum, a teacher I adored and who had helped heal the wounds of my exclusion from the Greek circle, introduces me to the concept of guilt and shame. Although she is careful to point out to the class that we were born in Canada and are far too young to have been involved in the war (this is 1970), she forgets that our fathers (and Werner's and Achim's mothers) were born there, and that they were alive during the war. I never again look at my father in the same light. His crooked hands, which he caught in one of the machines he repairs for a living, are no longer symbols of the daily sacrifice he makes for his family. They resemble the swastika that Miss Goldbaum held up. They are twisted the exact same way. When he is in the shed doing "things," I can no longer imagine him fixing ordinary household items, like bikes and chairs.

He is experimenting, destroying, cooking up evil concoctions. When he is stern, which all fathers sometimes are, he is being more than stern. He is showing his true genetic colours (a sentiment that Margaret Thatcher, beehive and all, would agree with: "They will do it again; it is in the blood"). I wonder if Werner and Achim look at their fathers this way too now, but I can't ask them because they disappeared soon after the stand-on-the-desk episode. They obviously told, but I was too ashamed to ever utter a word.

All these feelings about German I take with me to the German House on Cremazie, when my father and mother decide that, at the age of ten, I should become German. Finally, a tiny voice inside me declares, I am to have a culture. Yet I approach the experience warily, for many reasons. For one, I am not used to being the same as anyone else. I am more used to being different, to looking in, to listening in, to standing like a sore thumb in the wrong line-ups. The idea that I am being asked to become part of a group intimidates me, as it will continue to do even now. I am terrified. I try my best to take the German lessons seriously, and sing my young heart out during music break ("*Laterne, Laterne, Sonne, Mond, und Sterne*"), but I feel false, fake.

When I learn that Germans capitalize the German forms of you (*Du* and *Sie*) and not the I (*ich*), I immediately think that this is proof of goodness, of respect for others. I am too aware of trying to stack my deck, to undo the only impressions of Germanness I have gained until now. *Hogan's Heroes* is the most popular sitcom of the day. For half an hour every week people everywhere laugh at the stupid Germans (even my father loves the show). The villains in all our favourite Saturday morning cartoons sound just like my father and are obviously German. At *Bedknobs and Broomsticks* I cringe and cry in the dark. The villains, once again, are replicas of my father. In fact, as a child I had a hard time seeing my father as an individual, a separate and real person; he was a symbol, one that was replicated in so many negative ways.

At the German House I also have to learn to do proper German dancing, where a boy holds your hand and puts his other hand around your waist. The girls sit at tables and wait to be asked. When a boy finally does ask me, I realize I don't know the steps. I am clumsy. I am totally self-conscious twirling into these predetermined steps that are not mine. He tries to twirl me and I break like wood. He pushes me away and mutters some disbelief at my ineptitude. My parents sit behind me, waiting, I feel, for me to suddenly become German, as though the steps to the dance were somehow lying dormant in my genes, waiting to be released. I return to the table, awkward, heavy. I have failed. I refuse to go back. My father is angry, disappointed. I feel his anger is unfair because until that day he had never tried to teach me anything at all about his culture. Not a word. My mother didn't speak German either, so it was a completely foreign language. Greek was more familiar. *"Then thello naertho sto horo,"* I'm not going to the dance, I tell my friends.

I never again attempt to become German. I try to forget the whole issue, and for the most part do this until we take a trip to my father's hometown when I am eleven. It may be easy to block out the war in Canada, but in Europe this is impossible. The fact of the war screams out to me from every nook and cranny of the old town. It is in the sawed-off limbs of the old men who hobble on canes and crutches, in the bags of gout that old women carry under their chins from years of drinking tainted water. It is in the cracked-toothed castle that sits like a decrepit crown on the top of the hill at the centre of town. Green army trucks pump their way continually through the narrow-veined streets, the soldiers in the back calling out in a variety of languages, mostly French, Italian, and English. It is in the sadness of my father's eyes when he looks at his mother, and it is written in the deep lines on her face and the million wrinkles of her hands that seem immune to the flames that burst beneath them when she lights the old stove. But mostly it is in the deep hole that lies in the ground under the root cellar, hidden by a camouflaging heap of potatoes. It was there that my father and his brother hid their sister from soldiers. As an eleven-year-old I couldn't imagine why she would need to be hid, but later I understood that rape was common. Even later yet I discovered that this aunt of mine was really my father's half-sister and that her real father was Jewish, the most potent reason for hiding her.

It is during that visit too that I am able to add a dimension to my father that makes him less of a cut-out stock character. I pad his Germanness with curves and angles. I learn of the time he walked himself to the hospital (*krankenhaus* — sickhouse), doubled over with the pain of a nearly ruptured appendix. I learn of the betrayal he felt when his parents sent him far out into the country to pick potatoes, knowing full well that his life was in danger. I learn that my father and his brother cannot look each other in the eyes and reminisce without crying. I learn, that year, to be a little less ashamed of being German. I learn that the war, any war, is not just team A versus team B, but a million shades of A's and B's, shades that might save me, tuck me inside their shadows and hide me. But I don't get over (and never will) the discomfort that being of German descent elicits.

One last memory strikes me. The family that lived next door to my father's was so kind to us when we visited. The mother, who was my grandmother's age, baked us special cookies and gave me a fistful of mad money (Spielgeld). The old father, without telling anyone, put up a swing in my grandmother's backyard, attached to a high branch of one of her sturdy trees. That afternoon he pushed me on it, obviously thrilled to watch my happiness as I pumped myself higher and higher towards the orange-tiled roof of my father's home. That night my father told us that that couple were the chief informants in their town: true, one hundred per cent Nazi sympathizers. The next day my mother looked the swing over carefully, as though she thought he might have cut gashes into it, and was just waiting for me to fall, break my neck, and die. Then she wanted to take it down and give it back, but my father refused to let her do this. It would have been rude. The neighbour had given it in kindness. The war had ended twenty-five years ago.

As for me, I continued to use the swing, but never again as freely as on the first day. I never again swung so high. The episode filled me with questions. How could my father have lived beside such people? What relationship did his family have with them? How could an evil man benevolently build a swing? What if I had been related to them, instead? How could anyone really know anyone? How could I look at this person and smile in a friendly fashion unless I was totally able to disconnect him from his history? Could such a manoeuvre be done?

These are the questions that run through my mind the day we leave my father's hometown. Across from me on the train my father is crying, sobbing, the tears running over his crooked fingers, down his palm, soaking the cuff of his shirt. Outside, on the platform, my old grandmother runs beside the train under our window. She is waving a white handkerchief, as though she is surrendering.

And then suddenly we are back in Canada, a place with so little history, a place where people are always in the process of remaking themselves, redefining who they are. A place of newness, or improvisation. I see it everywhere in my neighbourhood, this blending, this criss-crossing of culture. And it is what I gravitate towards: the mix, the blend, the anomalies, the hybrids.

The first thing I do when I get home is call Elli. She asks me about my trip to Germany. I tell her I had fun, but I don't tell her about the man next door, or the root cellar, or the way my father cried. She asks if I brought her anything, but I didn't. It is not a souvenir type of place. When she went to Greece the year before she brought me back a plastic Acropolis paperweight. What would be the German equivalent? No, the most salient parts of my trip and the impressions left on me are destined to remain private, relegated to a back corner of my mind, as concealed as the root cellar, but just as deep.

Elli cannot wait for me to meet their new border, Costa Rica, who doesn't speak a word of English and arrived a few days ago from Athens. He is exotic, incomprehensible, and when Elli's mother isn't home he tries to fondle our little breasts. I take comfort in his difference, preferring, as I will for the rest of my life, the aspects of him that I can't know, will never know or relate to. My upbringing in Park Extension has left me with that — a preference for difference over similarity, a discomfort with belonging (since belonging was never an option). It is a legacy that leads at times to a sense of isolation, but at others to complete connectedness with everything and everyone, since one can always be an observer.

* * *

The fact of having a German heritage is one that most of the time means very little. My father was right. Our family did blend in with the mainstream far more than the families of any of my ethnic friends. We don't have any equivalent to the large Italian wedding, the Passover Seder, or the Sunday afternoon picnics of the Filipino community in the park across the street from my old apartment. I used to watch them with that familiar mixture of awe, envy, and relief. They would number at least one hundred, ranging in age from ancient to newborn, the families all mixing and blending together, brought there by the ties of their blood and the meat sizzling on the barbecues. Such ethnic identification is completely foreign to me. The ability to be so at one with my background would also be completely impossible, given the complexity of feelings that being of German heritage has always caused.

Just nights ago at a potluck dinner a woman told a story of a despicable woman who had recently become a decent man's girlfriend. Through her whole discourse she referred to the woman as "that German." Nobody at all who was listening seemed to recognize this as a racist comment, except for me. The amazing thing was that the teller of the story is an enlightened and well-educated young woman who works for refugee organizations in Montreal. She is well known for her tireless crusades to aid the downtrodden and needy. Yet she could say "that German" with impunity, in a way that I've heard the word German used a hundred times before. It would have been unthinkable for her to pepper her story with "that Italian" or "that

Chinese" or "that Mexican." But "that German" is seen as acceptable because of what German still represents.

Such derogatory utterances don't even sound wrong or jarring to the ear, unless one is German, I'm sure. Funny that when she was telling the story my mind drifted back to the beautiful blue and white costume for the Greek Easter parade that I never did get to wear. I could see it hanging on the wire fence, as though it had been waiting all this time for someone to claim it. At that moment, I would have gladly crawled into it, to camouflage myself and take on a new identity. I wondered what it would be like to be able to lay claim to a heritage that one could be one hundred per cent proud of, that was above reproach. This, of course, is probably just an idyllic fantasy. Perhaps all people are embarrassed by some part of their culture, and perhaps everyone has a parallel image of that blue dress, a symbol of otherness that they sometimes wish they could easily adopt.

That night, at the potluck, I never did point her racism out to her, and if it happens a hundred times more I probably never will. I will always, in some ways, be the ten-year-old child standing on a desk, completely immobile and burning with shame, listening to the adored teacher tell stories that are difficult to hear.

PRESENT COMPANY EXCLUDED, OF COURSE . . . REVISITED

•••••••••••••••••

STAN ISOKI

When I originally undertook to write "Present Company Excluded, of Course" for this book's first edition, I embarked on the task with a particular mindset and a less-than-subtle agenda: I wanted to make the "Canadian public" aware of one person's experience with systemic racism, and all its attendant problems. I believed that in talking about and describing the varying ways in which people experience our society, we could develop a co-operative approach to ensuring that everyone is presented with an equal opportunity to succeed. (I am struck now by how laden and value-implicit many of the terms I used really are. Words like "co-operative," "presented," and "equal opportunity" all conjure up, for me, images that the dominant culture within my society has prescribed as desirable.)

The task I have set myself this time is to examine the context in which "Present Company" was written and analyse some of the anecdotes described in it. Where my initial article provided a description of growing up in Canada, this time I intend also to explore another way of looking at some of those incidents. My new notations are set in the italic font.

It wasn't until I was in school that I realized I was both highly visible and also totally invisible. It was a lesson learned in the most subtle way; a lesson taught by a series of the unlikeliest teachers; a lesson incapable of being unlearned. It has made an impact upon all personal and professional aspects of my life.

One of my first lessons occurred in the corner store in Thunder Bay (then Fort William), Ontario. Non-metropolitan Canada abounds with across-from-the-school, corner variety stores where people can purchase almost anything from pantyhose to penny candies. The stores have a character and ambience not found in Toronto or Montreal or Vancouver. The regard their patrons have for this type of entrepreneur is reverential. And the backbone of the institution is the child — the child who, clutching pennies, nickels, and dimes, represents most of the profits. No wonder then that a special relationship exists between the proprietor and his prepubescent clientele.

Trying to break into this special relationship was impossible for me. My "Excuse me, sir, can I have three cents' worth of bubble gum?" was usually met with a hostile glare or, worse yet, an indifference that negated my existence. At seven years old, I couldn't understand why my three cents wasn't as valuable as that of my friends, who always seemed able to get the owner's attention. I most often resorted to having my friends buy my candy for me from this same man who taught me that in some way I was less valuable and valued than my peers. I'm not talking now about the kids-versus-adults kind of invisibility. Kids are used to being ignored by store owners when a more lucrative transaction with an adult can be made. I'm talking about the kind of invisibility that set me apart from other kids in my own age group, an invisibility that sapped my fragile self-esteem and gave rise to self-doubt.

Another assault on my self-image occurred when my grade five teacher, a woman whose apparent wisdom and stature were unquestionable, put me and the only other "different-looking" child in the class on either side of the front row in order to take the class picture. I felt honoured to have been chosen for this special place, but I also felt a little confused. In every other class picture I had been placed somewhere near the middle because I was usually the smallest kid. Later, when the anxiously awaited picture arrived, the reasons for her actions became graphically apparent. Neatly framed between two different-looking children was the "real" class, those children for whom the school system existed. I think I realized even then that my humanity was, at the very least, inferior. I felt that I had been left on the periphery, looking in. I have that picture still. It serves to remind me not only of the subtlety with which a teacher or parent or adult can harm a child, but also of the vigilance that must be maintained to avoid the damage that can be so easily perpetrated.

I have no doubt that my grade five teacher knew exactly what she was looking for or that she single-mindedly set out to achieve the desired effect in the photograph. What I do question is her sensitivity to the needs of the children who formed the bookends in that picture. Was she unaware of the possible negative impact of her actions, or did she underestimate or dismiss the probability that we would notice the result? My experience with most elementary teachers is that they are caring, sensitive, and compassionate people whose major concern is for the well-being of their students. I can only conclude, therefore, that this teacher, this woman whose "wisdom and stature were unquestionable," did not or would not concern herself with the sensibilities of her only two minority students.

Other examples of failed attempts at assimilation (and at that age I wanted nothing so much as to "fit in") seem insignificant by themselves, but cumulatively they had a devastating effect on a child's developing psyche. It is easy to doubt one's worth when there is what appears to be overwhelming evidence that one is invisible. I remember a birthday party where I was the only non-white child. What fun it was to watch the children bob for apples and to make hilarious, uncoordinated attempts to pin the tail on the crudely drawn donkey. But when it came my turn, what a disappointment to discover that the cake was in need of cutting at that precise moment and that we would have to wait to complete the game. Inevitably, the game was never completed, nor was the elusive tail ever pinned. When my mother came to pick me up and asked the obvious question, my reply was an enthusiastic, "Yes, I had a really good time, Mom." I couldn't admit that I had been overlooked by my friend's parents.

It was around that time, or perhaps a little later, that I began to question my rationalizations about what seemed to be a series of coincidences. Store managers seeing through me, friends' mothers ignoring me, playmates often not knowing me when other friends appeared: these were all occurrences far too apparent to ignore. Did I exude a peculiar odour? Was my breath inordinately foul? Was I just plain stupid? These were questions I asked myself in my futile attempts to deny the obvious. And yet . . . And yet . . .

And yet, I had friends who never denied me as myself. The small town and smaller community in which I spent many of my formative, impressionable years had a relatively large proportion of Canadians of Japanese descent. It was with these friends that I felt most comfortable and most valued as a person. Perhaps it was because I was so young that I did not realize that my comfort came from their unconditional acceptance of me. I was being treated as though I belonged; as though my being who I was mattered. And I was denying a fact I did not want to know. People treated me differently because I was different. But at that age, I wanted nothing more than to be the same. I had internalized the values and norms of a society that systematically denied the validity of my cultural heritage and denied me access to the opportunities for success that are purported to be the right of all Canadian citizens.

My being Japanese Canadian was and is a major determinant in who I am; but, lest the reader assume that I have idealized the Japanese cultural community in Thunder Bay, let me point out that the feelings of acceptance and comfort originated not from any sense of solidarity or unity within our group, although that may have been a factor, but from the fundamental fact of our being "visible minority" people in a white-dominated culture. All the petty jealousies, rivalries, and misunderstandings that characterize human relationships existed; and economically we were as disparate as any other community, albeit very likely earning an average salary far less than other groups in town.

The issue of salary raises another point that I did not deal with in my original article: that is, socio-economics and how it intersects with race, and ultimately how it is an integral factor in perpetuating the systemic racism that not only still pervades our society but also, in many parts of this country, is strengthening its Vise-Grip hold on the Canadian psyche. If I was unaware that I was both invisible and visible, I was even more unaware that we were an extremely poor family. For that act of grace I thank my loving parents, who, like so many other marginalized parents, through self-denial, frugality, and tremendous sacrifice sustained our extended family through the leanest of postwar years.

One of the last incidents that led to my realization that I was invisible came as a Scout. The Boy Scouts of Canada is an organization devoted to making responsible, dutiful, loyal, honourable young men out of boys. The problem with that definition is that it omits the word "white." To be successful one must subscribe to the ethical values explicit in the Boy Scout motto and attempt to live by them. I was able to pass without much effort the tests required to attain the badges, and I enjoyed immensely the diverse activities sponsored by the organization. But, again, I was troubled. Was I required to believe every word of the motto? I had also been taught that by dint of hard work and striving, I would rise quickly and become a leader among the boys in my troop and that eventually I would be able to help with the younger boys in Wolf Cubs. Now, having risen as far as I could and having become a Queen's Scout, I was still not asked to lead the Cubs, although I had made my willingness to do so well known.

In retrospect, my naiveté is appalling. This organization's Poet Laureate had penned the words "Take up the white man's burden." How could I have expected it to recognize any leadership potential in a non-white person? Or, more insidious still, were the parents afraid that I might instil unacceptable cultural values in their children? But these questions were too perplexing, and, with the optimism of youth, I thought I would have many, many years to answer them.

For me, other, more direct examples abound throughout my life, but I have deliberately chosen to outline the more obscure ones from childhood memories because they seem to me to be the ones that only the victim will remember as significant. The perpetrators would have almost certainly dismissed them as unnoteworthy or, at the very least, as having had a different intent.

I feel it is important to note the dichotomy existing between intent and result. Most Canadians have good intentions. I believe that their intent is not to wilfully harm another individual. The results of some thoughtless actions or words, however, are far different from those anticipated or unperceived by the instigator. From my recollection and analysis of the feelings associated with those recollections, I can assure anyone that the child, and later the man, who were forced to deal with those feelings were lonely and confused. Invisibility is not a happy state; it embodies isolation, self-doubt, and often despair.

One incident left me agitated and confused for months. I couldn't understand, given my transparency, why I had been so ill-used. More often than not I was accustomed to being seen through rather than being noticed. I was about fourteen years old and, like most teenagers, had begun to feel the first vague stirring of rebelliousness that characterizes that age. Several of my friends and I had decided to "play hooky" and skip classes to go to a movie playing in a downtown theatre. To get there we had to take several buses and make two or three transfers. The second time we changed buses, the driver informed me that my transfer was invalid. I explained in a less-than-obsequious tone that since he had accepted my friends' transfers and since the previous driver had punched all of them together, I couldn't understand why he would not accept mine. His loud retort — "You people are all alike — trying to get something for nothing" — left me speechless, and I immediately retreated into invisibility and meekly paid another fare. I was faced with an apparent duality in my existence.

Looking back, I weep for the child whose attempts at assimilation, whose desire to be like everyone else, were among the dominating factors of his childhood. How could he realize that the act of assimilation in itself is a concession to the systemic racism that pervades our society as well as a denial of our own culture, which, for better or worse, has shaped our psyches? In the desire to be accepted by the dominant culture, minorities willingly accept an inferior position that maintains the status quo. "Let's live in harmony" translates to "Don't rock the boat," which in turn means, "Keep your rightful (inferior) place in our society and we can all live in harmony."

Several decades after my recognition of invisibility, I learned not only that I was not invisible, but also that I was a member of a visible minority. That underlying contradiction has informed my life: I am both visible and invisible at the same time. Of course, there had been times as a youth that I had had my differentness thrust on me, but I wasn't ready to recognize that my life had any more facets than I could understand.

Much later, as an adult, I began to build expectations and foster hopes for myself and my family. Having gained some measure of success, I optimistically began a conscious effort to bolster my self-image and to succeed in my society. During that period, my visibility and self-esteem grew.

Armed with fledgling confidence, I sought work and there encountered more striking examples of how my society perceived me. In the final year of my undergraduate degree in English language and literature, I looked for a teaching position with one of the school boards in Metropolitan Toronto, secure in the knowledge that the dearth of teachers would help me find a job I was qualified for. I went to the "cattle auctions," the mass hiring procedures of the day, at Don Mills Collegiate and was promptly offered several positions in Toronto. Unfortunately, none of them were ones I could accept. The interviews began with the usual background questions but ended abruptly when, in every instance except the last, the hiring official asked me whether I was interested in teaching mathematics or science. Here were high-ranking school-board officers who automatically, and to them quite naturally, assumed that because I was Asian I was a math or science major. All stereotyping has a negative aspect. Expectations, the ways in which we view others, and how we react to others are all shaped by what we think we already know about one another. What if I had not been able to acquire a position because people in power made those assumptions about me?

Finally, however, I managed to obtain a job. I mark the beginning of my second, more painful "education" from that moment. Less than two weeks into my first term, one of the more experienced teachers, possibly in an effort to make me feel accepted and at ease with the faculty, related a "humorous" story dealing with a common stereotype about Asians. According to him, because of their slanted eyes Asians couldn't tell the difference between a harbour in Hawaii and a human being and therefore ended up bombing the human. As if noticing me for the first time, he said, "Present company excluded, of course." Those words have come to symbolize for me the insidious affliction that permeates our society. This educator, this shaper of our children's minds, this well-educated man, apparently believed that by mouthing those five meaningless words, and by dint of his maleness and whiteness, he had earned the right to disseminate a racial stereotype that was both harmful to the whole race and demeaning to the individual in whose presence he felt no discomfort in telling the "joke." Looking back, I recall that I laughed harder than the others and I am shamed at my naiveté and my relief at what I thought had been acceptance by the faculty. I felt much like Dudley Moore's character in the movie *Arthur*, who in a drunken state was informed that he was with a prostitute and exclaimed, "Are you a hooker? I thought I was just doing great with you."

As my years of experience in teaching grew, so too did the stockpile of present company excluded jokes, anecdotes, and generalizations; so too did my realization that I was, in fact, not "doing great." I learned through experiences — sometimes humiliating, sometimes bitter, often humorous, but always enlightening — that somehow I needed to try harder to achieve the same successes that seemed to come so easily to those for whom the rules of my society had been made. I had been optimistic enough to imagine that merely by trying harder, I would be rewarded for my efforts. And now I am constantly saddened by many of my "visible" students who believe, infused with the freshness and optimism of youth, that our existing institutions and networks have changed enough so that they will be given the same opportunity as everyone else. I am consumed by the ambivalence of teaching these young people, without fostering a sense of hopelessness, that we live in a country that still requires a great deal of learning, maturing, and changing before it can live up to its claim that we are all equal. The task often seems overwhelming, and I feel much like the politician who would have his country go to war for peace.

But the essence of the human spirit is to strive, and in that striving I encountered another type of behaviour from a source that, although obvious, I had not anticipated. One day in the staff room of my high school I was being subjected to yet another generalization about how "all Asians whom we allow to come to our country take the jobs away from our own unemployed" when our principal came in. The speaker immediately enlisted his complicity, but the principal refused to participate. Instead, he hastily excused himself and left the room. The incident itself was, I am certain, insignificant to both administrator and perpetrator. It served to reinforce for me, however, the latitude that the educational institutions of my province allow in interpreting what appears to me to be a straightforward document, The Ontario Human Rights Code. If silence implies consent, and even if it doesn't, did that principal's silence not give the appearance of agreeing with an unfair and inaccurate stereotype? It is unconscionable that through inaction a respected figure, who possesses the power to discriminate, was a party to the dissemination of harmful stereotypes.

By that time in my career I was secure enough to voice my disagreement with the stereotype, but my effort was dismissed as "just another malcontent who can't take a joke." And he was right. I cannot, nor must I, listen to another joke or generalization that impugns or discredits another person. It is my responsibility, as a teacher and as a member of the human race, not to allow such thoughts or attitudes to go unchallenged.

I see now that this principal's actions and the words of my long-ago colleague who excused his racial slurs and racist attitudes with that loathsome phrase "present company excluded" were merely a harbinger of the practices that would be taken up in the 1990s by, among others, Ontario's provincial government. I suppose the official "stamp of approval" has been bestowed upon policies that tend to exclude and marginalize the poor, the minority groups, the special needs portions of our society, women, and any group that has traditionally been without systemic power or influence: that is to say, all those who are not part of the long-standing power structures upon which our current society has been built. White privilege remains a dominant factor in Canada, and the governments that set legislation bear witness to this fact.

In case I sound like I'm condemning all educators or the entire educational system, let me explain that the examples cited are from my life and are particular to me, although I believe that any person of colour can corroborate, and indeed add to, this compilation of incidents. The point is that none of these situations should have occurred, nor would they have occurred had I not been a member of that part of our society which, through racial background, manifests a discernible difference in habits, looks, speech, or method of worship. Of course, to be different implies a "norm" from which to differ; and that "norm" in North American society is white and Eurocentric, and it has dominated this continent since it was forcibly imposed upon the First Nations of this country. That "norm" carries with it all the privileges that our society has gone to great lengths to deny it possesses.

I have stated before that I believe most people would not intentionally hurt another human being, and I fervently hope that explaining the degree of unintentional anguish caused by the privileged position of some unthinking individuals will serve to enlighten those people and provide some insight into the repercussions of their thoughtlessness. Most teachers I know are sensitive and kind, but even they have difficulty recognizing that if they are white, of European descent, and additionally male, they are endowed with privileges that, having been scrupulously hidden or assumed for so long, have become, for them, a right. For example, I am curious about how many white, Anglo-Saxon Canadians have been asked to speak for people of their race; or to write an article explaining their experiences in our society; or to go into a history class and explain how their parents were interned by their government; or to anglicize the spelling of their names or even change their names so they could be more easily recognized and pronounced; or how many opportunities were made available to them through no virtue of their own. However, the controversy over what is a right and what is a privilege is easily settled if one remembers that in our democracy, the rights of one must be the rights of all. And that reality is patently a myth.

Yet another, more recent, example provides startling insight into how some people think. Not long ago, as a former internee in a British Columbian internment camp, I received the Canadian government's redress payment along with a letter of apology and a formal acknowledgement of the mistake that had been made. Having been born in Canada and considering myself Canadian in all respects, I was thrilled at the thought that my government had been capable of admitting error and was taking measures to rectify the injustice. Naturally, I felt that other Canadians would share my elation and perceive the action as right and just.

Unfortunately, I had overestimated the vision of some of my teaching colleagues. In an initially casual conversation about the redress issue, one individual in our group remarked that it was only because "we," meaning white Canadians of European descent, had allowed the Japanese Canadians to assimilate so easily that "they" had managed to bring the issue to a beneficial conclusion. When some others, perceiving the unreasonableness of the assertion, would not allow that he was correct, he immediately shifted to another line of attack, which was to point to the inequity of redress for only one group. We all agreed and stated further that if the Canadian government was serious in its efforts to be equitable, it should consider redress for all the groups who had been wronged, especially those people who had the least influence. He persisted by stating that it was only the Japanese who would take advantage of having been educated in "our" country and then would use that education to subvert Canada. My argument that rather than subverting the country we had made it more truly democratic and responsive to the needs of its people fell on deaf ears, and I was left with a feeling of frustration and despair.

Obviously, my antagonist had no interest in an intelligent discussion and was interested only in expressing his views and having them accepted by the present company. However, in this case the present company had not been excluded; it was, in fact, the very target for his vituperation. As is so often the case when people discuss matters pertaining to race, ethnicity, and who belongs, his emotions rather than his intellect had seized control of his arguments and rendered them easily assailable. But he was adamant. No amount of arguing or reasoning would sway him from his convictions. His philosophy that Canada would be a much better place if "those other people" had not been allowed to immigrate was as hard and unshakable as the lump forming inside me as I listened, by now silently and sadly.

Perhaps because it occurred relatively recently, perhaps because the person involved is well educated and holds a responsible position in our society, this particular incident left me unusually depressed. Had we come such a short way in such a long time? Can we ever hope to generate an understanding that will attenuate the rift between the ideals of our nation and the reality of discrimination and prejudice that still flourishes here today? I still believe we can.

Looking back, I notice that most of my examples are negative. I cannot, however, apologize for my choices, for they have been made consciously and with much thought. Let me say, though, that while I can remember some positive examples of incidents resulting from my race or appearance, even they, upon analysis, seem to be based on a tokenistic or at best patronizing approach to me as a person. Overall, the "warm-glow" memories are the result of my relationships with people from other minority groups as well as other Japanese Canadians, and only a very few result from my interactions with dominant-culture Canadians.

I have come to believe that the colleague who participated in the 69 redress conversation is not well intentioned, nor is he a caring, compassionate individual. I believe he is a person who, like many who share his ideals, is becoming increasingly more anxious as minority groups, despite systemic barriers to success, become more vociferous in their demands for equality and fairness. He represents what I fervently pray is a minuscule group of teachers who continue to perpetuate the myths of white dominance and superiority.

I believe that education is the route to attenuate that rift, and I believe that true strength does, indeed, lie in diversity. As a teacher I have attended many workshops and teacher in-service sessions dealing with anti-racist education and equity issues. I have been astonished at the vast numbers of well-informed and well-intentioned people from all cultures, ethnicities, and races who are working together to re-create a vision of Canada that is truly multicultural. Much remains to be done, but with current ministry of education mandates to school boards on equity issues, as well as the growing awareness that our educational and other institutions systematically exclude a wide variety of individuals from enjoying the advantages of other groups in our population, we have begun a process that could lead to a truly equal society. I'm not sure how long the process will take, but I do know, to paraphrase Bob Dylan, that the norms, they are a-changin'. And the people, they are a-waitin'.

My belief that we can eliminate racist behaviours and eventually racist attitudes and that we can create a country based on principles of fairness and human decency remains unshaken despite the directions that many of our institutions appear to be going in. When I first paraphrased Bob Dylan I did not imagine that the norms would change to the extent to which they have; nor did I imagine the way in which they would change. For, like Dylan, I imagined a shift towards mutual tolerance, acceptance, and co-operation as well as an impetus to begin building a truly multicultural nation. Instead, what appears to have transpired is a regression to the insular, suspicion-laden times most evident during the war years and immediately after. The rift between those who possess power and the ability to succeed in our society and those who do not possess it has become much greater in the meantime.

I also stated, mistakenly, that "with current ministry of education mandates to school boards on equity issues, as well as the growing awareness that our educational and other institutions systematically exclude a wide variety of individuals from enjoying the advantages of other groups in our population, we have begun a process that could lead to a truly equal society." What has actually happened in Ontario is that the Equity Department has been dismantled and funding for equity issues has dwindled immensely. Apparently, the provincial government believes that there is no longer any need to address issues dealing with fairness for all students, including those with special needs and with linguistic challenges, or those who are recent immigrants. But schools must continue to try to meet these needs because the needs will always be there and, I believe, the human spirit will endure and outlast any misguided notions or uncaring, unresponsive regimes.

I hope that no one any longer believes that there are no racists in Canada and that all Japanese Canadians are inscrutable, polite, and humble . . . present company excluded, of course.

PART III

ROOTS OF IDENTITY, ROUTES TO KNOWING

Revealing Moments: The Voice of One Who Lives with Labels

....

Didi Khayatt

Moment # 1

The year was 1981. I was a graduate student at the Ontario Institute for Studies in Education, working on my Ph.D. I was also a novice feminist, listening to the words of my professors and fellow students and absorbing the ideas that were changing my life and my thoughts. We were being taught to attend to the words of other women, and to locate ourselves in our research. That day in class, the discussion centred on immigrant women. Students were attempting to grapple with the new (to us) sociological methodology that began from the standpoint of the oppressed, in this case, "immigrant women," and not from a defined sociological category. The debate had been raging for close to an hour when finally the professor was asked to give her opinion regarding what constituted an "immigrant woman." The professor smiled, looked in my direction, and said, "We have an immigrant woman in our midst, why don't we ask her what she thinks?" Following the professor's example, the whole class focused on the space where I was seated, and, likewise, I, too, glanced behind me, trying to find the "immigrant woman" to whom the professor was referring. In my astonishment at being included in that category, I was rendered speechless. It had never occurred to me that I could be perceived as an "immigrant woman," a category that, to be precise, did include me because I had emigrated from Egypt in 1967, but one that did not fit me any more than it did our "immigrant" British professor.

Why did I reject being included in the category "immigrant woman"? Why did I feel the label did not fit? We had just been told that people who originated in white, Western, industrialized countries were not considered "immigrant." I came from Egypt. Why did I think I did not qualify?

In Canada the term "immigrant" technically refers to any individual who has a legal status of landed immigrant or permanent resident as opposed to being a citizen. It is a temporary category intended not only to represent a period of adjustment, but also to include an interval during which those who are being considered as potential citizens can be evaluated. Individuals are given rights and privileges in areas of work and education but are not yet able to vote or carry Canadian passports. Indeed, historically, immigration policies were traditionally tied to labour needs and the political and economic imperative of populating certain areas of Canada with communities of skilled and unskilled labour. However, as Roxana Ng suggests, the term is used in government documents to suggest all persons who are "foreign-born," regardless of their citizenship status. She continues: "In common-sense usage, however, not all foreign-born persons are actually *seen* as immigrants; nor do they see *themselves* as 'immigrants.' The common-sense usage of 'immigrant women' generally refers to women of colour, women from Third World countries, women who do not speak English well, and women who occupy lower positions in the occupational hierarchy." I agree with Ng that there is a disjunction between the legal government definition and the common-sense notion of what comprises an "immigrant woman."

Moment # 2

I was recently going up the elevator with one of the cleaning staff of my building. Since I often saw her, smiled, and had always greeted her previously, it was appropriate that in the time we had to go up nineteen floors we would engage in a short conversation. I asked her where she was from. She answered, "Me from Korea." I informed her that I was from Egypt. She smiled at me and said, "No, you Canadian, me Korean." I laughed and insisted that I was from Egypt. She was adamant. She kept shaking her head and repeating, "You Canadian, me Korean," right up to the floor where I got off.

What had this woman seen in me that was Canadian, that denied my assurance to her that I came from Egypt? Evidently, she perceived me as assimilated, as having power, and, in her eyes, as undifferentiated from those people who fit her notion of "Canadian." Although not all immigrant women are "visible minorities" (another state-originated term) like this Korean woman, and not all visible minorities are foreign-born, often both categories are *perceived* as almost interchangeable. Frequently, as Ng points out, the situations of Canadian-born visible minorities and immigrants are similar in many respects because of the race and class biases inherent in the social structure.

In her analysis of theories of race and class oppression, Caroline Ramazanoglu argues against the notion that racism can often be reduced to class. She rightly points out that Black women and, I add, women of colour, "are not uniformly oppressed and they can have contradictory interests in which race, class, ethnicity and nationality cut across each other." Furthermore, she asserts that colour "is not a static or universal category of disadvantage that transcends all other sources of social difference which determine the quality of people's lives." Although I agree with Ramazanoglu's position, I suggest that colour is *perceived* to be a category of disadvantage, as are other labels, such as "immigrant," "visible minority," "refugee," "person from a developing or Third World country," and so on. This perception does not just stem from bigotry, but is in keeping with official government ideology that has designated individuals who fit into state categories of gender and/or of multiculturalism[1] as disadvantaged minorities who should be protected from discrimination and assisted in maintaining equal access to Canadian standards of living. The state, for the most part, has defined those categories, and as such they have entered the currency of institutional language. They each have a state-produced definition that is designed to signal difference but at the same time to protect those included in these classifications from social and economic discrimination in this society.

It is precisely because of the perception that these categories are of disadvantage that I am concerned with indiscriminate labelling of individuals. To call me an "immigrant woman" or a "woman of colour" is to trivialize the very real oppressions of those who are within these categories and who are disadvantaged. Moreover, those "benign" categories themselves, although useful for state-supported policies of employment equity or legal bases for human rights complaints, are not as effective for the individuals themselves who are named within them. They often do not locate themselves in that manner precisely because the categories emphasize what seems to be an inalienable difference between themselves and the rest of the population. These classifications are significant when they are appropriated to provide a feeling of belonging to a community, where this self-labelling may develop into an accepted identity, or whenever these terms are taken up by the women so identified and transformed into a political identity. For instance, being referred to as a "woman of colour" merely because a person belongs to a particular ethnic group, regardless of whether this individual shares any common concerns, becomes more a means of slotting people to force containment; whereas in self-labelling, even if the same term is applied it is used by the people themselves to achieve a cohesive community of support based on shared concerns or political perspectives.

Here I want to use my own experience to discuss the intersections of sex, race, class, and ethnicity. I am interested in examining how, in the process of assimilating into a new culture, one finds the self-definitions that will eventually comprise one's identity. I shall also investigate the distinctions made between the various expressions of dominant white culture and minority groups within the social contexts of Canada. Finally, I shall demonstrate how the categories used to describe race and ethnicity operate differently to keep certain groups oppressed when particular elements are present. These include such factors as sex, religion, sexuality, class, language, financial situation, education, and relative darkness of skin, combined with an individual's particular history.

I came to Canada in the late sixties to do graduate work. At the end of my first year in this country, I decided I wanted to stay and I applied for immigration status. At that time, the process included an application form, a set fee, and, most important, an appointment with an immigration officer who would assess, based on a predetermined point system, whether I, as a candidate, was suitable to become a landed immigrant. According to Alma Estable, this hurdle consisted of assigning points to different categories, the most significant of which were employment skills and professional qualifications. Immigrants were also "assessed on the basis of their personal characteristics (such as age and professional qualifications), education, possession of a skill in demand." Because it was quantifiable, this system was supposed to be neutral and equitable. However, it should be

77

noted that the linking of citizenship with occupation points to a system located within the dynamics of capitalism. Canada needed (and still needs) young, skilled immigrants; therefore practical training and work experience comprised the category that yielded the highest points. For my appointment with the immigration officer, I dressed up and made a special effort to look "good," not that I had any idea what would really make a difference. I presented myself at the appointed time, and we proceeded with the interview. On the one hand, my age, my very fluent English, and my education, as well as my knowledge of Canada's second official language, French, gave me a certain number of points. On the other hand, my chosen field of anthropology did not rate at all on the priority list of needed skills, nor did I gain any points because of professional capacity. I had never worked in my life, not even at a summer job. The education officer questioned me regarding sponsorship by a relative, an organization, or a company. I had none. Did I presently have a job? No. What kind of work was I capable of doing? I was a cultural anthropologist; my choices were limited. The poor man obviously wanted to give me the points, but I was clearly ten short of the required number and no amount of prodding into my professional experience could produce one single point more. Finally, he just looked at me, smiled, and said, "I know. I shall give you ten points for charm."

Would I have obtained these points had I spoken English haltingly? Would he have had the same measure of patience with my lack of skills and work experience had he perceived me as a visible minority? The accredited "charm" that the immigration officer appreciated relied on a combination of social relations that are not quantifiable, nor were they meant to be. Points were based on very practical state-defined occupational categories as well as potential characteristics that would eventually lead to job proficiency. I was assigned ten points based on nothing more functional than class and gender. I was located as a woman with no colour. My differentness was invisible. I was perceived as posing no threat to the ruling white system. As a woman, my potential for work was trivial when compared with my youthfulness, and thus my procreational capacity. Therefore, I would suggest, what he saw was a woman of the right age and class to marry well, after which my assimilation would eventually be complete.

The assumptions implicit in the categories of "immigrant woman," "woman of colour," and "visible minority" conceal real differences in experience and do not account for or distinguish between the various levels of oppression. They assume a homogeneity of background amongst all people who fall into those various groupings. As

Linda Carty and Dionne Brand point out, these terms are "void of any race or class recognition and, more importantly, of class struggle or struggle against racism." Who is entitled to determine who we are? How are those labels made to apply to various people? What do the labels really signify, and how does that translate itself in the experiences of the individuals to whom they are applied? The question becomes not who we are, but who we are perceived to be. It is not my identity that is of concern, but the appropriate label that can be attached to me and can decipher what I represent. The labels are applied by those in power to differentiate between themselves and those they want to exclude, and they accomplish this on the basis of race, class, ethnicity, and other factors. Or, as Carty and Brand suggest, "State policy around issues of race, class, or sex can be characterized as policy of containment and control."

When asked how I identify myself, who I am and where I come from, my responses vary according to: a) the questioner (who is asking me, what I perceive is her/his interest in knowing, how she/he is going to use the answers and how I think they will be used, what the relations of power are between the questioner and myself); b) the context of the questions (an interview, the topic at hand, the discussion that frames the question); and c) the circumstances under which the questions are asked (friendship, intimacy, making acquaintances, first meeting, and family, for instance). In each case, my answer will be different, and the differences will be generated from the relative safety of the situation and the interest of the questioner. My answer will contain elements of pride, uncertainty, political correctness, concealment of aspects that can be misconstrued, or that are threatening; in the same way, it will include aspects of my social self that I feel will make my listener think the best of me — at least for a moment.

Therefore, in disclosing my identity to you, I will say this: I am a woman. I am an Egyptian Copt. I come from the upper class. I am a feminist. I am a lesbian. Your labels for me may include: woman of colour, immigrant woman, Third World woman. When I asked a friend recently what she thought was the difference between "identity" and "label," she answered with little hesitation, "Identity defines, labels limit." To me, identity is that part of me that needs to fit into a group, the need to see a reflection of myself in that group. It is the safety of belonging. What you choose to call me, the label by which you refer to me, may have little to do with what I call myself. It has more to do with how you treat me, with how you treat the group with which I identify. Mistreatment on the basis of a label is discrimination. It may be against one individual or aimed at all those included within the disparaged category. However, the distinction between identity and label may become blurred when the label is threatening in a way to marginalize or exclude the one labelled. For instance, I may have been sexually involved with women, but have chosen not to identify as a lesbian. Or, conversely, I may identify as a lesbian, but be afraid to disclose it publicly.

Moment # 3

Several years after I obtained my landed immigrant status, I was finally granted citizenship. By that time I had qualified as a secondary school teacher and had been gainfully employed by a Northern Ontario board. The day I was supposed to be sworn in was finally at hand and I presented myself at the local courthouse. The judge had come all the way from Toronto for just this occasion, to oversee the transition from immigrant to citizen of several people. There were only five of us: a Chinese family of three, an Italian man, and myself. After the ceremony, we were all invited to attend a tea given by the I.O.D.E (Imperial Order Daughters of the Empire) where they were to present us with a few mementoes, a Bible, and a Canadian flag, to commemorate the occasion. I crossed the street from the courthouse to the church basement and found myself surrounded by older women bent on making me feel "welcome to Canada," my new land. Since the other four people had great difficulty with English, I became the centre of attraction, the one queried about conditions in my "old" country. The gist of the conversation was to make me articulate how I had left behind a dreadful situation to come to this land of plenty. The questions revolved around how we dress in Egypt, what and how we eat, do we have cars, or is our public transportation based on camel power. I thought they were joking. I believed that they spoke in stereotypes on purpose, and I played along. I laughed at their references and exaggerated differences, all in the name of fun, until the moment I left. Since I was the only Egyptian for miles around in that Northern Ontario town, people often made humorous allusions to pyramids and camels in order to tease me. It never occurred to me that these women were deadly serious. I did not take offence at the conversation.

I did not translate the exchanges as a level of racism. I knew my background, and therefore I did not perceive their presumptions about Egypt as being anything more than lack of information. Many years later, when I understood the language of racism, this incident fell into place; I recognized their benevolent attention, not as welcoming me, but as relegating me to my "proper" place as grateful immigrant. Racism is not about colour, it is about power. Racism *is* power. It is not only a recognition of difference, but also the explicit emphasis on difference to mediate hierarchy based on colour, ethnicity, language, and race. Those women would probably not have seen me as particularly distinctive if I had met them socially without mention of my cultural background. Within the framework of my class, they had no power over me, which is why I took no offence at their words. I was neither destitute, nor was I essentially dependent on Canada for my well-being. I had emigrated for personal reasons that had more to do with the necessity of finding myself than the urgency of earning my living.

In a recurrent discussion with my friend Marian McMahon (where she plays devil's advocate) she suggests that just because I am not conscious of racism does not mean that I do not bear the brunt of racist attitudes and remarks. When I interject that racism serves to place an individual in a vulnerable position, that, like sexism, it is flagged as a fundamental difference to highlight hierarchy and therefore justify discrimination, she agrees, but argues that as with those women who say they are not oppressed, my inability to feel oppressed is a denial of my status as a woman of colour, indeed, is in itself a form of internalized racism on my part. I take up her discourse seriously. However, I see that because of my privileged background I can hardly qualify as "a woman of colour," and it would be inconsistent with the spirit of the common-sense usage of the word for me to assume that label when I have never been submitted to the anguish of discrimination, the alienation of being slotted without my consent, or the experience of being silenced.

Moment # 4

In 1967 I enrolled in graduate studies at the University of Alberta, Edmonton. I was twenty-three. My entire formal education had been in English up to this point, and I spoke French and Arabic as well. Shortly after my arrival, the chair of the department in which I was enrolled invited all new graduate students and faculty to a party at his house to meet the rest of the department. I attended. I mingled. I exchanged pleasantries with many people. I answered innumerable questions about my country, our traditions, our ways of eating and dressing. When I thought it was appropriate to leave, I went to my host, who promptly accompanied me to find my coat and boots, scarf and gloves. It was late October in Edmonton. At the front door, in full view of a roomful of his guests, after he turned and winked at them in collusion, he offered me his hand to wish me good night. Since I was already dressed to go out I tendered my gloved hand, and, following the rules of formal social conventions I had been taught, I said, with all the dignity of youth, "Please excuse my gloves." At which point the entire roomful of people who had been watching our exchange burst into laughter. I looked at them in surprise, and left without bothering to give or receive any explanation. To my youthful, naive eyes, these people proved to be boors without redemption. Not for a single second did it occur to me that my behaviour was inappropriate, or that I needed to feel self-conscious. To me, they were simply amiss in their manners.

Laughter and humour, when aimed at a certain person who is not "in the know" because she is new to a culture, or is different from the rest of the group in some way(s), is a method of ridicule or mockery. It is particularly so when the person being laughed at is not included in the jocularity. If I had not had the assurance of privilege, the knowledge that my manners were impeccable, the assumption that my class background transcends most Western cultures, I would have withered in shame, wondered at my possible faux pas, and wilted from the insensitivity of these, perhaps, well-meaning strangers. However, I did not give them a second thought. In the same way that I knew the term "immigrant woman" did not quite apply to me, I did not experience this incident as a humiliation or negative comment on my race or ethnicity. Even though I had just arrived from Egypt, a country considered "Third World," even though as a new graduate student I was at the bottom of the intellectual hierarchy in that department, and even though I was probably perceived as non-white, I had the composure of class and the confidence of privilege to protect me from the exclusion to which I may otherwise have been subjected and of which I may have been made an object.

From a very young age I was taught that I was a daughter of privilege, from a family of a certain class, from a particular city in the south of Egypt. Managing class is not just the knowledge that one is born to privilege, but also the understanding that this privilege may transcend different social and cultural changes. For instance, it did not come as a surprise to me when one day, as I was shopping for a sofabed in Eaton's department store in Toronto, the salesman recognized my family name. He came from Egypt and asked me the inevitable question to verify whether I came from that certain city in Upper Egypt and whether I was a Copt. Even though I was living on the limited means of a graduate student, he was immediately deferential. It was not me personally that he recognized, but how class operated in Egypt. The major discount he gave me was, perhaps, a reflection of his acknowledgement that, even in this new country, he had not forgotten the conventions of our past lives, that we both belonged — if differently — to a distant past, that in the vast sea of Canadian foreignness, we shared a common history.

The formation of my identity includes my class, colour, ethnicity, sex, sexuality, and religion. These factors seem to have been constant since I was old enough to identify myself. They are my location. However, other elements just as important are variable, their relevance modified by changes in personal politics, circumstances, age, career, current ideologies, the general political climate.

I came to this country over three decades ago. I could speak both official languages fluently and with minimum accent. The relative lightness of my skin colour combined with my privileged class background has spared me from experiences of discrimination or prejudice. At best, I intimidated people around me; at worst, they found me exotic. Even though "exotic" is, broadly speaking, a form of racist categorization, the word is often used to imply a kind of difference that is coveted rather than scorned. Although I claim not to have suffered racism, I am often made to feel aware of my differentness. Strangers regularly mispronounce my name, but then people in North America often stumble over names that are not simple to spell or are uncommon. When I refuse to use my first name, Madiha, it is because of the way in which it is frequently butchered, and because it is seldom remembered (even when people comment on "what a pretty name" it is). Moreover, as a result of its foreignness, if my name is being called out so I can take my turn at being served, it is often presumed that I do not understand English (especially if I hesitate before answering). I am addressed, therefore, in that loud, overenunciated diction that assumes that volume will make up for language. But it takes only a moment to set people straight. I would maintain that those incidents are very minor, that if they constitute racism they, essentially, do not have any recognizable consequence on my life.

I have been assimilated well. I do not stand out. I have had to adjust to Canadian cultural significations, not to prevent discrimination against me, but to avert feelings of inadequacy that may spring from lack of communication. I have had to alter my British accent, to tone down my formal manners, to adapt to many Canadian customs and traditions. I have learned to use cultural referents to project the messages I want to convey. Consequently, I become invisible because I am recognizable. What is concealed is my history; what is hidden is my Egyptianness. However, I am in a position to produce my history when it suits me, when it adds a new dimension to my qualities, and certainly not when it can be held against me. Can it be said that my very insistence on assimilating is itself a response to levels of internalized racism? Is the invisibility of my foreignness precisely an indication of racism? I have argued that I do not suffer racism because of class and skin colour. This does not deny that racism exists, but it does suggest that, given certain other factors, I am not touched by its virulence. My assertions contain elements of contradiction because they stem from a complicated issue. The fact remains that I am spared, that in the ability to define my own identity, to convey a specific persona, to contain these contradictions, I can control how I am perceived. I choose to make myself invisible only in that I want to blend; I do not want to stand out. Consequently, although I can be heard, a part of me is silenced.

Rigid definitions of race and ethnicity, which do not account for the fluidity of the categories, are not useful in that they mask the differences of class and location. They fail to respect individual identities or to take into account lived experiences. Conversely, gender as a category, when considered a basis for discrimination without accounting for class or for race, conceals distinct and intelligible levels of oppression within the category. And yet, Catharine MacKinnon reminds us, "To argue that oppression 'as a woman' negates rather than encompasses recognition of the oppression of women on other bases, is to say that there is no such thing as the practice of sex inequality." It is also difficult to forget an early comment by Audre Lorde, who informs us succinctly, "Black feminists speak as women because we are women." Feminism transcends yet recognizes difference. As a feminist, I bring to the discussion of race and gender the specificities of colour and class. Unless the boundaries of race, gender, class, and sexuality intersect to make visible the various nuances of each category, the usefulness of each becomes lost in a hierarchy of oppressions. In other words, if we isolate each characteristic in an attempt to make it visible without taking the whole framework into consideration, we are, in effect, rendering invisible the significant factors that combine to produce situations of oppression and discrimination. We are reduced to piling one oppression onto another to show the extent of discrimination, or we attempt to debate which form of oppression — race or gender or class or sexuality — is more potent.

Gender, race, class, and sexuality have to be considered together and at the same time. They must each convey specific location without denying the distinctiveness of individual experiences.

If I have personally ever felt the alienation of national identity, it was not in Canada but in Egypt. Egypt, situated in what Europeans called "the Orient," is anchored in people's minds as "a place of romance, exotic beings, haunting memories and landscapes," but, as Edward Said continues, "The Orient was almost a European invention." In Egypt, where colonization by the French and English has reworked class structures to incorporate Western notions of "culture" and "education," upper-class society demands an understanding and consideration of, and an affinity with, the conquerors, with their locus of power. Some of the questions Said addresses in his book are appropriate: "What . . . sorts of intellectual, aesthetic, scholarly, and cultural energies went into the making of an imperialist tradition? . . . What is the meaning of originality, of continuity, of individuality, in this context? How does Orientalism transmit or reproduce itself from one epoch to another?" I am a product of this problematic. Despite my pure Coptic origins, each member of my family sports a European name: my father Andrew, my uncles Albert, Maurice, and Robert, and my aunts Edna, Margaret, and Dora. My generation was defiantly christened with Arabic names, another conqueror, but closer in geography and culture. It is in Egypt, where I have never properly learned my native tongue, that I feel like a foreigner. I have never read Egyptian literature except in translation. The literary imagery that informed my youth is that of distant lands. I recited poems on daffodils when I had never set eyes on one. I described fields, streams, and forests while living in a land of intensive agriculture and wasted deserts. I knew of snow but had never experienced it. I enjoyed Western toys, bought real estate in London playing British Monopoly, and donned clothes made in Europe. I attended French and English schools, and a U.S. university. I walked the streets of Cairo and felt I did not belong because I spoke my own language with the exaggerated enunciation of one who is not using it continually; my idioms are outdated, my expression forgotten. When I return to my native land, I stand as foreign, am perceived as alien. I was never assimilated because class demanded a perceived difference from the masses. In Canada I am integrated because my survival depends on my being like everybody else.

Finally, living in Canada, I have had to adjust to Canadian culture so as to be seen and as a way to be recognized. However, for me to include myself in a category such as "immigrant woman" or "woman of colour" would be to deny the very real experiences of oppression suffered by those who are truly disadvantaged within those labels.

Furthermore, within the framework of politically correct discourse, I would be given legitimacy to speak if I were to mention that I am a woman of colour. I would be granted even greater licence as a lesbian woman of colour. However, I do not believe in a hierarchy of oppressions. I do not want to be heard through a label imposed on me, through white guilt, but rather because of the validity of my words — whether I am a woman of colour or not. I do not want to be erased as a consequence of an assumed identity. As a woman, I have too often been silenced. As a lesbian, I have frequently been paralysed. As an immigrant, a woman of colour, I might be given a voice because of the current political climate. But this voice is not mine; it belongs to those who live with the daily burden of those oppressions.

Afterthoughts

Since this article was first written, my thinking has shifted on several issues. Indeed, I would say that I have moved away from the whole theoretical framework of the original article. Firstly, I do not see identity locations as fixed categories that define us. Therefore the concept of "intersections," which relies on the notion of a stable identity, ceases to make sense. I now understand that identities are unstable, that they shift relationally, and that they need a context to frame them and give them meaning. I also believe that individuals are multidimensional, complex human beings with identities that are unsettled, that grow, and that are contextual. People embody their gender, race, sexuality, ability, and so on, always at the same time; it is those who are labelling or merely observing who put one or more dimensions in the forefront.

Secondly, I claim in the article that I do not consider myself a "woman of colour." This odd notion came from the realization that because of my relatively light skin colour I often pass as white. I could not see myself claiming an identity when I had not paid "my dues." My skin colour does not trouble people. It does not shock them into recognitions of difference. While my "Egyptianness" is exoticized, it does not disrupt the taken-for-granted whiteness. So, while I recognized that I was not white, I also did not feel that I deserved to claim the identity of "woman of colour," especially at a time when universities were nodding in the direction of affirmative action policies that favoured non-white hirings. Today I insist on being seen as a woman of colour. I claim my brownness for political reasons and because I recognize that even if my skin does not necessarily indicate difference, my ethnic and cultural background certainly does.

Thirdly, although I hint at issues of social class in the article, I do not confront the difficulties I have with some of the notions that define class. I state throughout that I come from the upper class in Egypt, but I do not analyse how this has influenced my life in Canada, except anecdotally. I have always had trouble with how class is defined and framed, especially with respect to recent immigrants. Even socio-economic factors are not good indicators of social class. An individual, for instance, could have been a poet in his/her country of birth but is a "blue-collar" worker in this country. The underlying assumption in the article is that all people who are brown are taken to be working class. I did not delve into this taken-for-granted notion.

Finally, in the opening story of the article, why did I not recognize myself as being in the category of "immigrant woman"? We had just been told that people who originated from white, Western, industrialized countries were not perceived as "immigrant." I came from Egypt. Why did I not think the label fit me?

I understood even then that one of the reasons for my inability to recognize myself as an "immigrant woman" had to do with the category "immigrant" and how it was understood in Canadian culture, but still I would analyse the moment differently today. I know of at least three ways of taking up the term: the first is the legal definition, which refers to any individual whose legal status in Canada defines them as "landed immigrant" in accordance with the Immigration Act. It is a temporary category intended to indicate a period of adjustment and evaluation. Individuals who fit into that status are given the rights and privileges of a citizen of Canada in areas of work and education but are not yet able to vote or carry Canadian passports.

The second defining concept of the term "immigrant woman" is the common-sense interpretation that shifts the understanding of "immigrant" from anyone who is "foreign-born" to anyone who relocates in Canada from a "developing country." Roxana Ng (1987: 29) suggests, "Not all foreign-born persons are actually *seen* as immigrants; nor do they see *themselves* as 'immigrant.' The common sense usage of 'immigrant women' generally refers to women of colour, women from Third World countries, women who do not speak English well, and women who occupy lower positions in the occupational hierarchy." Finally, a political understanding of the term "immigrant" would recognize on whose land we are settled, and therefore, as Celia Haig-Brown (2000) reminds us, everyone who is not of Aboriginal descent is an immigrant in this country.

That day in class it was easy not to see myself in the term "immigrant woman" because the common-sense understanding of the term precludes someone like myself, who is upper class, educated, and relatively white-skinned, from recognizing herself in that term. Furthermore, I ask myself, how many people who are white and middle class, and speak either English or French as a first language, ever think of themselves as immigrant, especially if their family has been in Canada for several generations?

Acknowledgements

I gratefully acknowledge the support and ideas of Marian McMahon, Frieda Forman, Linda Carty, Peggy Bristow, Mary Lou Soutar-Hynes, and my sister, Dina Khayatt. They should get the credit for refining my thinking, although I take the responsibility for my words.

A version of this paper appeared in *Canadian Woman's Studies*, vol. 14, no. 2 (Spring 1994).

Note

1 "Multiculturalism" is a term that expresses the varied ethnic heritages of Canadians. *The Collins Dictionary of Canadian History, 1867 to the Present* by David J. Bercuson and J.L. Granatstein (Toronto: Collins, 1988), p.143, states that the term was first heard in the 1960s "as a counter to the emphasis on Bilingualism and Biculturalism that characterized the Liberal Government." The authors explain that the "ethos of multiculturalism is that every Canadian, whatever his or her origin, has the right to honour his or her heritage in Canada." However, the dictionary also notes that government policies of multiculturalism were subsequently perceived to be a political tool to remove francophone concerns from the limelight by introducing those of other rapidly growing ethnicities. This strategy promoted a politics of divide and rule by using federal funds. Marjory Bowker distinguishes between two versions of multiculturalism, in the first of which "all cultures are allowed to prosper and flourish amongst their followers; that nothing in the law be allowed to impede the personal enjoyment and enrichment to be derived from one's ethnic heritage." The other version, like the above, "concerns government funding for ethnic programs which tend to divide rather than unite, resulting in a loss of cohesiveness and eventually a fragmented Canadian culture." Marjorie Bowker, *Canada's Constitutional Crisis: Making Sense of It All* (Edmonton, Alta.: Lone Pine Publishing, 1991), p.87.

German-Japanese-American-Canadian: Chapters in a Twentieth-Century Life

••••••••••••••••••••••••••••••

Gottfried Paasche

I

In the early days of 1991, the winter after Saddam Hussein marched into Kuwait, when the United States was escalating its threat of retaliation, even though I had no sympathy for the Iraqi I found my spirits falling every time President Bush hurled an ultimatum at Saddam. I told my friends and colleagues in Canada, where I had been living for twenty-five years, that my America was a kind, generous place; Americans were not a warlike people. Then, as I was walking across the campus of York University, where I teach sociology, it struck me that I myself had once been conquered by the Americans. I was identifying with the object of American wrath! Immediately my spirits lifted and I assumed a more rational stance towards the conflict. I was finding out that I had quite an ambivalent, conflict-laden sense of identity when it came to the United States, where I had lived the formative years of my consciously intellectual life.

I was born in Japan in 1937 to German parents who were in self-imposed exile from Germany. We lived through the Second World War in rural Japan. At the end of the war, when all my Japanese playmates felt the pain of national humiliation, in order to come to terms as a child with the defeat of Japan I embraced my U.S. conquerors as all good. During the war my parents had withheld the nature of their own loyalties from me, and they had also not given me any help in making my own belated transition once the war ended. Many years later Canada seemed to be a kind of solution for me, unwittingly grasped, because it was neither Germany nor America. I thought I had laid to rest my earlier Japanese identity.

Here I will explore how three parts of my life, divided into infancy and childhood in wartime Japan, boyhood and youth and education in postwar United States, and maturity and professional life in Canada, were entwined around a long, almost-invisible stock of German parentage and heritage, and how each made its own demands on a spirit that was pulled many ways.

II

In March 1948, three years after the end of the Second World War, my family emigrated to the United States. I spoke Japanese before either German or English. I learned German from my parents in my immediate family, and English in nursery school in Tokyo. Although I have lived significant segments of my life in Japan, the United States, and Canada, one constant throughout has been the German language.

It was part of the Japanese ethos of that time that foreigners in their land maintain their own language and identity, in effect, their own place. One of the first decisions a foreigner made in Japan was whether to live in a Japanese or a Western-style house, and whether or not to live in a part of town or a region in which there were many Western homes and institutions. My parents' inclinations, and the circumstances that brought them to Japan, predisposed them to live only marginally among other Germans. It led them to live among and associate with the Japanese themselves, and with others from non-German or non-conventional (for example, non-Nazi) German backgrounds. Hence my early acquisition of both the Japanese and English languages.

My memory of playmates and friends begins mostly after 1941, when all those foreigners whose countries of citizenship declared war on Japan and who could leave had left Japan. I had one playmate whose parents were German (of a family that had roots in Japan), and the rest were Japanese. I don't recall being aware of being German, or of being different from the Japanese. I grew up identifying deeply with Japan. The isolation of war, and the difficulties of daily living that we shared with the Japanese around us, probably made it easier to be and to feel Japanese.

On the street my sisters and I played with neighbourhood children. There were all kinds of games to be played. However, our more intimate family associations tended to be with families that had Western educations and connections. For instance, we were very close to a family that held a leadership position in the local Christian community. Although we were not particularly Christian, it did serve as a common bond in contrast to the majority Japanese society. I spent endless hours in the midst of this family that lived completely in a Japanese fashion.

I was sometimes thrown into conflicting situations. On the same street along which I joined village children in playing highly dramatic and intense war games, I was also followed by gangs of children yelling *"gei jin, gei jin"* ("foreigner, foreigner"). Later, when I was of school age, I would sometimes be the centre of attention because of my exotic — in the Japanese context — physical features. I would be asked to close my eyes only to be greeted by a burst of giggles, or I would be entreated to allow schoolgirls to touch my soft, blond hair. I don't recall these experiences causing me any distress. I felt Japanese. Wartime is a time of mobilization. I read the Japanese children's comics, which featured the struggle against the "foreign devil." I had an older friend in the army who, when he came home injured, visited me.

An additional but crucial context for my childhood in Japan was my parents' own particular relations to Germany and Japan. My parents had left Germany to distance themselves from the Nazis. My mother's father, Kurt von Hammerstein-Equord, was prominent as part of the German military opposition to Hitler (who characterized my grandfather, whom I never knew, as one of his most dangerous enemies). Von Hammerstein was chief of the general staff of the German Army from 1930 until December 1933, when he was replaced. He was an aristocratic Prussian soldier, nicknamed the "Red General," and one of two reforming generals in the turmoil between the beginning of the Depression and Hitler's appointment as chancellor. My mother herself had a wide circle of Jewish friends and acquaintances. In 1934 she went to Palestine with my father to visit her Zionist friends from Berlin and to explore immigration. She soon found herself under increasing pressure from the Gestapo. Had she stayed in Germany she would have had to choose between endangering her family, her father in particular, or betraying her Jewish friends and colleagues. On my father's side was a Jewish grandfather, whose son — a pacifist German naval officer and photographer and author of note — was assassinated after the First World War by military fanatics. His son, my father, was in turn forced to give up the study of law when the first Nazi anti-Jewish laws were introduced. Instead, he turned to the study of Japanese. After deciding against emigrating to Palestine, the young couple made up their minds hurriedly in 1935 to travel to Japan. They were attracted to Japan by my father's interest in the language and culture, as well as by its position in the world. They did not anticipate Japanese military ambitions and Japan's alliance with Germany, and were later horrified and threatened bodily.

Although my parents managed to leave Germany in the early stages of Nazi domination and the realization of military ambition, they did not manage to leave Japan in 1941, when it attacked the United States and many of their closest friends departed. They began as exiles from Germany and ended up in internal exile in Japan.

III

Among the Germans in Japan, a portion were Nazi sympathizers. My parents had to guard themselves against these Germans. Once the Japanese were allied with Germany, my parents had to guard themselves as well against representatives, open or hidden, of the Japanese government. The situation for them was fraught with danger. One protective strategy they used was to maintain total silence about the nature of their sympathies with respect to the combatants in the war. As children we grew up knowing little about our parents' politics. As a child during the war, I did not know that my parents hoped and prayed for German defeat or, more importantly, that a Japanese defeat would be linked to German defeat. My sympathies, insofar as I was able at that age to understand the situation, were with the Japanese. And, partly because we were separated from our parents' families, and also partly because of my parents' caution, I knew almost nothing of my families in Germany. I was not given a sense of who we were.

Their difficulties with the other Germans in Japan had an impact on us children. Very early on we were aware that my parents were shunned by them. We didn't know why. We simply knew that our parents were not accorded the respect we felt was due to them. A particular experience occurred in the one year in which I was sent to a German school. My older sister tells me that I was called names and that stones were thrown at me, and that she had to defend me. We did not finish the school year. My parents subsequently hired private tutors or gave us lessons themselves.

I have had a lifelong ambivalence about my German background as well as a fascination with it. I think this is rooted in those early experiences and circumstances in Japan. My Japanese identity was more clearly available to me than was my German identity. When we left Japan in 1948, when I was ten years old, I went through deep mourning; I assiduously studied my Japanese characters on the ocean passage. I consumed every scrap of Japanese news for several years and cried over the terrible natural disasters that hit Japan so severely in the postwar period. In California I tried to speak Japanese to people I thought were Japanese, only to find that they would hurry away. I had not heard of the wartime internment camps for Japanese Americans.

There was a specific day when I knew that my ability to speak Japanese was slipping away. I lost the verb forms first, followed by the nouns. I retained an interest and admiration for the Japanese and things Japanese, but what I learned after the war also made me critical of Japan during the war years. I retained the language of gestures: body language. I often find myself misinterpreted because I sometimes respond in situations of social interaction in a Japanese fashion. For instance, I laugh in situations in which it is culturally inappropriate here — that is, when I am feeling discomfort or sense discomfort in others. I find myself bending my upper body forward in the Japanese fashion when I say goodbye, and so on.

My Japanese childhood taught me how to make foreigners feel at ease, especially in adapting English speech patterns in such a way that I am more easily understood by non-English speakers. I speak a somewhat differently intoned English when I speak to someone from Japan or from other non-English-speaking countries. Part of my Japanese heritage is that I feel at ease with people from other cultures and am able to make some of the adaptations necessary for easier communication.

My later ambivalence about being an American and living in the United States was rooted in my years in Japan and in the nature of the contact with Americans. When I was eight, as a Japanese (and a German) I was defeated by the Americans, but in no time I joined them and then ventured into the "belly of the beast." In Japan I started visiting the U.S. tank company that set itself up not far from our home in Chigasaki. A kindly, older sergeant had a uniform made for me, complete with insignia. I became a regular. I helped out with English-

Japanese translation at the gates of the camp. I was allowed to use the mess hall and the club, enabling me to bring food to my family each day. I rode around in tanks and jeeps, unless forced out by an officer. In this way I was, at the age of nine, an eyewitness to a major military exercise (only a short distance from where we lived) simulating the U.S. invasion of Japan. Because of my connections I was able to arrange our transportation to the ship that would carry us to the United States. My father found work in the headquarters of the U.S. Occupation in Tokyo, and later decided that to complete his university studies he would emigrate to the United States with his family.

I was ten and a half when we landed in San Francisco. Overnight my Japanese background became largely invisible to others. I was never asked in school about my knowledge of the Japanese language or culture. I may have collaborated here. We were keenly aware that Japan had just lost a war to the United States, and that our Japanese background might meet with hostility. People knew us as refugees and as Germans.

My German identity was a kind of void at that point. I spoke German within the family and could read and write the language, although formal German schooling was limited. I doubt that I knew where Germany was, nor did I know any of its history, including its immediate past. And I knew very little of my own family history.

I found myself poorly prepared for suddenly having my German background highlighted in America. I was at an age, however, when I needed a sense of family and background. I began by inventing a past. I recall telling an older girl, when I was about twelve, that I was related to the German imperial family (in an effort to impress, undoubtedly). I did this on the strength of the name "Maximilian," which I had heard in connection with my father's family, and my mother's own aristocratic origins. There was, in other words, an emptiness that I was taking the first steps to fill. That need has turned into a lifelong quest.

There was also the headlong rush to be an American, indistinguishable from other Americans, at a time in history when there was absolutely no doubt that to be in America was to become an American. It was seen as natural to become naturalized. There was never any question in other people's minds but that we would become Americans. I suppose it had something to do with California itself. People did not concern themselves with our past, only with our present and future — except that the time was also the dawn of the Cold War, a period of a spreading fear of Communism. The Immigration Service and the FBI did take an interest in us.

My parents were repeatedly questioned by agents of these services. They were especially interested in my mother's purported Soviet Communist connections. I still marvel at the image of my mother sitting in a simple California living room, in a rundown house, in a rundown part of town, being questioned about reports that in the early 1930s she had run off to the Soviet Union with the military attaché of the Soviet Embassy in Berlin. The agents were basing their information on Soviet diaries later proven to be fakes ("disinformation").

There was also the situation of my mother's older sister, who had chosen to live in the German Democratic Republic (as the Soviet zone of occupation was later to be called), and who earned her livelihood there as a lawyer. It was always said that this circumstance blocked my father's career in the United States. He later worked in the Chinese-language section of the Library of Congress in Washington, D.C., but without the possibility of security clearance and hence advancement.

My parents had been suspect first in Germany, then in Japan, and finally in the United States of America. Actually, given the historical circumstances of the twentieth century, this was a solid accomplishment on their part, it seems to me.

IV

This history and predicament of my parents had certain consequences for me. Although my family lived in California, I spent my high-school years at a boarding school in Vermont. In my senior year I was embarrassed when my father wrote a letter to my history teacher complaining about what he viewed as a pro-communist bias in the list of course readings. Most dramatically, in that last year of high school, I found that I had to answer questions from the FBI about my senior project in history. I had made a study of Lenin and the Bolshevik Revolution; somehow the FBI obtained a copy of my essay. In that same California living room in which my mother had faced interrogation, I was interrogated by two agents. This happened a year after I had become a U.S. citizen in a proud ceremony in the judge's chambers in San Francisco. I had been pleased that I was able to answer all his questions concerning the Constitution and form of government — for example, "How many senators are there?"

I have often thought that because of my family's winding odyssey through the mid-twentieth-century's flashpoints, the most innocuous documents and family records and histories have been carefully and curiously preserved in the archives of the Third Reich, the Japanese wartime government, the FBI and State Department, the House Un-American Activities Committee, the German Democratic Republic, and probably the KGB. Practically everything I might want to know about myself as a child and young man is filed in classified dossiers around the world. If a universal freedom of information act were passed, the separate pieces of a personal puzzle would only need assembling.

A lasting legacy for me of these dimensions of my parents' lives was a caution about joining any organized groups. For many years I worked on the margins of groups like the National Association for the Advancement of Colored People without actually joining. In the fall of 1956, during my first year at the University of California, Berkeley, for instance, I became interested in the work of the local chapter of the American Civil Liberties Union. After the chapter president asked me to take on the office of treasurer in the organization, my mother and father came to visit me on the campus and my father implored me not to join. I did not argue with or resist him. His experience with and fears about political persecution were in my bones. I continued to work for the ACLU, but without formally joining or accepting a title.

V

Despite these experiences, and the ambivalence and confusion that they sowed, I embraced America with open arms. America was to be our future. And at every turn in America we met with generosity from strangers, new friends, teachers, and many others. However, my parents had an exceedingly difficult time after coming to the United States. They were in midlife with a family of four children, the oldest almost a teenager and the youngest a preschooler. After one year of full-time work they entered into the life of graduate students. My father studied and worked part-time — including nights in a tomato-canning factory and, once, as a butler — and my mother had various full-time jobs. She worked as a cook, a house cleaner, a secretary, and, finally, a research assistant. Later I felt a bitterness at the harshness of the life my parents encountered in the United States. I learned that immigration favours the next generation, the children, not the parents.

But I plunged into believing in America. The country that defeated my "team" had to be perfect. Paul Robeson's singing of "Ballad for Americans," a poignant and expressive celebration of American ideals of diversity and equality, captured my imagination and feeling about my new country. I encountered contrary evidence in books. My eighth-grade teacher gave us Steinbeck's *The Grapes of Wrath* and Richard Wright's *Native Son* to read. I was amazed and moved by what I learned in these books about American life. And there were personal experiences with poverty, and the difficulties my family had with housing, health, and the finding of decent work.

Ten years later, in 1959, when I made my first trip to Germany, I was struck by how thoroughly I had drunk of the American Dream. It was the era of school desegregation (on which I was to base my doctoral work), and of racial violence against Blacks in the South. America was uniquely a society, I tried to convince my German acquaintances and fellow students, that had the capacity to overcome all social obstacles.

VI

In the early years in the United States, although I was busy creating an American identity, I was also groping towards my German identity. I did not present myself as German; I kept it very close to myself. In my teenage years, when I found myself far from my family, I would go alone into the woods to practise my German. I avoided situations that would draw out my German background. It was a kind of secret. It was almost as if by exposing it, I would lose it. My German identity was a fragile thing. I recall learning about the Holocaust in high school and finding it totally incomprehensible. I had no context for it. Who were these Germans responsible for such unspeakable crimes? What was my connection to them? I had not yet fully understood my parents' own background in Germany and why they had left for Japan in 1935. I remember the high school being shown a film about cultural differences narrated by Margaret Mead. I silently noted that the German children shown in the film were characterized by obedience. It ate at me. I was inwardly ashamed that the whole school saw this as what was typically German. Just as in Japan, I was finding that identifying as a German in the United States was a double-edged sword. I also recall feeling irritated by an American stereotype of Germans that I often encountered, a stereotype of loud, beer-drinking, sauerkraut-and-sausage-eating boors ("Oktoberfest"). In university I was to learn that this caricature of Germans grew out of a conflict in the late nineteenth-century between newly arrived German immigrants and native supporters ("Nativists") of the so-called "Blue Laws" (restricting the purchase and public consumption of alcohol). But at the time I responded by having nothing but contempt for any such Germans. I knew very few Germans, and had never lived in a fully German environment, and none of the Germans I knew fit such a stereotype, least of all my parents.

I still remember my first encounter with Germans that seemed to fit some of these stereotypes. It occurred during a holiday with my parents in a cabin in the Blue Ridge Mountains of Virginia. A group of Germans who seemed to me to be behaving just like the stereotype passed us on the trail just on the other side of the cabin. I was mortified. Incidentally, I learned later that my father agreed to vacation at the cabin only because it was the time of the Berlin Crisis, and he found it wise to get out of Washington for fear of a Soviet attack.

In my last year of university I chose to do my main project on a history topic — this time, under the influence of my professor, on the foreign policy views of the nineteenth-century German daily newspaper in Dayton, Ohio. This was part of a pattern in which others would assume I had an interest in things German or would mobilize me because of my German language skills. I resented this, but it was a no-win situation. I was interested, but found it irritating when others took the initiative. I wanted it both ways, but only I could decide when I was to be German. This history project, as it happened, taught me a great deal: that large parts of the United States were once heavily German in their institutions (schools, newspapers, churches), but that the First World War wiped all this out. And while doing my research I came upon a notice announcing a talk in Dayton by my great-grandmother Paasche, during a North American tour with my grandfather, on the evils of nicotine and alcohol.

VII

An important chapter in my struggle with my German identity occurred during my first trip to Germany in 1959. I was then twenty-two. My ship docked in Rotterdam and I made my way by train to Bonn. As I stepped off the train I found myself looking around for Nazi soldiers, just before being welcomed by my mother's brothers.

The ostensible purpose of my visit was to study at a German university. My underlying intent was to try to find out whether, and to what extent, I was German. Over the ten months I spent in Germany I concluded that I had become a North American in several important respects. I felt the shortness of the distances and saw the extent to which young people my age were already tied to a particular career track. I found that I had been shaped by the geography and the flexibilities of culture in North America. For example, I was dumbfounded that after I had spent several weeks visiting my grandmother in

Berlin, the police came around and informed me that I had to register if I intended to make my stay longer. At the time I felt this to be very contrary in spirit to my American experience.

Being in Germany for the first time was also an opportunity to strengthen my ties to family and place. Of this I took full advantage. I discovered what it was to have an extended family and to have my family name recognized and respected, even by perfect strangers. One of the things I missed in living in the United States and later in Canada was the absence of any kind of name recognition. In other words, the history of my family, or even just the names we hold, had no meaning for anyone. At times this was also liberating, of course.

In the German university where I studied for two semesters I took part in the first set of lectures and an accompanying seminar that focused specifically on the Nazi era. To have been among German students being confronted for the first time in an intimate and thorough way with the historical materials of those years was a rare privilege. I found myself able to take both the insider and the outsider position. My own parents had left Germany as opponents of the Nazi regime, while my grandfather and several other relatives had participated in the resistance. The seminar leader commented after the conclusion of the course that I had seemed to feel free to identify sometimes as a German and sometimes not, depending on the issue and historical moment. He had picked up on the love/hate relationship to Germany that I felt at the time, and occasionally feel today. I am fascinated and drawn to my German background, while at the same time repelled and distanced. This tension has surfaced in a variety of ways over the years.

VIII

Later on, during my first years in Canada, I had experiences that also related to identity. For instance, one quite trivial but for me eye-opening situation occurred in the first telephone call I made to the university library. I was responded to in German, and taken aback. Something like this had never happened to me in the United States. I felt completely American in this respect. Suddenly this stranger felt free, unasked, to respond to me in German. Here I felt was a Canadian difference from the United States. It was all right to speak in other languages. This was a revelation.

Another experience that reflected my ambivalent sense of German identity resulted from a senior professor at my university presuming that I would want to do research on the recent German immigrants 99 in Toronto. I was hurt. I felt he was imposing in an area in which I wanted to be free to make my own decision. However, I went along. I was a junior member of the research team and had much to learn. This research had the unintended consequence of allowing me to make peace with ordinary, "beer-drinking, sauerkraut-and-sausage-eating" Germans. I had already learned about the pleasures of drinking beer, but now, as a result of the field work, I became fond of sauerkraut, sausages, and other German foods. Later, in another context completely, a descendant of pre-revolutionary German soldiers and their families, who settled in the Mohawk Valley of upstate New York, taught me how to make sauerkraut, and I have been making it every August since. The research project also taught me something about the variety of backgrounds, including Germans from the Volga region of Russia, among the Germans who emigrated to Canada in the postwar years.

IX

Being of German background is, in my case, a complex matter. The effort I have put into knowing and understanding my family history, as well as German history itself, has been motivated by my desire and need to come to terms with my Germanness. Could I have simply turned my back on it? I don't think so. That initial void, the departure from Japan, as well as the particular circumstances of my immediate and extended family, impelled me to take on the challenge of my German background.

I have often wondered how I would have responded and coped had my parents or grandparents and other relatives been Nazis. Everything would have been different for me. My family has served as an island of safety for me. It insulated me from "ordinary" Germans. Recently I have become more aware of this and have tried to extend my network in Germany and among Germans in Canada. I am privileged to have been born into my German family. It has enabled me to find and cultivate a connection with Germany. It has also at times made me feel superior to other Germans in a way that has not been constructive, and it has prevented me from knowing people I might have learned much from. In Canada I often seek out conversations with travellers from Germany, especially young people. I find them quite fascinating, even exotic. This, of course, suggests that I am the outsider looking in; but I am a very particular kind of outsider, the outside-insider.

X

Although my children may look at our family odyssey as complete, I can never be anything but part of a transitional group. My generation straddles the political and diplomatic world of a period in which refugees from upper-class, middle-class, and working-class backgrounds shared the experience of loss, dislocation, disorientation, and resettlement. This article has been largely concerned with my late-realized German identity. But withal I have also had to come to terms with my American identity. I arrived in Canada from the United States, after all, not from Germany. In the 1970s, when there was great agitation in academia about the threat of U.S. domination of Canadian universities, I was sympathetic. I quietly became a Canadian citizen. But it was a low-key event. I did not take any family or friends along. Impulsively, as I watched the proceedings in the courtroom, I resolved to take advantage of the right to swear my allegiance to the Queen and the nation in the French language. French had always held a privileged position in my father's family. By doing this, it seems to me now, I was, in effect, distancing myself once again from a firm identity, this time the Canadian one. Or was I just emphasizing a difference from the United States? That I did not bring anyone else along, most of all my children, also suggests something about my feeling about citizenship in general and Canadian citizenship in particular. My motive in becoming a Canadian was that I did not want my U.S. citizenship to become an issue for my students. For it to become an issue would have been ironic given my underlying ambivalence about the United States. I did not intend to make any public statement about America when I became a citizen of Canada. I was making a personal statement; my relation to the United States was even more complex than I myself was aware of at the time. But I also had wanted to spare my students in Canada my own ambivalence. They were to have a solidly Canadian education. I did not want a passport to come between me as teacher and my students.

But how times had changed. It was easy for me in 1966, but in 1938 my father and mother could not even immigrate to Canada from Japan. When I told my father in California that I had taken up Canadian citizenship, he was not pleased. He told me that Canada did not take strong stands internationally, and was compromised morally. This response and comment puzzled me. It is only recently, after his death, that I have been able to gain the context. I discovered that my parents had attempted to obtain visas for entry into Canada in 1938, when they first realized that it was wise neither to return to Germany nor to remain in Japan. Friends of theirs, who had English roots and who had emigrated to Canada from Berlin, provided them with references. The attempt was unsuccessful, however, and the visa application was turned down. I knew none of this until I had been a Canadian citizen for many years. What irony: just as I might have grown up in what later became Israel, I could have grown up in Canada. I can only imagine the feelings of my father when I moved out of the country that did eventually give him refuge and took out citizenship in the country that had refused him.

From earliest home life, to family language, to family roots, my Germanness has served as the most constant identity in my life. It has been the thread tying together past and present. So what does it all mean for my routine life in Canada now? Most of the time it is probably irrelevant. Other things have a heavier impact on my life — issues such as profession, income, gender, and age. Still, issues around my German identity crop up unexpectedly even in very small ways. Just recently I collided, unwittingly, with the issue of identity. I was calling a business that repaired telephone message machines. I noted that the woman at the other end had a distinctly non-English accent, but one that I could not place. When I brought my machine in and gave my name, she said to me, "European, isn't it?" I concurred, but left it at that. I had suddenly become guarded; what if she were Jewish, or even a Holocaust survivor? For me to have added "the name is German" was to have taken the risk of offending this person, or at least putting her off. Later, when she volunteered that she was Greek, I felt a kind of relief.

In other words, I had felt it necessary to hold back the knowledge from her of my German background. Lots of people have German surnames without having any German identity or background. Why was I so guarded? The answer probably rests in the importance of the identity to me, and the continuing tension between what attracts me to it and what repels me about it. I still want to be free to pick and choose the moments when I am German and am not German. But I also want definitely to be both a Canadian and a German. I do not in any sense feel like a "German Canadian." I see them as distinct and separate identities.

XI

Whatever my Germanness is, it is open-ended. By this I mean that I am continuously learning about, and feeling through, my encounter with the German in me. That German in me impels me to learn more of German history, as well as to confront the contemporary face of Germany. It is a living thing. I have a love for language, and being familiar with more than one language feels like a blessing.

I dream of going back to Japan to see the places and even some of the people from my childhood. Of course, the only unchosen part of my past was the Japanese sojourn, and although I have a tender spot for it I could never really be Japanese; the indigenous culture prevented it. My subsequent habitations have had an element of my concurrence or choice; they certainly were receptive of me. They were residential and national identities that I could choose: the United States, postwar Germany, Canada. Living in Canada has allowed me to look up to the colossus and to see it without the instinctive patriotism that floods the heart when "The Star-Spangled Banner" starts up. After all, one cannot hear four national anthems with equally distributed emotion. It has been said that nationalism is the epidemic scourge of the twentieth-century. With my patchwork quilt of nationalities, I like to think that I have been inoculated against this disease. If I can demonstrate a more practical and benevolent patriotism, one that demands virtue of a nation's citizens and not just national prejudice, then my diverse twentieth-century life may stand forth as a paradigm rather than an anomaly.

It Was Always There? Looking for Identity in All the (Not) So Obvious Places

••••••••••••••••••••••••••

HOWARD RAMOS

Identity is a complicated matter. Everyone has one, but rarely are we aware of how we get one. We rarely know the boundaries that we build or the symbols and language that make those boundaries stand. Somehow we forget the seeds that germinated into our perception of self. Here I will attempt to find my seeds and cherish them. In doing so I will tell you about an experience I had on the side of the road and share the thoughts that it provoked.

The road trip

One summer recently my father and I went on a road trip. We drove through the Maritimes, spending about two and a half weeks cruising through Nova Scotia, Prince Edward Island, and New Brunswick. On our way back home we ended up having car problems. We were zooming along somewhere in northeastern New Brunswick when the car stopped zooming and began to lose speed. As the car slowed, my dad pulled it over to the gravel shoulder and eventually we rolled to a stop. I remember being quite worried. The only thing I could think about was the endless lines of trees all around us. I could not recall the last town we passed or a sign telling us how far the next one was. Thoughts of being stranded were running through my mind, as I am sure they were running through my dad's.

My dad got out, walked to the front of the car, and opened the hood. I joined him, and we both looked at the engine with curiosity. I am not sure what we expected to see, as neither of us knew much about cars. My dad smiled and didn't look too worried. He must have realized I was a bit nervous. He stood in front of the car, and as cars sped past he waved his hands. A couple of cars flew past with no signs of stopping.

Just as I was giving up hope and beginning to think about the wild animals that must inhabit northeastern New Brunswick, a pickup truck came along. My dad flagged it down and it stopped. In the truck was a man and his wife. The man walked over to our car, asked my dad what had happened, and, thinking that the problem could be the battery, asked if we had jumper cables. We did, and he pulled his truck around and tried to give us a boost. Nothing happened. The car still didn't start. When the man offered to drive to the next town and send a tow truck, we accepted thankfully.

Before the man walked back to his truck, my dad thanked him and offered his name — "Segundo Ramos." The man responded with a very Canadian question: "Where you from?" My dad answered, "Toronto." The man seemed a bit perplexed, probably because he had noticed that my father had an unfamiliar name, spoke with an accent, and did not "look white." Unfortunately, such a response represents an all too common occurrence in Canada — the constant need to ask those who don't fit our perception of *Canadian* where *they* are from. The man asked again, "Where you from?" My dad corrected himself, "Actually I'm from Etobicoke." The man looked even more puzzled, so my dad added, "It's part of the new megacity, it's really part of Toronto."

The man looked at me, and I smiled. He told us he was from the town up the highway, gave us his name, and ended by saying, "And I am a French Canadian." It seemed strange to me that he felt it necessary to mention that, but as I thought about it later I started to think that he was trying to ask my dad where he was *really* from. The man set off in his truck and soon enough a tow truck arrived. The car was eventually fixed, and we zoomed back home.

On the way back the experience on the side of the road stuck out. Even after we got back I continued to think about it. I tried to make sense of it, knowing I had learned something I had not realized before

— but I was not sure what. At first I was a bit surprised at my father's response. I thought it was interesting that he identified so strongly with Toronto. I was a bit disappointed that he didn't attach a hyphen to his name and opted to be a Canadian rather than maintain at least part of his former identity.

The luxury of choice

I was disappointed because my father decided not to identify with his country of origin, but instead with the country he had been living in for the last thirty years. It seemed almost a shame that he didn't tell the man on the side of the road that he was originally from Ecuador. I wondered why my dad identified so strongly with Canada and why he insisted, even after being asked a second time — given the chance to change his mind — that he was from Toronto. Part of the answer can be explained through the notion of cognitive dissonance, or, as one dictionary defines it, "the simultaneous holding of incompatible ideas, beliefs, etc." In this case it can be understood as not biting the hand that feeds you. It represents the desire to identify with the dominant group, to try and acculturate or be a part of the mainstream in order to reap the profit of the dominant group. In wondering why my dad identified as Torontonian, I began to think about the decisions and choices he had made in coming to Canada.

When he arrived, my dad believed that "when in Toronto, you should do as the Torontonians." Over the years he increasingly began to change and mould himself into the settings around him. He began to follow Canadian politics, learn about different areas of the city, and eventually began taking courses in French so that he could be a "bilingual Canadian" — it was as if, speaking Spanish and English, he was not one already. My dad felt that he needed to learn the "official" languages, the ones legally and socially recognized as being Canadian, the ones that carry status and importance. He realized that language is a symbol that acts as a boundary distinguishing between who is and is not seen as Canadian.

In trying to be a part of the mainstream he dated Canadian women and went to Canadian clubs. Eventually he met my mother, and they had me. I am perhaps a good example of his efforts to become Canadian. I once asked him why he named me Howard. He said he wanted to call me Harold, but my mother did not want people calling me Harry. He added, as did my mother when I asked her, that he wanted to name me something English, something *Canadian*, something that would allow me to be a part of the mainstream. They saw an English Canadian name as a key that would open the door to success and stability; they associated it with mobility and achievement. My parents believed that someone hearing or seeing my name would think of me as Canadian, and that being seen as Canadian would deflect discrimination in employment and daily life. They saw *Canadian* as being Anglo, and they thought that if I could not be Anglo the next best thing would be to have an Anglo name, at least in part.

My father's decision to join the mainstream was a way of gaining upward social mobility. Although he did not realize it, he was trying to avoid being trapped in what John Porter (1969) called the vertical mosaic. Porter argued that new immigrants' mobility was confined to the limits of their ethnic community and that the highest levels of success tended to be reserved exclusively for English and French Canadians. My dad was able to see that success as a mainstream Canadian was different than success as an immigrant or as a part of a minority group. He wanted access to all the things that made Canada different from his home country. He wanted to see me break past class and ethnic barriers, achieve my wishes, and more importantly have a stable and financially prosperous life. My father wanted us to get a piece of the Canadian pie.

In identifying with Canada or Toronto and trying to "do as the Torontonians when in Toronto," my father avoided being trapped in an ethnic enclave. By and large his strategy worked. When he moved to Toronto he lived in the downtown area, renting a room in a boarding house. After he met my mother and I was born, the family moved into a house on Dufferin Street in the west end of downtown Toronto. When we moved there, the neighbourhood was mostly Portuguese, Italian, and South American immigrant families, though in time the ethnic demographics changed. My father worked hard at his job, often taking classes to improve his skills as a telecommunications hardware worker, and he kept up with the rapid changes in the industry. When I was a teenager he bought a house in the suburbs and left the noise and commotion of downtown. Over the years he was promoted in his job, and his salary provided us with a modest middle-class lifestyle.

Although my dad managed to make a comfortable life in Toronto and got to taste some of the pie, I have wondered what cost he paid for doing so. Part of my disappointment in his identification with Toronto was that he was cutting away from his past. He was selecting the last thirty years of his life as the point of reference for his identification and as a result seemed to turn his back on all that had gone before it. When I was growing up most of the references my father made to Ecuador were laced with a comparison between it and Canada. Of course, he always showed that Canada was more prosperous. It had the brighter future, and it was safer and more beautiful. He reminded me that Ecuador was poor and that its governments were riddled with conflict and corruption. I wondered if he had lost a part of himself in his drive to be Canadian and to fit in — if he had closed the door on my chances to identify with his history. It seemed as though he thought he could not be Canadian and still identify as being from Ecuador. Instead he seemed to think that he had to be one or the other, and he chose to be Canadian.

Even so, as I thought about it more, it became less than clear. Did he really have to make such a bold choice? Or were things actually more subtle? Did he forsake one identity for another? Or was it a matter of time? I wondered why I expected him to identify as anything other than Torontonian. After all, he had been living there for thirty years. He had been away from Ecuador for so long that I imagined he had little in common with the place he used to live. Things don't stay the same. Language and culture, not to mention people and identity, are always changing.

Time has an amazing effect on memory and identity. It allows us to forget, to re-create, and to sow our seeds over and over again. Along such lines, Ernest Renan (1945) and Benedict Anderson (1983) argue that identity and nation-building represent a cyclical process of forgetting, misinterpreting, and re-creating symbols and markers of identity. In thinking about time and the process of maintaining or perhaps more appropriately re-creating culture, I wondered why I had expected my father to hold onto his identity as a foreigner for so long. How long do people have to stay in Canada before they are Canadian?

The answer to the last question has long evaded many scholars. Part of the irony of our experience on the side of the road was that my dad identified as Canadian, but the man asking him the question did not see him as such. Frederik Barth (1969) argues that identity is enclosed by cultural and symbolic boundaries. He argues that ethnic and national groups use features such as accents, mannerisms, physical characteristics, or other differentiations to distinguish people who belong to a group from others who do not belong. In my father's case, he speaks with an accent, has a name that is not considered common to Canadians, and looks different from what most Canadians would think of as a *Canadian* look. Identity is a two-way street, and, unfortunately, to choose to be Canadian does not necessarily make you one. Instead, identity is a contested issue that is reflexive and negotiated.

The man asking the question did not accept my father's answer and then asked the question again — offering my dad the chance to give a different answer. My dad elaborated, maintaining his identity, and the man on the side of the road was in turn forced to adjust his perception. The way he adjusted was by walking back to his truck and accepting my dad's answer. In thinking about this I realized, like the man who asked the question, that I did not really accept my dad's choice. I did not see him as Canadian . . .

He isn't but I am? Or am I?

It was strange that I was offended by the interchange on the side of the road, both at the man for asking his question and at my father for answering in the way he did. The paradox is that I saw myself as Canadian, but did not see my father as such. Somehow over the years I had bought into the belief that being Canadian meant that you speak with a Canadian accent, that you speak English, and that you are born in Canada . . . and so my father was not Canadian. Even so, I was, I am, Canadian — when friends ask me what I am, I always answer Canadian; it always seems unimaginable to be anything else. For example, when I moved to Montreal a couple of years ago, people would ask me: "Where are you from?" I would answer, "Toronto." Somehow I thought that answer was appropriate for me, but not for my father. In justifying my belief I thought of the little things that make the two of us different. I thought of his passion for soccer, my passion for hockey, my dad wearing long johns in winter, the embarrassment I had in wearing them as a kid, his assertion of manliness, my dislike of machismo . . . and the list goes on. We were different, we are different; somehow I always accounted for those differences by thinking of him as being not from Canada. I thought it was novel that he insisted on being Canadian, that he wanted to be from Canada, but I was not convinced that he was.

I was not sure what he had to do to *be* Canadian, but I had created a subconscious list of things that excluded him from being so. In thinking about the question the man asked on the side of the road, I thought about times that I had been asked what I was or where I was from. Despite my ready answers — "Canadian" or "from Toronto" — there were times the response did not work.

For instance, when I was a teenager my mother and I moved to Winnipeg, where I spent my high-school years. The high school I went to was in the city's North End and had a large cohort of Filipino students, many of whom were first-generation immigrants. At my 109 high-school graduation ceremony we had to line up in alphabetical order. In seeking out my place I found two other "Ramos," both children of Filipino parents, and according to the procedure I was supposed to be between them. One of the Ramos told me that I was in the wrong place, that they were both Ramos and I should be either in front or behind them, not in between. I told them that I was also a Ramos. They looked a bit surprised. One asked, "So how did you get a Filipino name?" When I said that my dad was from South America, they said, "Oh?" Another time I was at a friend's house and his father jokingly asked me, "So are you related to Fidel Ramos [the former Filipino president]?" When I said no, I wasn't, he said, "If you are ever in the Philippines, make sure you say you are not related, Filipino politics aren't very friendly." In dealing with both instances, I deflected the question of identity by saying that my father was Ecuadorian, that because of him I had an Hispanic or Filipino name; but I would think to myself, I am not Ecuadorian, I am Canadian.

In thinking about my Ecuadorian identity I have always thought of the markers and symbols that exclude me from it. I don't speak Spanish, or at least the little I do know of the language does not serve me well. I have never been to Ecuador, and what I have read about it in the newspaper or heard through my dad is not appealing. For example, I remember a couple of years ago reading (in *The Globe and Mail*) that in an election campaign for the presidency, one of the candidates said that people should vote for him because the other candidate had watery sperm. Such rhetoric is unheard of in the conservative realm of Canadian politics. I cannot relate to such experiences. By and large I have lived a modestly comfortable Canadian life; the things I hear about my dad's country are foreign and strange; it feels fraudulent to think of myself as anything but Canadian.

But to say that I know nothing about my dad's country would be a lie. I have a certain affinity to read about it when I see a story in the newspaper. I go out of my way to ask people from Ecuador about it, and I ask my dad to tell me stories and give information about his country. I also exchange letters with a cousin, Patricio. He writes in Spanish, I write in English, and we manage awkwardly with the translation. He tells me odds and ends about Ecuador and I try to tell him about Canada. Both of us share the exoticness of each of our experiences. I have managed to learn about some of the foods and dishes that are traditional in my father's country, like *fritada*, *plantains*, or *uca*, and try to include them in my regular diet. I even know a number of folk stories and a bit of the country's history. Nevertheless, I always seem to be aware of the boundary that divides us, that distinguishes me from my father and my cousin. I am not Ecuadorian, South American, or Hispanic. It feels strange to think of myself as such. Just because my father was born in another country seems an odd reason to consider that country a part of my identity and experience, but it is equally strange not to think of it as a part of me.

Fitting in? Dancing the tango

In thinking about why I was not Ecuadorian, I came to realize that I have identified with Canada and Canadianness for many of the same reasons my father has. I have spent my whole life in Canada. It is where I was born, and it is what I have experienced. I have done it unconsciously. For the most part, no one has questioned me when I said I was from Toronto or Montreal. Unlike my father my skin is pale, I speak with a Canadian accent, I speak French, and I know the little oddities and cultural quirks that come as badges of Canadian experience. Unlike my father, I do have the luxury of choosing my Canadian or Ecuadorian identity. Unconsciously and later manifestly, I identified with mainstream Canadian goals and identity. I want what I was shown through school, the media, and the state: I want a comfortable middle-class lifestyle. I have identified as Canadian, because in Canada it is the way to fit in.

But in Canada what does fitting in mean? Supposedly we have a multicultural society, but how multicultural is a society that is constantly asking people with dark skin, accents, different mannerisms, and ways of dressing where they are from? As I think back on what fitting in *is* in my experience of Canada, most of the people involved in this experience are like my dad: they speak with accents, they look different, they were born in other countries, they are immigrants, they are Canadians. I think of my aunt who immigrated from Russia, or the kids I look after whose mother immigrated from the Philippines and whose father is Québécois. I think of my friend and his boyfriend who come from Saskatchewan and Cuba, or the people I go to school with who come from all parts of the country, different parts of the world, who have varied lifestyles and share a Canadian experience. Some people have argued that the *other* now lives in the dominant society and that in fact the dominant society is filled with *others*. Stuart Hall (1991), for example, notes that because of globalization, immigration, and increased travel, borders have become fluid, in turn forcing the deconstruction of the hegemonic identity of industrial societies. Likewise I have come to realize that fitting in, in Canada, is not clear-cut; we don't all look the same, we don't have the same

111

dreams and aspirations, and we don't have the same experiences. If we did, life would be boring and we wouldn't spend so much time trying to figure out who is what and where people come from.

I have realized that fitting in is not so much a matter of looking and being Canadian; it is not a matter of being the same. Instead it is a matter of identification, a matter of acceptance, and a matter of learning the steps to the tango of questions like "Where are you from?" I have been luckier than most, in not having to dance that tango so often. It is clear that some of us have to dance more than others. My father, for instance, knows the steps all too well. Fitting in is learning to deal with the Canadian obsession with identity, which manifests itself through the conflict between Canadian and Quebec identity, our inferiority complex with the United States, and our attempts to define a multicultural Canadian identity. In each instance we create categories of identification and boundaries of inclusion and exclusion. The problem with our obsession is that it tangibly and materially impinges on and excludes people(s). Evidence of this effect can easily be seen in the cases of Aboriginal peoples, Quebec, and discrimination in immigration laws, as well as in the vertical mosaic that excludes some ethnic/racial groups from getting ahead. Fitting in is working with and against our cultural or social categories of inclusion and exclusion.

At that point in my thoughts, in thinking about the question the man asked at the side of the road, I felt like a dog chasing its tail. I began to see that my dad was Canadian, that, like Descartes, he thought he was Canadian, therefore he was . . . Yet at the same time I became aware of his identification with his home country and the subtle transmission of his culture to me. I realized that identifying with Toronto did not have to be an all or nothing process and that identity or identification is far from a clear-cut matter. I realized that all the little things that made my father different from me, that made me think of him as an Ecuadorian, were the things that made him both Canadian and Ecuadorian. At the same time I was convinced that a metaphysical, cultural, ethnic, and geographic boundary did not make me Ecuadorian. And these subtle distinctions had prevented me from allowing myself to see my dad as Canadian. It was the invisible boundary that people cross and dance with as they identify with the world around them and project themselves into it. It was the invisible line that the man who asked the question tried to establish with my father, and it was the line, which my father crossed, showing that he and the man who asked the question were within the same place. As I thought about it, the distinctions and boundaries that included and excluded became less and less clear. I was not able to figure out what they were, or which ones allowed me to see myself as a Canadian and my father as an Ecuadorian who wanted to be Canadian. I could not see the boundaries that prevented me from being Ecuadorian. I could not explain the distinctions that prevented me from seeing what was always there.

Was it always there?

My final realization made me think of a story my dad once told me. There was a man who asked his son to take three mules into the market to sell. The man told his son, "Whatever you do, don't ride the mules, and make sure they get there in good health." The son headed off to the market, walking with the mules. After a half day of walking the son realized that it was a long journey and decided to ride one of the mules despite his father's orders. He mounted one and was spared the discomfort of walking barefoot the rest of the way to the market. He got so comfortable that he fell asleep on the mule, which walked along the path with the others following. As it approached the market town the mule slowed, which woke the boy. Realizing that he had fallen asleep, he quickly counted the mules. He counted two. He counted again, and still there were only two. He got worried and realized that his father would have his hide. But instead of panicking, he figured that he would go into the market and sell the two he had and then look for the one that had disappeared. When he got to the market, the livestock salesman asked the boy, "Do you want to sell any of your mules?" The boy said "Yes," and the livestock salesmen asked how many. The boy answered, "Two." The salesman asked, "How about the one you're riding?" The boy realized that the third mule had been there all along. It had not disappeared. He did not have to look for what was already underneath him.

Like the boy on the mule, I realized two things that had always been there: my father's answer was justified; and a part of me is Ecuadorian. My father's desire to get what everyone else has, the time he has spent in Canada, and his feelings of attachment all make him Torontonian or Canadian. Although Canada claims to embrace multiculturalism and diversity, the exclusion and lack of recognition of people like my father make that embrace more a matter of ideology than a reality. Instead, people on the side of the road, in the bank, in our everyday lives, still question the legitimacy of other people's Canadianness. Only when people are able, every day, to accept diversity, to accept everyone who chooses to *be* Canadian, can we say that

113

we have become a multicultural society. The process of accepting such symbols and markers involves our own acceptance of what has always been there. It comes through the acceptance of the stories, people, and histories that have filled our Canadian experiences.

In the end I discovered that to embrace my Canadianness is to embrace the stories I know, the relations I have. It is to embrace being asked about my last name, to embrace my Ecuadorian identity. What I discovered is that identity is a mucky thing. It is like walking around in knee-deep mud wearing rain boots; you pull, you slide, sometimes your boot gets stuck in the mud, and at times you end up pulling so hard that your foot comes out of your boot. The question the man asked on the side of the road was an experience that led to me pulling my foot out of my boot. It forced me to think about my relationship with my father, about how he sees himself, how I see myself, and how we both project ourselves to others around us.

THE ELUSIVE AND ILLUSIONARY: IDENTIFYING OF ME, NOT BY ME

•••

CAMILLE HERNÁNDEZ-RAMDWAR

I live in Toronto now. I live here, but I am not from here, I did not grow up here. I grew up in Winnipeg, during a time and in a place where I was an anomaly. I don't know if that is still the case today. I don't visit Winnipeg much anymore. It is not "home" to me. My whole concept of home is problematic, which I expect is because I was born into a climate, a space, in which I felt unwelcome and unbelonging.

I have written a lot about my experiences of growing up in Winnipeg, but I believe that this time I am writing from a different perspective, perhaps, than I did earlier on, in my twenties. I am in my thirties now, and I have lived in Toronto for over a decade. I am raising my two children here and feel a certain distance from the life I led as a child and teenager on the prairies. I am, I find, even allowing myself some nostalgia for certain things — the rivers, the clean air, the safer streets, the lack of big-city dirt and crush. But other than that, I do not miss Winnipeg. I would not choose to raise my kids there. It is more than the overbearing winters, the floods, the predatory mosquitos. It is a perception I have of a suffocating and engulfing

115

whiteness that prevents me from returning, from naming Winnipeg as "home." It is only the Aboriginal presence that redeems Winnipeg for me, but because I myself was never a part of that world my memories are primarily of trying to fit into a scenario in which I was unwelcome.

In the language of children that sense of being unwelcome is inarticulated but overt. Children verbalize sensations with ease; they do not often know why or how they have reached certain conclusions. They simply spew. Why is your skin that colour? Where are you from? Why is your mom white and you're not? I faced these questions alone. I developed ways in which I shielded myself from their invasiveness.

At first I tried elaborate explanations. My father is from Trinidad, of mixed origin — Indian father, Spanish (pañyol) mother, her descendants from Venezuela, incorporating generations of mixedness and silences around mixed heritage. My mother was of Ukrainian origin, born in Canada, raised in small-town Manitoba. So I heard this from my parents: "You are Spanish and Indian and Ukrainian." I thought that sufficed. But to my peers my dark skin placed me in other categories: Nigger, Darkie, Paki, Injun. I would come home crying — "They called me nigger!"

My father, clearly understanding the term in a Trinidadian context, in a colonial context, in a context in which hair texture and shade of skin and proximity to whiteness meant points, would retort in indignation "You are not Negro!" I would be coached to teach those (white, though he would never say that) kids a lesson in genealogy and racial typography and be sent back to the schoolyard, armed with my definitions.

"Nigger!"

"I am not Negro. I am Spanish and Indian and Ukrainian."

"So? You're still a nigger!"

End of lesson.

What my father failed to understand (or perhaps he did, but kept secreted in utter and exhausting denial) was that in Canada we were all niggers. If you were dark, you were Black. If you were dark-skinned but didn't have a dot in your forehead, wear a turban, speak English with a strong accent (and my father's accent was 90 per cent British colonial subject and 10 per cent Trinidadian), you were Black. If you were brown-skinned but didn't wear braids, feathers in your hair, drink rubbing alcohol or Lysol, live in the North End, or frequent the welfare office (all the negative and stifling perceptions of Aboriginal identity to white Winnipeggers), then you were Black. Winnipeg, at that time, and in the middle-class white residential neighbourhood I grew up in, sorely lacked an imagination as to the varieties of humanity existing in the world. My peers saw people who looked similar to me on TV — African Americans, straightened hair, light-skinned — and saw no difference. I became Black. I understood that, after years of failed explanations, I had no choice. Become Black, or become invisible.

Not that being Black was such a bad thing. It just jarred with my father's plans for me — after all, he had married a white woman, and how could he now have a daughter who called herself Black? The more I adopted the stance — dressing as a Supreme, false eyelashes and all, to go to my school prom, or later experimenting with Rastafarianism (all my attempts at fitting into existing images of Black identity) — the more I heard, "You're not Black": my father's only comment. Not "This is what you are, we are mixed, we are many things, you have this to hold on to, this to be proud of," but "This is what you are not." I became a negation. This has stayed with me — the feeling of being in limbo, of not belonging anywhere; the feeling that I am "passing" as Black if I claim that identity. Know that I am not white (seen as or desiring to be), although that is half my ancestry.

Thinking back, I realize that my experiences would have been significantly different had a number of circumstances been otherwise. Had my parents affirmed an identity for me, rather than leaving me with what appeared to be none, I think I would have been able to defend myself better and have a stronger sense of identity. Likewise, had I not grown up in a predominantly white middle-class neighbourhood, had I seen other reflections of me, had I been able to choose among a number of identities, perhaps I would be a much different person today. Similarly, had there been more representation of mixed-race identities in popular culture, and in my schools (with teachers, and in books, for instance), that also might have made a difference.

I know that for me at a certain point escape seemed to be the only alternative. By age twelve I knew I would have to leave Winnipeg if I wanted to remain sane. I longed to live in a place where I blended into the landscape, a place where I would not be singled out for my difference, my seemingly unusual appearance, where I wouldn't be exotic or despised. It troubled me that I had been born in the very centre of North America, in a landlocked terrain of extreme climate. What possible reason could there be for this isolation? I wondered. I set my sights on righting the wrong of my birthplace. This created in me some very strong feelings about birthplace and identity, 117 particularly towards people who subscribe to natal-nationalist notions of birthplace and belonging. We do not choose where we will be born. To ascribe some inherent identification to one's birthplace is problematic for the very reason that the individual may feel no connection to that birthplace — in fact, may be treated as an unwelcome intruder in the land of birth. The many challenges I have received — particularly from Caribbean people — on the issues of authenticity, identity, and birthplace have been too numerous to count. I think it is time that people re-evaluate their allegiances to these ideas, particularly considering that a great many "Caribbean" people now reside outside of the Caribbean. They are having their children in the diaspora and are raising them in ambiguous spaces.

Toronto, in this sense, has failed to be "home" for me either. The polarity I experienced in Winnipeg becomes a kaleidoscope of racial identity politics in "T.O." The necessity of carving out niches, of scavenging over the pittances tossed to communities of colour by government bureaucracies monitored by white, bilingual (Founding Fathers' bilinguality) and racist staff leads to a divisive and bitter mentality. We become typographed and policed again, this time not by the colonizing gaze of the plantocracy, but by ourselves. Your hair too straight? Too kinky? Nose long, broad, straight, flat? Eyes round or otherwise? And colour? Can you pass? Have you? Do you change colour seasonally? Are you dangerous, suspect? Are you pure? Can you pass for pure Other? How many racial slurs have you been subject to in your life? Where were you born? Are you whitewashed? Half-white? Near-white? White-identified? Do you sleep with white people? Have white children? A different kind of segregation. A different kind of hostility. More closed doors.

To survive as an Other (because the option is to be white-identified, to seek solace in a community and comfort in the very society that sets the rules against you) you realize you must choose an identity, a racialized community, a moniker to get you through some door, even if you're not entirely welcome in the world it opens into. So we (multiracial people) become Black, South Asian, Asian, Aboriginal, and then make attempts to inject our multiplicity into arenas where purity and loyalty and allegiance demand clear-cut and defined boundaries. In the event that we are allowed to name ourselves as "mixed-race" we must append a further definer to fit within the representative festival, history month, panel, conference, course, workshop. Therefore, one becomes Black Mixed-Race or Asian Mixed-Race or Caribbean Mixed-Race or a Mixed-Race Woman — something plus mixedness. As if the mix itself weren't enough.

Despite the divisions, there have been some moments in Toronto in which, sharing moments with other mixed-race individuals at some of these events, feelings of solidarity and shared experience bring us into some semblance of community, or at least empathy. Of course, there have also been moments of strain and tension. Some mixed-race people have very different ideas than others about the meaning of mixed-race identity. At one such event I participated in, the MC who had been chosen for the evening proceeded to launch into a series of rather racist and offensive self-deprecating jokes, although he himself was mixed-race. Another participant and myself were both disturbed by this, and addressed the organizer. We were informed that this was not meant to be a "political" evening, that it was a "celebration" of mixed-race identity. Our discomfort turned to outrage. For some of us, our experience as mixed-race people has been nothing but political. We are not interested in celebrating or investing in some idea of a utopian rainbow identity and the ensuing global wave of coffee-coloured children that will, in some magical, fairy-tale way, eradicate racism. This has not been our experience; this is not our vision.

Another experience involved participating in a documentary on mixed-race identity for national television. Given that the program was being produced by South Asian men, I was concerned about how I would be read, as a mixed-race Caribbean woman of partial South Asian descent. I insisted on asserting my multiple identities from the onset. I spoke eloquently and at length on camera about my research into mixed-race identities and my own journey of self-discovery. I invited the crew into my home, subjecting my family, my children, to scrutiny. I participated in an on-camera discussion with an interracial couple and my mixed-race partner at the time about mixed-race identity and racism. I read a poignant poem over and over again for the director, who, in typically distanced fashion, gave no response but "Again!" I invited former Caribbean students of mine to participate in an on-camera discussion with me. The result? A documentary in which my identity is skewed by the framing of my voice. I speak about mixed-race identity, but it is not mentioned that I am also pursuing a doctorate degree, that I had already produced a Master's thesis and have done a significant amount of research and writing into mixed-race identity. Instead I am framed as a mixed-race wife and mother of two mixed-race children. The discussion with my students and the poem were simply omitted. The conversation with the interracial couple was edited in such a way that my partner and I were seen to be agreeing with their benign, "love-thy-neighbour" Christian

119

outlook on racism and the raising of mixed-race children, when this, in fact, was not what took place. The documentary continues to circulate on the airwaves. People still stop me and comment that they saw me on TV. I wonder about the perception they have come away with — of me, of the issues.

Over time I have become less enthused about participating in such events or projects. In many ways the final outcome sabotaged my intent. I was silenced — by the context of the event, the sound bites that cut out the fullness of my expression, the clever editing to frame my experience as pathological. I felt used — used by both white people and "legitimate" people of colour to satisfy their own discomfort with mixed-race people, children, families, identity, and voice. It seemed that the more one spoke out — about identity, lived experience, pain, anger, racism, exclusion — the more one was open to attack. Like many before me, I have looked to "safe" places to explore my issues. I focused on writing.

Even here, there have been moments when, in discussing my work among others, I have been subject to attack. One evening I was invited by another writing friend to meet her editor, who was visiting from out of town. At the gathering, mainly of Caribbean academics, I knew most of the people and felt relatively safe. We began to go around the room to discuss our work, what we were writing about and researching. When it was my turn I began to discuss my research into Caribbean identities — how they are transnational, fluid, convoluted, complex, how one's racial identity can change according to locale, time, situation. At a particular point in my presentation a colleague of mine jumped up, exclaiming and protesting that I was "born in Canada" and that my "mother was Ukrainian." He seemed quite outraged — by what, I was not sure, but his hostility was not unfamiliar. I was being "outed" as unauthentic, tainted, suspect, diluted — God knows what — but I had been there before. I controlled my temper as best I could, explaining through gritted teeth that my identity was a primary reason why I was engaging in this work in the first place, and that it was sorely needed. It was only afterwards that the editor herself, whom I had come to meet, drew me aside and defended my position while denigrating my colleague's behaviour. She offered that her daughter was struggling with many of the same issues I had raised, and she thoroughly supported my endeavours.

It has been moments like those that have encouraged me to continue to speak out about mixed-race identity and experiences. For every attack, sabotage, misunderstanding, or dismissal, there have been many other instances of support, of shared pain and laughter, of conversations of frustration, and moments when the feelings of isolation and alienation are lifted because someone else spoke the words you may have said to yourself time and time again. It is still disheartening to me, though, to encounter prejudice from other people of colour who feel threatened by the presence of mixed-race people in their circle. Although I understand well the history — of colonialism, colourism, and privilege — that those sentiments come out of, it is still very painful to feel rejected by people who may be the closest form of community available, a community in which, in a white supremacist world, we tend to seek safety.

For now the path of isolation continues to be the option of choice, if only to maintain my integrity and security. It is frustrating and at times debilitating to operate in what sometimes feels like a vacuum, but the external climate of race relations in Toronto does not seem to be improving. On the contrary, the struggle continues between self-preservation and longing for community. Communities are fragmenting, destabilized, eating themselves from within under an oppressive political regime. We outsiders seek sanctuary, seek safety in a variety of places, but we are often invisible. The work, though, continues. Perhaps, in time, a public face can be put to a private struggle once again.

Is It Japanese Artist or Artist Who Is Japanese?

●●●●●●●●●●●●●●●●●●●●●●

Lillian Blakey

About twenty years ago, *he* changed my name. And I became a split personality. All my life I had been called by various forms of Lillian — Lil, Lily, Liliane, even Lilika — all of which were more or less acceptable to the real me, all of which identified me as myself, to myself. One's name is intimate, a cocoon that gives comfort, familiarity, and security in a world that can be hostile. It is with you all of your life, or so I thought before I met *him*. Even changing my surname upon marriage did not affect me a great deal, but allowing someone to change the name that is the essence of me was like giving all of myself away. "Wait!" I cried silently in panic, "I've changed my mind. I don't want my name changed!" Too late. He told everyone he knew immediately. I felt myself slipping away, like a mist dissipated by the sun's overpowering heat. And the people who had known me before this name change looked at me in amazement, as if I had had a sex change.

He was my first husband. He was quite a forceful individual in his own way. On first impression, he appeared to be like a clumsy teddy bear who somehow inspired everyone around him, especially women, to look after all of his needs. We *all* gave in. I fell into the trap of agreeing to the change of my name, even though I was, deep down inside, very unwilling.

Right from the beginning, he felt that my Japanese name,

Michiko, was much better than my English name, Lillian. And he decided that the shortened version, Michi, was the best of all. The only problem was that he changed the pronunciation to Meeshee, because to his ear it sounded more poetic. To my ear, this name was weird and foreign; it was not even Japanese. But like hosts of women before me, I allowed myself to be manipulated. I could not bring myself to contradict him because he was so pleased with himself. The truth is, I did have a choice, but I blew it. Because I said nothing, he interpreted my silence as approval. I now know that being Japanese had a lot to do with my choices, and less to do with his pushiness.

It's funny that, although I am so far removed from being "Japanese," much of my behaviour is still influenced heavily by a Japanese mentality and code of ethics, which can be a handicap in this country, where people's values differ so greatly. What can be good manners to one group of people can be insulting to another, because common understandings of appropriate behaviours are lacking. Of course, now the problems are compounded because of the increasingly large number of races, religious beliefs, attitudes, and cultures that make up Canada. However, for most of my experience, there were white people, and then there were a few of us who were not white. I always felt as if I had one foot in the boat and the other foot on land. Very odd, at times. Most often, I found myself taking the role of observer in both worlds, rather than as a full participant in either.

The Japanese mentality obviously took over when my husband announced the name change. I found myself deferring to the male, who makes all the decisions in a Japanese household, where it is the women, not the children, who should be seen but not heard. All my life I had watched my father decide what clothes my mother should wear, how she should wear her hair, what furniture she should have, what her job should be, and who her friends should be. It is no wonder I grew up thinking that men should make up my mind for me. My only saving grace was that my father had no sons. I became the son he should have had; therefore, the message was unclear whether I should behave as a Japanese male or as a Japanese female — or both, depending upon the situation or my father's inclination.

In addition, Japanese manners also dictate that, when confronted with a particularly embarrassing situation, you are not supposed to mention the problem. Embarrassment is to be avoided at all costs, even if it means disaster to you personally. You must allow the offender to save face because it is a matter of preserving his honour. Honour is so important that even enemies are courteous to one another. Hence, the inscrutable Asian. For a long time, my feelings used to be 123 hurt by non-Japanese because I did not understand that people have some very conflicting modes of behaviour that can lead to enormous misunderstandings. And obviously, although I am not Japanese, I had inherited this very deeply ingrained mentality without even realizing it. It is only now that I am beginning to understand my cultural inheritance and to deal with it successfully in my life.

And so, I had allowed the name change because I would rather have had him do this than point out his insensitivity to my feelings and his blatant lack of respect for me. The way he looked at it, though, was that if I did not like what he was doing, I should have said so. Instead, my resentment seethed under the surface because I felt he ought to have known how I really felt. The marriage did not survive.

It was only a matter of time before I exploded and stopped repressing my real self, because the other half of me was pure Canadian. This other self had very strong beliefs about equality for women at work and at home. I was among the earliest advocates of equal pay for equal work — not quite a suffragette, but not a doormat either. This duality of Japanese female subservience and Canadian feminism has continued to haunt me to this day, and it has taken me all of my adult life to come to terms with it. It has deeply affected my attitudes, beliefs, and relationships.

Growing up, I had taken virtually no interest in things Japanese. In Toronto in the 1950s my sister and I were the only Japanese Canadian children around for miles. My parents had avoided having much close contact with the Japanese community because of their reaction to the violent discrimination they experienced in pre-war British Columbia. My father always felt that part of the problem there was that the Japanese were such a close-knit group that they attracted suspicion and resentment to themselves. He decided that the best way for our future was to assimilate into the dominant culture. We were among the first to come to Toronto, and we lived apart from other Japanese Canadians, who obviously had the same idea. Unlike the Chinese, or the Italians, or the Greeks, or the Blacks, there is no definable Japanese community in Toronto even today. We had learned our lesson well.

My sister and I behaved like perfect children because we were encouraged to be invisible, to think white outside the home and to think Japanese in the home, and not to draw attention to the fact that we were Japanese. We were loved by our teachers and well liked by our friends because we worked harder than everyone else, so that we could be model citizens in a white society. Like the Avis rent-a-car slogan, "We try harder."

As a result, the only culture I really know is European. Somewhere in the process of growing up and being educated, I had learned to deny my Japanese cultural heritage and to reject an integral part of myself, a part that, sadly, can never be regained. Although in later years I have explored Japanese philosophy, art, social and economic structures, and cultural traditions, it is always as an outsider looking in — never as one who belongs.

The experience that first awakened my curiosity to explore my heritage took place at the Japanese Canadian Cultural Centre, which I had visited only once before, to attend a wedding reception. The Japanese Canadians in Toronto erected this sanctuary at great expense to preserve their cultural heritage. When you think of the effort, it was quite a feat to get people who were not a community to work so long together to fulfil a common goal. I remember my father contributing to this undertaking for years, although I do not recall his ever going there. He always used to say, "When I retire, I'll have time to go there." He never did retire.

One thing that has always impressed me about the second-generation Japanese Canadian people is their incredible solidarity on matters of loyalty and reverence. Never mind that they have never been to Japan. These people are more Japanese than the Japanese in Japan. Their lifelong dream is a pilgrimage to the land of their fathers. And even if they do not see each other for years, they are fused together in a bond of kinship, a part of the cultural link that is so precariously thin in the land that is home and yet is still alien to them. As a result, they rally around the flag with the rising sun in undertakings such as the building of the Centre, which is almost a shrine embodying Japan, the homeland they will most likely never see. Similarly, when one of their own passes away, as did my father a decade ago, suddenly out of nowhere come hundreds of people to pay their last respects. I remember thinking, "I don't know any of these people. When did he know them? I've been with him for thirty-five years and I've never seen them before."

The Japanese Canadian Cultural Centre itself inspired pride, partly because of its understated beauty and elegance, partly because it was designed by one of the sons of the Japanese Canadian community who had "made it" in a field dominated by white society. It was one of the earliest works of Raymond Moriyama, who has since become one of Canada's foremost architects. The building and its surrounding gardens were a true reflection of the serene, low-lying structures of Japan, and every feature of it spoke of good taste. Moriyama had envisioned a building that was in harmony with nature in the abundant use of beautifully crafted wood and stone surfaces throughout the inner and outer spaces. Behind the building was a lovely garden that inspired contemplation and inner harmony. In front of the main entrance was an incredible cantilevered fountain with a spiral of layered slabs of natural stone, landing as if flung by the hand of God Himself. Now, the beauty of the place has been marred by the addition of a paved parking lot around the fountain instead of a crystal-clear lily pond with goldfish. People rush into the building without even a glance at the creation that stands before them with mute pride.

Perhaps it was the aesthetic beauty of the place that inspired me to agree to take part in the annual arts and crafts show. As an artist, I could not resist the temptation. Ordinarily, I would never have agreed to create craft instead of art. But I thought to myself, "This is not your everyday craft show. After all, the surroundings are truly a work of art. It certainly is not your church basement craftsy show." What a terrible snob I was to distinguish between art and craft. I now realize that my vision was clouded partly by the brainwashing of the institutionalized Western philosophy of art education I had received at university. I also now realize, upon reflection, that this philosophy also casts doubt on the validity of all art forms not in the Western tradition. But it has taken me almost a quarter of a century of soul-searching to realize that the Western tradition always looks after its own and makes no room for the new kid on the block.

At the time I felt a little odd about taking part in the show. My feelings were mixed as I became acutely aware that I was not one of "them." And I certainly did not want people who came to the show to think I was one of "them." Inside I had become white, and I felt very uncomfortable in the presence of other people of my race. I was a closet racist. I had prided myself on my acceptance of other people's beliefs and values — people other than the Japanese, that is. Today, when I look back at myself, I am horrified at this totally insensitive me.

And so my art career was launched by this craft show. I decided to create "soft sculpture." They were really soft toys, but I called them soft sculpture, to elevate their status to the level of art. I threw myself into my work, sewing frantically eight hours a day in between running, like a fiend, after my precocious twin daughters. When they did sleep, they usually did so for four hours at a stretch. As they were being revitalized, I was creating art as if I were possessed by a demon. In one month I designed and sewed eighty pieces, each one unique, each one a work of art. No patterns for me. After all, if you were going to be an artist, reproduction was forbidden.

A few days before the show, I suddenly thought I would like to create a real art piece, an appliquéd wall hanging, which would form a suitable eye-catching backdrop to my display of soft sculptures. In a fit of inspiration, I was transported into a fantasy world of underwater splendour with imaginary schools of fish, plants, and coral, all positioned carefully to look spontaneous in a flowing design filled with movement and vibrant blues, purples, and greens. At that time, I had no idea that this wall hanging would change my life.

As I was sitting by my display during the show, a very chic woman in an immaculate cream-coloured suit, dark glasses, and a hat, which was tilted at precisely the right angle to give an air of mystery, approached me. I could not see her eyes behind the dark lenses. She reminded me of Ingrid Bergman in *Casablanca*. She glanced at the work and surreptitiously handed me her card. I looked at it. *Evans Gallery 123 Scollard Street Toronto Ruth Levinson, Director.* I looked at her. Without a hint of a smile, she said, "I'm interested in your work. Do you do anything besides children's themes?"

I replied, "Yes. I don't usually do children's art. I did these only for this show."

"Good," she answered tersely. "Why don't you bring me some of your other work. I'm looking for a fabric artist. By the way, what name do you go by?"

I do not know why, but when she asked me, I had a moment of anxiety. Which name should I give her? Instinctively, I knew that my professional name would be important. I blurted out "Meeshee, spelled M-I-C-H-I," and in a very small voice gave her my surname. I do not know why I said Michi and not Lillian, or why I was reluctant to give her my married name. Perhaps I subconsciously did not want to be tied to *him*. What flashed through my mind was that none of my fine-art friends would know who Michi was and that it would be very difficult to change a professional name after a reputation was established. I probably chose Michi because it is the sort of name that could be used by itself, with no surname, but Lillian by itself would look stupid. However, as time went on, I regretted my decision, for each time I had a show, people would stumble on the pronunciation and ask me what it meant. All I knew was that the literal translation of *Michi* was road, and *ko* meant child; so I replied, "I guess it means child of the road." But in my mind this response always evoked connotations of being a streetwalker's child, and I would feel a smirk forming on my lips each time I was asked this question. In actual fact, I discovered a far more esoteric meaning much later. *Michi* is the way of the cosmos, not just a set of ethics for the artist or priest to live by, but the divine footprints of God pointing the way. I like this interpretation much better.

My heart was pounding as the chic lady walked away. I could not believe that someone actually thought that my work was good enough to display in one of the Yorkville galleries. I felt like Eliza Doolittle being discovered in *Pygmalion*. Things like this simply do not happen in real life.

Right after the craft show I got busy with my first real art piece, producing it within a week. I am still mystified as to why I chose to create a non-representational piece of art. "White Night" was an abstract landscape completely created in varying tones of white fabric. Upon reflection today, I find myself thinking that this is an odd way of representing night. The other strange thing is that the abstract expressionism of the sixties had never been of intrinsic interest to me. As I grew older, I searched for meaning increasingly in the world of realism. Today I paint only those images and people who are special in my own life.

There were many things that struck me as superficial in the art world. After the sale of that first piece, which really reminded me of an interior decorator's choice for an all-white room, it was decided that I should be half of a "two-man show." Today the word "man" would be replaced by "person," of course, but at that time, women were not exactly plentiful in the world of art. Another thing I found objectionable was that I was now part of a "stable" of artists. It made us sound as if we were livestock to be disposed of at will. The director also decided that we had to get rid of any implication that my work was craft; therefore, my work was advertised as stitched fabric sculpture. They were not really sculptures. Stripped of all embellishing descriptions, they were appliqué wall hangings that were puffy and would pass as sculptural, perhaps. But, being Japanese Canadian, I said nothing and smiled politely.

One of the most difficult things I had to do was to play the role of artist on display on the opening days of my shows. People come to drink wine, ask questions, see who else is there, be seen, and perhaps buy a piece. I am a very shy person who values private space, and it almost killed me to be packaged, publicized, and put on display for public scrutiny.

One absurd question repeated by many people, after the initial fumbling with the pronunciation of Michi, was, "And how long have you been in this country, dear?" I replied, "I was born here. So were my parents. And my grandparents, all four of them, came when they were very young." The answer was invariably, "Oh, my goodness, that is a long time." What this question had to do with my artwork defies logic. Perhaps it was the choice of the name Michi that triggered the train of thought that led to things foreign. It seems as if people automatically assume that one is a foreigner when one does things such as showing artwork, looking as I did, and with a name that they cannot pronounce.

Curiously, for ten years after the show, no one asked this question; now suddenly it is being asked again quite regularly. The people who are now asking me are the new Canadian Asians. It took me a while to catch on to why they were asking me where I was born. I kept on saying, "I was born here." And they would walk away, looking puzzled. I realized after a time that what they were searching for was another familiar person with whom they might have something in common in this totally alien culture. At first, I was reluctant to say that my family originally had come from Japan when the question was asked by a Chinese or Korean person, because of the inhumane treatment their countrymen had received at the hands of the Japanese. But I was relieved to find that they harboured no resentment. Any Asian, even a Japanese, was better than none.

A few years before this art opening, I had experienced the same odd feeling that this question had evoked. It was in my first year of teaching art that I was confronted by the night-school pottery teacher, a nosy, chatty Englishwoman in her fifties, who always knew what everyone else should be doing.

"Why aren't you doing work that is more Japanese? Japanese art is so lovely. It really is a shame that you are not following your own heritage."

Immediately, I felt a prickling sensation on the back of my neck. Why should I be producing a hollow imitation of Japanese art when I am not Japanese? I merely happen to be an artist who looks Japanese. I found her suggestion patronizing, even a little insulting, for in her zeal to praise Japanese art she had assumed that all artists who belong to a specific racial group should adhere to the art styles produced in their native countries: to each his own. I guess she felt that all Blacks should do African carvings and masks, all Ukrainians should decorate eggs, and that all Egyptians should make pyramids.

What people like this woman fail to understand is that we are all products of an extremely complex set of influences, and that we are changing all the time. Nothing stands still, frozen in time. What she failed to see is that I am the product of two cultures, and neither wholly of one nor wholly of the other, and therefore my work, which is the expression of my particular view of the world, is bound to be   129 different from the art of my ancestors. In fact, all true artists aspire to make an original contribution to art, not to rework glories of the past. It is absurd to think that I should be producing eighteenth-century Japanese woodblock prints.

The Japanese mentality in me was at work again as I answered politely that she was right. One should never ever criticize or disagree with someone older. Age gives a person the right to say the most outrageous things while maintaining a position of honour and respect. I still have trouble dealing with older people who are wrong.

Ironically, while I never attempted to make Japanese woodcuts, I did eventually try to resolve the dilemma of being two people in one through my art, and, ultimately, my work does have a Japanese quality about it. By the time my first art show was launched, I had gone through much soul-searching in a variety of ways, ranging from trying out a few religions to writing poetry, but for me, the most meaningful way was through my art. Thus, two pieces in that first show marked milestones in my gradual self-awakening.

The first piece, "After the Fall," was a dark, romantic work that depicted Eve after she had fallen from grace. I was under great stress in deciding whether to present a naked Eve because, as strange as it may seem, the Japanese are extremely modest about nudity, though they think nothing of taking communal baths. My father thought nothing of walking naked to the bathroom when I was a child, but when my toddler twins tried to peek in, he would roar with panic, shouting to get them away from the door. Even erotic Japanese art does not reveal completely naked figures. There is usually a veil or some other strategically placed prop. Sexual matters are implied, not blatantly flaunted, for such immodesty would cause embarrassment. It was extremely important to me that my parents should not be embarrassed at my show.

My fears seem, in hindsight, to be ludicrous, because for years in my fine-art studio classes I had drawn nudes, and I certainly was not embarrassed. We simply looked on nudes as subject matter, the same way we looked at bottles or flowers. Finally, I convinced myself that it would really be silly to cover Eve with a dress, or with leaves. This thought made me giggle, as it immediately brought to mind Dürer's "Expulsion," which shows Adam and Eve being hounded out of Eden, covering their private parts. Whenever I showed this work to my art students, they would roll with laughter. I am sure that Dürer never intended this reaction. All he was probably thinking about was the tragedy of loss of innocence.

What surprised me most about "After the Fall" was the review it received in *The Globe and Mail*, which described my work as appearing to be "heavily influenced by the surface decoration techniques of art nouveau. But closer inspection shows they go directly to the source that inspired art nouveau in the first place: Oriental art."

The strange thing about this observation is that I was not consciously following the conventions of either art nouveau or Asian art. All I was trying to do was to create harmony of design in establishing the profound sadness when one loses innocence and things can never be the same again. Hence, the dark, rich tones and the repetition of the lines mirroring the stillness, the timelessness caused by the guilt Eve felt after the sin. Perhaps there is a part of me that is so Japanese that it haunts my subconscious mind and manifests itself in how I perceive and interpret the world in my art. My second husband believes in the reality and persistence of race memory. Maybe there is something in his theory, after all.

For me, intuitively, the most important element in my work has always been spatial relationships. Not the actual subject matter. Not the colour. Or the form or line. The handling of space is what conveys the meaning. I have always concentrated naturally on the negative space, the space around the figures which, to the Western eye, is the space left over, the space that does not count. I feel that awareness is heightened if you concentrate on that which is not obvious. To some people, this is a very odd way of looking at things.

Perhaps this ability to focus on relationships is a gift from my Japanese heritage. The Japanese have always been masters at manipulating space in a peculiar way. In a tiny country so incredibly crowded with people, they are able to find enough private space to make tiny gardens and create the illusion of vast expanses — raked sand that appears as a wind-rippled beach where no man has trod, a tiny pool that takes on the dimensions of a large pond complete with fish, reeds, and lily pads, bonsai trees that are only a few inches high but deceive the eye and make you think they are full-grown trees.

I will always remember an artist friend's description of his first attempts at learning ceramics from a Japanese teacher. After many, many frustrating tries, the teacher took my friend aside and demonstrated. "What you are doing wrong," he said, "is that you are trying too hard to control the outer shape of your pot. Concentrate on the shape inside the pot, and the outside shape will follow naturally." Sometimes a different way of looking at a problem makes all the difference.

The second piece from my first show, "Mirror," is really a portrait of my two selves. At the time, I felt I had to write a preface to the work. In it, I explored my dilemma of being two people in one:

131

"Mirror" is an introspective piece which attempts to express my ambiguous feelings resulting from belonging to two very different cultures. It is a highly symbolic work. The two women are really one, as if one of them is looking at a mirror image of herself. Both are Oriental. One is in Western dress and the other is in a Japanese kimono. But who is the real person and who is the image in the mirror?

I have had many shows since this first one, and exhibited with many other galleries, but in 1980, with the death of both my father and my marriage, I decided that Michi must also die. I removed everything from the gallery and never really said goodbye. I simply said that I would be in touch sometime. It has been over ten years since I walked out of that gallery to begin my new life.

Since that time I have experienced much, but I have never sewn anything again. And it is probable that I will never sew again, because I had never really wanted to become an artist known for wall hangings. I had never wanted to be Michi and I had always thought of myself as a painter. At the present time I am painting images of people and situations that are part of my private world. Now I am faced with a dilemma of a very different nature. To show my work again means that I must be prepared to share my work with strangers and, eventually, to part with it. At the moment, it still belongs completely to me.

My work remains a study of space. I once wrote, "In silent spaces between the notes, I stand outside myself and watch." And it is the poignant space between the figures that carries the essence of the message I wish to convey. Am I, then, a Japanese artist, or am I an artist who is Japanese? Perhaps, ultimately, the answer to that question is heavily ironic; perhaps, ultimately, there is no distinction.

CORRIDORS:
LANGUAGE AS TRAP AND
MEETING GROUND

••••••••••••••••••••

ANGÈLE DENIS

In recent years I have moved frequently along the Quebec-Windsor corridor. I moved first from Quebec City to Toronto to study, then back to Montreal to study as well, and then to what I call Hullottawa. The last move was for work purposes, in an officially — as in Official Languages — bilingual environment. These frequent geographical repositionings corresponded to movements within and between languages — mainly French and English. Each of the cities has a different socio-linguistic reality that corresponds to social issues and mutations in my life. Meeting others and being elsewhere allow you to become conscious of your social and internal Daedalus: of what you are and of what makes you who you are. This movement also brings up questions about where one fits and where one is going, which is what I want to explore here. But what also concerns me, specifically, is the paradoxical character of language as both a trap and a meeting ground.

In reflecting on my experience as a young Québécoise francophone in Canada today, I note how through my moves I have become conscious of the constructs around francophone/Québécois and anglophone/Canadian identities in Canada. Indeed, human beings build;

we set up walls. We define — physically and symbolically — the space we evolve in, and we trace or follow certain corridors. We think along lines; *nous suivons le fil de nos pensées.*

Threshold warning

Language shapes identity and is like a system of corridors. Language fills the air of those corridors; it shapes its walls; it allows us to take some corridors and limits our access to others. Being a francophone in Canada means that I have to write this in English if most Canadians are to understand it. It means writing it in English because a translated version of French would not have the same flavour or imagery. Indeed, because language is also built on mechanics, thinking processes based on different languages invariably vary. Since the very character of what is said, and what is, is altered by the language we use, translation is problematic. The same principle applies to people: what we speak and what we "are" overlap. For this reason, wherever I go I try to learn the local language, since, having lived in English, I understand the loss of spontaneity that comes when expressing oneself in a foreign idiom.

Dangerous connections

Louis-Joseph Papineau was a leader of the 1837-38 rebellion of the Patriotes, crushed by Loyalist forces. He has passed into the popular Quebec imagination as having a particularly sophisticated intelligence. Indeed, Québécois say, when faced with a simple problem, *"Ça prend pas la tête à Papineau (pour comprendre ça)!"* (It doesn't take Papineau's head [to understand this]!) This expression has inspired the title of a book by nationalist writer Jacques Godbout: *Les Têtes à Papineau.* The fictional Papineau, a metaphor for Canada, was born with two heads. These two heads, two persons with a single body, have quite different personalities. Their most important distinction, however, is that while one speaks French, the other speaks English. The novel traces their growth to adulthood, when the Papineau brothers (so to speak) decide to undergo a critical operation that will regularize their existence: they decide to have their heads reunited into one brain made of French and English halves. At that point the metaphorical novel takes on prophetic undertones: the English half obliterates the French half, and the resulting personality is anglophone.

Since moving to Hullottawa, where living a bilingual existence has meant spending about 70 per cent of my time speaking English, I have found myself (still), not without paradox, a Québécois francophone. This situation makes me wonder whether I can escape Papineau's fate, and at this point in history the question remains pertinent not only for me as individual but also on the collective and political levels.

La porte étroite

I was asked, "Are you familiar with culture shock?" At the other end of the phone line was the woman who was interviewing me for an internship overseas. She could not see my smile. "I have experienced my biggest culture shock living in Toronto," I replied. After a pause (surprised?), she pursued the interview, asking how I dealt with it. Culture shock, experts say, is a process made of low and high peaks — a sinusoidal curve that goes from all-is-new-and-I-love-it to this-is-a-crazy-place-and-I-have-had-enough.

It was a fair September day when I arrived to learn (in) English. I wanted to gain access to Canadians' mental Daedalus, to understand how Canadians think, and I was determined to figure it out. In doing so I had to constantly examine, try to understand and relativize, what was happening around/towards/to me. Indeed, identity is both something that you define for yourself and something that others perceive of and place onto you. Toronto was the first in a series of movements and moments through which both the "inside" and "outside" aspects of "who I am" evolved. That is to say, identity is a relational and relative concept. It shapes and is shaped by one's surroundings and influences how one (evolves) in a given environment.

At first Toronto and its people were as diverse as I had expected, and I revelled in this difference. Diversity meant constant discovery and (re)adjustments to what were for me new ways of doing, thinking, being, and interacting. In my first week there I learned the word "tree-hugger" (it was the time of the Clayoquot Sound protests), took part in alcohol-pork-free parties, and was delighted to be anonymous insofar as a francophone accent was only one of the many accents of the crowd. I also soon experienced being called drunk or crazy for dancing tirelessly, and experienced being ignored in meetings when I raised my voice or gestured with my hands while talking. These were all things that had gone unnoticed "where I came from." With exuberance considered entertaining in social settings and embarrassing in serious situations, such as the "business-like" environment of student politics, I was quickly faced with the challenge of making my

135

voice credible and relevant. I made an effort to gain in subtlety in the public arena and relegated manifestations of *joie de vivre* to more personal domains, such as clothing.

After a few years of living essentially in English I found myself getting acculturated into "political correctness," the dominant ethos in my undergraduate environment. I met my first WASP friend, this dear Maxx who made me read Michael Ondaatje as his contribution towards making the "two solitudes" meet: I knew nothing of Canadian literature, other than a few names. I learned there was such a word as "jaywalking," which applied to when I crossed the street at the most immediate opportunity, which seemed like the natural thing to do. I discovered that one could claim to be part German, part English, part French, and part Scottish, and yet be perfectly at ease with the Queen of England as head of state. I realized that the CBC and Pierre Elliott Trudeau were the object of a cult among Canadian intellectuals — many of whom had lived here before the introduction of the Official Languages Act, and who believed that bilingualism and multiculturalism now actually did exist.

All of the things I was becoming accustomed to were expressions of a socially defined corridor, that of Canadians, which I had not known, and with which I could not identify. While I was faced with none of the outright hostility that many Québécois have come to expect, imagining that the Canadian on the street was as virulent against "those who want to break up the country" as some of their editorialists were, I was equally surprised by the general lack of interest for true reflection and discussion about the "Quebec question." It seemed that sovereignty could only be dealt with in one of two ways: either theoretically, by assessing whether the Québécois were a nation (invariably answering no); or emotionally, by expressing that "they would be sad should Quebec separate." Trying to present the issue as a matter of self-determination and local government was met with some sympathy by individuals from the West Coast and socialist radicals. The general refusal to engage in discussion was symptomatic of the lack of sympathy or even the latent hostility people in general felt towards Quebec.

Choosing to identify myself as a Québécoise first and talking overtly about the surprises, annoyances, and differences that I experienced led to me being singled out as a token francophone for an article in the "Cultural Week" issue of my college newspaper. At the worst times I was the qualified "Frenchie." In the best moments I was a oddity.

To be fair, I must say that I also appeared to be an oddity from the

Quebec point of view. For many of my relatives the "known" or safe world stops somewhere in the west end of Montreal, and, having lived in an overwhelmingly francophone environment, they have never experienced the necessity of learning a second language. Moving to Canada voluntarily and out of no apparent necessity was both an unprecedented occurrence and a bizarre choice for them. They could only see the discomfort that comes with being away from habit and familiarity. My moving to Toronto thus meant a repositioning for them too, as I was no longer bound to the standard path of a middle-class Québécois francophone. Experience-wise, I lived in a foreign world, Canada. Language-wise, I spoke a more "international" French, as opposed to joual or Québécois. The only people I would speak French with in Toronto, with any regularity, were non-native speakers. Nonetheless, my relatives were relatively impressed that I had not acquired an English accent in French. They were also impressed that I had successfully overcome the fear that prevents many Québécois from satisfying their desire to meet others — be they Canadians or people from elsewhere.

Soon I would realize that the awareness I had of boundaries/corridors was due not only to the confinement of my French communications, but also to the clear-cut separation between my francophone life/personality and my Canadian persona. It was as if I had grown a second head, one that was more socially acceptable and functionally suited to living in the (self-proclaimed) greatest city of the country. Indeed, the reality of Toronto — what it looks and feels like, how it functions — is very different from that of Quebec City. The cultural referents of the two cities' inhabitants are different. The differences meant that I learned to project a more polite and a less aggressive, epicurean character in Toronto. It also allowed me to gain a different perspective on a number of issues. Concerned with the environment, I found that Canadians are much more ascetic in their activism; they had an ethic that was applied to many more domains of their lives. As another Québécois said, almost without caricature, "Environmentalists in Montreal smoke and eat meat. In Toronto, they are complete granolas." I did find some of the arguments and habits reasonable and in harmony with my own beliefs, and thus adopted some of the Torontonians' practices and attitudes.

I grew a second head — an English one. Depending on the time or issue, I would inhabit one or the other of my two heads. But for many of my interlocutors, this meant at times exhibiting behaviours that appeared to be, or were effectively, "out of place" — that of a Québécoise in Toronto, and a somewhat Torontonian in Quebec. 137

While I had reached my goal of penetrating the Canadian psyche through mastery of its main language, I found myself socially sitting on a fence: in Quebec I was "no longer" a standard Québécois; yet in Canada I was politically marginal(ized) as Québécois and francophone. The latter was not new, but my experience made me conscious of what all this meant.

Even so, I had not yet fully realized the efforts needed to continue living in French within Canada. I would not have thought that a few years later, I would be writing about myself, and sometimes thinking to myself, in English. English was the language of the other — Canada — whose path was parallel and which was, until a hypothetical, successful referendum, a necessary annoyance. I would not have thought that I would be faced with Papineau's dilemma.

Québec, Québec (un long fleuve tranquille)

Raised in what was then a far suburb of Quebec's national capital, in a middle-class, francophone, Catholic family, I could not conjugate the verb "to be" when I arrived in secondary school. I already had, however, a rare mastery of French grammar, and I tremendously enjoyed the hours spent writing and reading, *seulement pour le plaisir des mots*. As I wrote a few years later, I cannot remember my life before books and pencils. I developed a particular affection for dictionaries and started collecting them, as I took part with some success in language games and competitions.

As some belong to the sports crowd, I was associated with the literary crowd: those who wrote, acted out written words, and spent their pocket money watching words put on stage. Not only was language for me a marvellous tool that allowed me to express visions, emotions, the world, but it also allowed me to penetrate the ways in which others felt or saw the world. I slowly realized that language traces the contours of one's world. For example, in English one looks at stained glass, while in French attention is directed to the specific craftsmanship, *le vitrail*. As I realized that other languages were other worlds, I realized too that I wanted to explore some of them.

My love of languages, however, was not enough to make me pursue literature or translation as an area of professionalization. I had been puzzled and angered by the arrogance of visiting Parisians, who considered that Québécois did not speak French (since they could not understand our "accent") and who did not realize the ridicule of "ze way in which zey speak Englishe." I had become conscious of the great gap between spoken and written French; between joual, French spoken by grandparents and relatives in the countryside or in my lower-middle-class suburb, and the French of my bourgeois classmates in secondary school, who had trouble understanding what Michel Tremblay's *Belles-soeurs* were saying on stage. I saw that apparently minor variations in pronunciation readily became a pretext to set up or delineate a fence between socio-economically or politically differentiated groups, even within the same linguistic and national group. I found that people were quick to confine themselves to known pathways within the fences put up by their group.

Obviously, this phenomenon is not limited to the joual-French-Parisian situation. I feel that a fundamental ethical problem exists in the hierarchization of cultures, xenophobia towards immigrants, and other remnants of colonialism. These concerns directed me to pursue studies in social sciences. In my daily existence, as in the life of Québécois in general, in any geo-social axis we chose to pursue, politics and identity were colliding at every twist and turn. In that context my decision to move to Toronto to study was seen as a very courageous move: I was exposing myself, I was told, to being called a "frog" every day, something that was even made to sound like a physical threat. In retrospect there were good and bad times in Toronto, there were cultural and emotional strains, but I rarely felt outright hostility from the people I interacted with. Nonetheless, I eventually grew tired of the city's smoggy atmosphere. I craved for an environment where I would not have to restrain myself and could get beer at the *dépanneur*, 22:57 on a Monday night, if I felt like it. I headed for Montreal.

Glass halls and slamming doors

While it was largely a place of internal reconciliation, Montreal life also challenged perceptions of my identity. Indeed, I had moved too far into the English labyrinth to simply go back. Montreal enabled me to be comfortable with my two heads. Breathing French as they speak it, people from Quebec City imagine that Montreal is or should be just the same as their own town, simply a bit bigger. The Montreal I experienced, however, was definitely a cosmopolitan city, with a large anglophone heritage and with languages as channels for people from different cultures to meet. This made Montreal a city of possibilities, a place where some corridors were transgressed and some walls shattered, where somewhat of a reorganization of one's mindset happened, where there was a third reality/way between French and English. That was where I met an approximately bilingual anglophone who insisted on 139 speaking French with me. It was where newcomers, refusing to be confined to one or the other linguistic labyrinth, put bilingual messages on their answering machines. And for me the place held the possibility of doors open to both sides of the city, of moving in and out of French and English — between *l'est du Plateau* and Westmount, between movies, between home and classes, between friends and lovers.

At the same time I also discovered a city with heightened daily language politics, one where some walls had been reinforced with armoured concrete, where attitudes were rigid and life was often blindly unilingual. I found that anglophones and francophones had a disdain for each other, to the point of incommunicability. As language shapes one's conception of the world, so too in academia it translates into distinct intellectual traditions, where even contemporary ideas and debates rarely cross the linguistic fence. It was experiences like meeting a perfectly bilingual anglophone refusing to speak French with me, and a McGill professor shamelessly saying that students of the university are allowed to write papers and exams in French "as a courtesy," that made me wonder. Both of these people refused to open passages between the linguistic corridors. And sovereignty was an endless and ubiquitously implicit topic of discussion, an inevitable item, and a point of contention in public debates, whatever the initial topic. Francophones and anglophones following parallel runways, paths on each side of a glass pane, just like Papineau with his two heads, had two different existences. Anglophones and francophones looked at each other's gestures with a distance, with little interaction or knowledge of each other's lives. A latent tension was everywhere. Rue St-Laurent was a virtual Berlin Wall; Montreal the microcosm of a greater ensemble — the real dividing line being elsewhere.

The one-way passage

Leaving Montreal was a pragmatic move with an economic motive. Hullottawa, I thought, would also allow me to keep my two heads and get the best of both worlds — I could live in Quebec and go back east for weekends. Instead, it heightened the paradox of still identifying myself as a Québécoise first, and it revealed where the dividing line is.

Spreading out from the banks of the Rivière des Outaouais/Ottawa River are the five bridges that connect Ottawa and Hull. For all geographic and many economic purposes, they really are one city. "Hull," as I was recently told, "has always been the slums of Ottawa." But as anglophones from the Ottawa bank of the river admit, if they step out of the Hull federal government buildings, where so many of them work, they find themselves "in another country." The cultural divide is obvious, yet rarely reconciled. People belong to one or the other side, and are only passersby on the opposite bank. This was made painfully evident to me once more when my conversation with another (rare) francophone player on an Ottawa sports field was interrupted by a sudden, "Hey, We're in Ontario here!" When I signalled my discomfort, the interjector would not acknowledge that his statement might have been inconsiderate. Rather than apologize and recognize that my being offended had some legitimacy, he affirmed being very upset at being called racist. It seemed as if all I was saying was going past him, and could not fit into any familiar scheme of information reception. Yet he had lived across the bridges from Hull for a number of years.

The situation in the region, then, is similar to the one I had seen in Montreal. It is Papineau *écartelé*, his body spread over the fence, each head feigning ignorance of the other. The administrative and political division is also clear-cut: halfway across Pont du Portage, drivers and passersby are notified that their 911 calls will be directed to the Ottawa-Carleton region. An Ottawa-Carleton Social Planning Council looks after the fate of the region on the Ontario side of things. Meanwhile, homeless people and wine shoppers cross the bridge without regards for the border — although the dividing line remains a concern for many, should independence be accomplished. Actually, I am always amazed at how seriously people consider this eventuality of a border gate: it is obviously already there in their heads, reflected in attitudes that I tend to find humorous. Many anglophones do not seem to realize that they (at least) equally share with Québécois francophones the ridiculousness of much of the talk around sovereignty. However, the rigid dividing line in people's heads is not inconsequential. Fearing the physical erection of a fence is enough to make it real.

Nonetheless, Hull is for the time being still a part of Canada. Giant flags on all the government towers for Canada Day, July 1st, clearly remind us of that. Posted in obvious sight almost a week before St-Jean-Baptiste (June 24th), *la fête nationale du Québec*, they were taken down on July 2nd: just long enough to boast, as if to tell Québécois living in the shadow of those towers, "You are not really a nation (but Canada is)." The second part of this affirmation is only whispered, because Canadian nationalism — a positive affirmation of existence as opposed to a definition of a people as being non-American — is only slowly losing its taboo status. It is not clear, however, what being Canadian means. It seems that bilingualism, multiculturalism, and inclusiveness would have a role to play there — but it is not altogether clear that the current institutional corridors can reflect these ideals.

The Folklorridor

Through my experiences I have come to believe that Canadian bilingualism and multiculturalism mean the "folklorization" of cultures. Folklorization involves the relegation of culture to the private domain, allowing "culture" to come into the public realm only during or for festivals. By definition, festivals are a breach in the regular order of things. Limiting the recognition of cultural differences to festivals is a symbolic recognition: it releases some of the pressure that would otherwise be exercised on institutions to change and formally recognize and promote differences.

Being able to speak French is part of this folklorization. But while a number of my colleagues proudly claim years of immersion education, they cannot sustain a simple conversation in French. They have, as an excuse, the lack of easy opportunities to engage with or in French activities, which makes it difficult to maintain and improve their language skills. However, it seems that collectively and publicly they hesitate to take the step between these facts and to admit that having a bilingualism policy in Canada is not enough to make bilingualism part of daily life and to create passageways between francophone and anglophone minds.

For practical reasons, there has been a recognition, in cities such as Toronto, that Canadians communicate in different languages. Therefore one can get information on the public transit routes in several languages. For some reason, the same thinking is not applied with regards to the needs (not to mention rights) of francophones living outside of major French-speaking areas of the country, nor is it applied to francophones travelling or moving to mainly English-speaking areas of the country. Of course, a law that is supposed to enforce this approach is already in place, but there are frequently repeated, documented problems and omissions in its application. There is a law, but it lacks spirit. There is a lack of respect for people who are not English-speakers — a lack of respect that is transformed into a lack of legitimacy. Thus, the folklorridor becomes a shameful one to be in, one that signifies being "out." The other facet of limiting recognition to the symbolic and folkloric one is a concrete violation of rights. It denies the possibility of existing in French in the public space.

This is best shown through the situation of francophones outside of Quebec. In a small community of Northern Ontario that takes about thirteen seconds to drive through on the Trans-Canada Highway, and where I got to spend some time, about 50 per cent of the population was francophone. Yet the town had no signs in French, and the only bilingual sign was that of the Bureau de poste/Post Office. Except in family settings, francophones tended to speak English. Francophones tended to be out of work, because the surrounding mines had closed. Parents were taking their children out of French school because they doubted the quality of the education offered and saw that English literacy made more economic sense.

Even in the absence of this class-language interaction, other francophones *hors-Québec* have told me of the limitations in the development and expression of their identity as francophones. They agreed with a statement made recently on Radio-Canada, that *"L'anglais ne s'apprend pas, ça s'attrappe"* (One does not learn English, one catches it) — with its implicit analogy to a flu and a non-spoken comparison with French, for which mastering even basic grammar requires significant work. They told me of parents bringing the family to church, as do a number of immigrant groups who have their own religious services in big cities, "because that was the only place to be a francophone community."

The latent nationalism that is the corollary of folklorization is also visible in the persistence of Canadians in designating Québécois, Acadiens, Fransaskois, and other francophone groups in Canada as French Canadians. Such is obvious in the recent creation of a Semaine de la francophonie canadienne, which is culturally folklorized to become, in its English version, a Celebration of French Canadian Heritage.

The Canadian folklorization/nationalism ethos has led to the neverending *"société distincte"* bind between Ottawa and Quebec. Indeed, the concept of a different society is oxymoronic and thus has no legitimacy if the society in question is not recognized; and if Québécois are seen as an ethnic group, a cultural heritage, rather than as a living nation and a group with a political identity with geo-historical roots. As a Québécois francophone, I don't necessarily want people, Canadians, to frown upon my accent. Instead I want institutions that are supposed to represent me reflect the society that I belong to. I want the institution to reflect not only "French heritage" but also the living reality of millions of people who live in French. This is not too much to ask, given that Canada already has a Constitution that embeds French as one of its two official languages.

A reason why the folklorridor is a political dead end is because Canadians, and in particular Ontarians, who are the power centre of   143

Canada, suffer from the "white male" syndrome; their culture and biases are assumed to be neutral or default categories. Since they are considered "normal," anything else demands consideration and adaptation in response. But, obviously, it is always easier to lean against a wall than to make an effort at moving or getting rid of it. An anthropological analysis would quickly show that British Canadian folklore is embedded in Canadian institutions, and thus (rendered) invisible. The next step in this chain of reasoning, and the most difficult to admit to and deconstruct, is that, because it is invisible and assumed as a default, British Canadian folklore becomes normative and coercive. It means that being anglophone, in truth or in disguise, is a condition of being upwardly mobile.

Once this realization is made the difficult thing for non-anglophones is to refrain from falling into bitterness, and to try and locate possible avenues for the future. I believe that those avenues lie outside the current mould/walls. Therefore, I again arrive at my original question: can Papineau's fate be avoided? Can one live with two heads, or can two heads be brought into one without one person being obliterated?

Highlighting the mind corridors, the lines of fracture, conflict, discomfort, and incommunicability that characterize the situation of Québécois and francophones in Canada, my experiences remind me that identity is a matter of constant repositioning and choices. There are pernicious impermeable walls that most of us are unaware of most of the time. Consciousness and current debates alert me to the necessity of working through our historical differences. We should not a priori close the door to the other(s). Yet asymmetries between francophones and anglophones have to be resolved. We have to learn to respect each other, not just as a matter of political correctness but as a true appreciation of each other's particularities. For true bilingualism to be realized, one has to be in a context in which people are free to express themselves publicly in the language they are most comfortable with. It means they do not omit or compromise their words with translation.

The challenge is that maintaining an ethno-linguistic and cultural identity remains pertinent, but it continues to be seen as a threat to institutions that the dominant, British Canadian group treats as sacred cows. This attitude is primitive. The Anglo-Saxon establishment will have to learn to live with the mutations that the English language faces as it becomes a tool of communication for people of different cultures. This resolution includes accepting mannerisms, enrichments, and transformations. The same can be said of the retrograde Académie française, which persists in resisting the feminization of French titles and the progression of the language towards a non-sexist grammar. These linguistic struggles are profound normative fights with transformative implications; they mark the reorganization of the public domain and a definite redistribution of visibility and power. The issue is only heightened when a similar normative and political struggle takes place *between* languages. Nonetheless, taking part in these — on the information highway, in university halls, in policy-making and policy implementation work — and learning new languages are a means of escaping Papineau's fate.

As they are fence- and corridor-builders, human beings — as Bruce Chatwin beautifully traces — are also nomads. The corridors we pass through are made up at once of walls and space. They are a place, and at the same time lead us to a place. Fence-sitters are privileged observers but have limited power as cultural mediators. But as human life is about transgressing and transcending borders, we all have to move within our own heads; to meet in new ways and to consider the creation of spaces rather than barriers. True engagement and respect are things that have to be developed and nurtured. Accommodation, and hierarchies of power, are antimonic. Encounters, through glass walls and in corridors, are really starting points, not the end of the journey.

Public spaces that promote and protect diversity have to be built, so that encounters between francophones, anglophones, and others can take place. Diversity has to shape public spaces. Single heads should be sported without arrogance. Being two- or three-headed, having one composite head, should become the accepted norm, and corridors should be replaced by open spaces. Being critical of ourselves, of institutional mannerisms, and of the coerciveness of the institutions around us is a first step. Accepting transformation and engaging in it will be a second. Between seduction and pragmatism, if we have the will and are ready to make the necessary efforts, something should emerge.

Acknowledgements

I want to give credit and heartfelt thanks to howard ramos, who, as an effective, attentive, encouraging, and generally great editor, helped me to complete this article. I also want to thank Carl James for giving me the opportunity to write this article in the first place, and for bearing with me through the process.

For the section "The Folklorridor," I am indebted to my friends and colleagues Arianne Dorval and Attiya Ahmad, with whom I discussed the main ideas presented there.

A Black Canadian Woman
of Diverse Ethnic Origins

•••••••••••••••••••••••••••••••

Marlene Jennings

Let me begin at the beginning. I was born in Canada in the early 1950s. My father, an African American, immigrated to Canada from Alabama in the mid-1940s to work on the Canadian Pacific Railways as a porter. He met and married my mother, a Franco-Manitoban who, like so many French Canadians of Manitoba, was of Belgian and Métis origins. My mother's father was a Métis; his Aboriginal ancestors were of Cree, Algonquin, and Attikamek Nations, and his French ancestor arrived in La Nouvelle France from Oren, France, in 1668. My mother's Belgian mother immigrated to Canada in the late 1890s with her parents under the Canadian Homesteaders' Act. The parents returned to Belgium in the early twentieth century because they found the Canadian West too inhospitable; she, my maternal grandmother, remained and married my Métis grandfather.

I know little of my father's ancestral roots other than that he was a descendant of African slaves and possibly had some European roots. I know this last piece because one of my sisters has blue-grey eyes, and the little biology I learned informs me (and her) that for a child to have blue, green, or grey eye colour both parents must carry the recessive gene. Evidently I know all this about my mother because I have been able to research my family tree on my mother's side (at least the French and Belgian side), while it is virtually impossible to do the same on the African and Aboriginal side of the family.

I have gone through the gamut of expressions when defining myself: Black, Black Canadian, Afro-Canadian, African Canadian, and, finally, as either an African Canadian or Black Canadian woman of diverse ethnic origins. I use the terms African Canadian and Black Canadian interchangeably, because both of them accurately describe at certain times who I am and how I think of myself. The term Black has so many connotations in our society: descendant of African slaves, or a recent African immigrant or refugee to Canada, or the colour of my skin and that of my friends and family members, regardless of the actual shade or hue.

I describe myself as Black when I want to drive home the fact of slavery, racism, and discrimination based upon the colour of my skin and that of so many other Canadians. When it is important to me to make the point that racism does differentiate between "visible minorities" who are "Black" and those who are of other origins, and that racism is not colour-blind, nor is it void of the historical implications for a society that practised slavery and institutionalized and legislated discrimination, then I define myself as a Black woman. When, instinctively, the issue appears to be that of discrimination generally, and not just racism, I define myself as an African Canadian woman. To me the term African denotes an ethnic group, notwithstanding that there are many ethnic peoples living on the African continent.

Ethnicity is more a construct of language, culture, and traditions than it is of historical life conditions. Race, however, does not depend upon language, culture, or traditions. It is a societal construct that aims to explain and prop up inequalities that have been legislated to provide unequal advantage to one group, to give that group privileges denied the other group. I am sure that most people characterized as being "visible minorities" in Canada never thought of themselves in those terms prior to their arrival in this country. They have usually defined themselves by nationality, ethnic origin, or both — not by skin colour. To me that is clear and convincing evidence that race has more to do with racism than it has to do with who one is and how one identifies oneself and those of the same group.

I am married to a man of Italian origin, and we have a child. She is now seven years old, and when asked about her origins she has described herself variously as an African, Italian, French, Belgian, and Native Indian. She has never, to my knowledge, described herself as being Black, but she does accept others defining her as such. She also will accept others defining her as Italian. When we talk to her about 147 how she sees herself, she invariably states that she is "like Mommy." My feeling is that her self-image is primarily based upon her ethnic origins. That may change with time as she begins to experience racism, and I do expect that at some point in her life racism will rear its ugly head. When that happens, she may begin to describe herself as being Black in order to capture the essence of the racism she has experienced.

My daughter's life experience and her view of herself at the present time and in the future are a good example of how the terms "race" and "ethnicity" are played out in our society. My daughter moves comfortably between her different ethnic groups; she is as comfortable interacting within my family as she is with that of her Italian father. She has integrated as well within the Black community in Canada as within the Italian and Native communities. What I find interesting is that while the Black and Italian communities appear to accept her as "one of them," the same does not appear to be true for the French Canadian community, which in general appears to view her as an outsider. Even though French is as much a mother tongue for her as English and Italian are, and one of her maternal grandmothers was a French Canadian, she does not appear to be included within that societal ethnic group. This is interesting given that the Black community considers one Black grandparent sufficient for inclusion.

Essentially, I believe that race is about more than just the colour of one's skin. It calls forth the history of many peoples, and of many different ethnic groups. The word explains, describes, and exposes our combined histories of colonization, slavery, discrimination, servitude, and finally racism; and racism embodies all of the other terms. Ethnicity, though, also explains who we are and why we look the way we do. Our actions, thoughts, and behaviours are related to both our race and ethnicity, and ultimately to our cultural practices. These terms are used interchangeably, but we need to be cognizant of their different meanings, recognizing that they both describe how racism has become so imbedded in our society and our collective psyches. After all, today people never use the term "yellow" to describe those of Asian origin — unless, of course, they consciously want to make an insult — and the only terms of colour that seem to be socially acceptable in today's society are white, Black, and brown: these tendencies are a real statement of how racism has left its indelible mark on society. The roots of slavery, then, have spread wide and deep within the social dynamic of everyday life.

Part IV
Race, Privilege, and Challenges

"I've Never Had a Black Teacher Before"
••••••••••••••••••••••
Carl E. James

"I've never had a Black teacher before": the statement was offered over and over again as a supposedly credible explanation for the complaints, questions, challenges, and disruptive behaviours that I experienced in my classes, largely made up of white students. With this declaration students expected me to understand their dilemmas and sympathize with their struggles of knowing how to relate to me, or what to expect from me: it was their first experience with a Black teacher. Why is this information important for me to know? Why is my race a factor? What does race have to do with my role as a teacher, anyway?

I do not want to question the comment, because, after all, it expresses the students' experiences and reality. It is what is implied by this statement — what is not said — that I want to discuss here. In doing so, I am drawing on my more than fifteen years' experience as a Black male educator at colleges and universities in southern Ontario. In referring to their comments, I will discuss how the preconceived ideas of students (both whites and racial minorities)[1] inform their expectations of and interactions with me as a racial minority teacher, and how these expectations and interactions in turn have an impact on teaching and learning.[2]

The role of race in teacher-student interactions is a significant challenge that must be acknowledged and examined. For as Patricia Williams (1991: 83-84) writes in her book *The Alchemy of Race and Rights: Diary of a Law Professor*, "Race isn't important because it isn't important; most of us devoutly wish this to be a colour blind society, in which removing the words 'black' and 'white' from our vocabulary would render the word, in a miraculous flash, free of all divisions. . . . Often we have to use the words in order to acknowledge the undeniable psychological and cultural power of racial constructions upon all our lives." And as Cornell West (1993) writes, "Race matters."

"Initial opinions"

Upon entering a classroom, all teachers are subjected to evaluations based on students' personal experiences with teachers. These evaluations will also be a result of assumptions and stereotypes based on such things as the teacher's dress, sex, accent, voice, social class, and race. If students associate Black people with a lower social class, and concomitantly lower levels of education, and with welfare and crime, these associations will influence how they perceive a Black teacher. One of my students, for instance, expressed the following opinion: "My initial opinions of Carl were negative . . . his black skin 'surprised' me . . . [and] his accent annoyed me. The idea of having a black teacher quite intrigued me, but having to cope with a poorly educated black teacher seemed to be asking a lot."

This assumption of my educational background also has to do with a prevailing construction of Caribbean people. The student continued: "I was . . . surprised when I later found out that Carl has a Ph.D. in Sociology. Somehow that did not fit my stereotype of a Black person especially from the Caribbean. (However, I could picture an American Black person having a doctorate.)"

That I did not "fit" the stereotype not only surprised some students, but it sometimes also contributed to feelings of anger. For example, one student wrote: "No one in the class told me our teacher was Black and for some reason I felt angry that no one mentioned this to me. . . . Carl is very dark and black and I have had problems with dark black people in the past."

The anger that this student felt can be related to the source of her surprise. It was a surprise that the teacher who walked into the room was not white, something that understandably many students had come to expect and accept as a given. If all of their elementary and high-school teachers had been white, it would only seem logical to them that their post-secondary teachers would also be white. My presence therefore was an anomaly — a deviation from the norm; it was something for which the students were unprepared, something that, as some of them would have us believe, they were unable to handle because they had no previous experience to call upon. This lack of experience can contribute to feelings of confusion and uncertainty and expressions of anger as individuals seek ways of dealing with the new situation. But individuals are not blank or vacuous, or totally without some experience in relating to Black people (if only in terms of the information they acquire from television or newspapers). Hence, any encounter with and judgement of a Black person will be informed by acquired biases and stereotypes. This frame of reference might explain why one of my students assumed that she would most likely have problems with me because she had "problems with dark black people in the past."

The student's comment also raises an interesting question: should the background of the teacher, educator, or professor be communicated to students beforehand as a way of preparing them to deal with the encounter? As faculties in post-secondary institutions become more diverse, students will be in for more "surprises"; and, as the comment indicates, previous experiences with minority teachers are no guarantee that students will be more accepting of the faculty member. If the students had heard about me, or had been able to guess my racial, ethnic, and/or religious background from my first or last names, would the encounter be any different? (Of course, given the history of British colonization neither of my names gives an indication of my race or ethnic background.) It is possible that such information would contribute to a decision to drop the class or willingly, as opposed to reluctantly, take it. The students who reluctantly take a course are a challenge to work with, because they are often resistant, not only to me, as the above comments indicate, but also to the materials, the ideas explored, the pedagogical approach, and, possibly, many other aspects of the teaching. I have taught compulsory courses that turned out to be very difficult because of the complaints and criticisms that had to be addressed. In a few courses, after the first two or three classes participation shrank to about one-half. Both situations can challenge anyone's morale. In my case I have spent a considerable amount of time thinking about how best to handle my first class. Indeed, like the students, I come into it loaded with my previous experiences. But this problem is not just a matter for myself or other minority teachers to address on our own; it is something for the institutions to address. Disclosing the background of the teacher does not remove the problem — the underpinnings of which are inequity, racism, classism, sexism, and stereotyping, all of which must also be addressed.

The initial "surprise" and resultant uncertainty are also experienced by racial minority students. Like their white peers, they have also had limited experience with racial minority teachers and have come to expect that their teachers will be white. As one Black student typically said, "In all my years of attending school I had never met a black teacher. Even though I myself am black I felt a bit uneasy, and unsure of how to react towards this teacher." For some Black students, that initial sense of surprise and uneasiness is followed by ambivalence and antagonism born of particular expectations.

"Where are you from?"

Within either the first hour of my first class or the first two weeks, students usually ask me, "Where are you from?" or "Are you from Jamaica?" In earlier years I used to say, "I am from the Caribbean," and to the Jamaica question I would say, "I'm not from Jamaica." And when I ask, "Why the question?" or "Why do you assume that I am not Canadian, but an immigrant?" the response is, "Because you have an accent."

Nowadays usually I do not answer the question, because I want to challenge the tendency of students, like many other Canadians, to associate being Black with being an immigrant. That tendency is an example of how individuals, consciously and unconsciously, reaffirm difference and remind those of us who are constructed as "other" — because we do not "look and/or sound Canadian" — of our "outsider status" (see James 1999). Is it any wonder, then, that, when asked, we mention our ethnocultural origins, hyphenate our identities, and/or continue to identify ourselves as immigrants rather than Canadians? In doing so, we avoid the further questions, "But where are you really from?"

In some circles the question "Where are you from?" is considered a "friendly" way of initiating a conversation, of indicating an interest in the background and experiences of the person, and/or of showing that the questioner sees "difference" and is not "colour-blind." I am aware that students sometimes ask this question because they are interested in establishing a "friendly" rapport with me. But my response (or non-response) to the question does not mean that I am being unfriendly; rather, it is a way to have students, and whites in particular, recognize that all of our interactions, and indeed the educational process we engage in, are mediated by our race and other

153

identities — their own as well as mine. Race and racial difference, then, are not the only, or even the most, significant factors around which interactions are built. I am not suggesting that students ignore our differences with regard to race — surely, we all see colour — but I want them to recognize, in my reactions to the question, my resistance to how my "otherness" is reinscribed and the not-so-subtle ways in which they make evident their privilege and power in our encounters.

In my experience with racial minority students, and Blacks in particular, the question is sometimes a way of establishing a connection or creating distance. In attempting to create distance, the question would be a way of demonstrating to their peers that there is a difference between us — I talk with an "accented" voice and they do not, because they are Canadian (born). What is partially communicated here to me and their peers is the idea that although we are the same in skin colour, there are important differences that must be taken into account. Thus they protect themselves from any embarrassing situation that may arise with me as their teacher.

"You have an accent"

Because I am a Black immigrant person "with an accent," people assume that I am Jamaican. This stereotype of Caribbean immigrants is a reflection of the homogenizing practices of individuals and the failure, premised in part on racism, to recognize the diversity among us — the Caribbean is, after all, a large region with many islands (and I am sure most people are aware of this). Another construction of Caribbean people and by extension me, based on accent, is illustrated in a comment by the same student who spoke about "having to cope with a poorly educated black teacher." She wrote:

> My assumption that Carl was poorly educated stemmed from the fact that he has an accent. Now, if Carl had had a British accent I would have probably assumed that he was quite well educated. British people "sound" well educated to me simply because of their accents, not because they are in fact, more educated. Conversely, Caribbean accents, which have a different grammar structure than the English I speak, arbitrarily "sound" less educated to me. In reality I know that there is absolutely no correlation between accent and level of education, but this knowledge has never stopped me from making unfounded first assumptions.

154   Indeed, there is "absolutely no correlation between accent and level of

education," but nevertheless people often make this association. Our colonial legacy is so pervasive that despite evidence to the contrary, we hold onto the myths that help to construct some people as educated and others as not. The "some" whom we construct as "educated" — in other words, intellectually superior, articulate, and well-spoken (in this case having a good command of English) — are people of a particular physical type. We cannot assume that *all* people with British accents are "well-educated." Certainly, while she did not articulate this point, the writer must have been well aware that accents are not homogeneous; in this regard, she is probably referring to a particular "British accent," most likely the one that indicates privilege based on class, race, immigrant status, and other characteristics.

Interestingly, the student did not say "if Carl had a Canadian accent." Is it that she thinks Canadians do not have accents? It has often been my experience that "Canadians" (I think here of white English-speaking Canadians) tend to think that "other" people (including Newfoundlanders [see Tilley 2000]) have accents. Yes, I have an accent like everyone else, and it is informed by the national, regional, social, and historical conditions — in short, the cultural contexts — of the Caribbean and Canada. That I have lived in Canada longer than I lived in the Caribbean has influenced my accent; and evidently accounts for how, when I am in the Caribbean, people there suggest that I have a Canadian accent. How is it that students do not identify my accent as Canadian? (Interestingly, in both contexts, my accent is attributed to the other place I have lived in.) Surely, my accent is Canadian; it is one of the many "Canadian accents," all of which are related to social class, language, country of origin, schooling, and other factors. Surely, all of us have accents, and these accents exist in relation to listeners' accents. No accent is neutral, and those who claim that they do not have accents are discounting the codes and tones that govern their communication, which, as Dean Barnlund (1988, cited in James 1999: 193) said of cultural differences, are "unconsciously acquired and automatically employed."

Furthermore, accents take on specific meanings and significance in particular contexts. So what students think of my accent, and the association they make between my accent, colour, Caribbean origin, and level of education, are related to the cultural norms and expectations of the Canadian society generally, as well as to the classroom context in which our interactions are taking place. The culture of the classroom is one in which supportive relationships with peers establish norms that all students are expected to follow. These norms help to govern students' expectations about and participation in the 155 educational process, and their perceptions of who is best able to assist them to achieve their aspirations with the least amount of work and problems.

On this basis, and depending on the experiences, biases, and listening skills of students, the accent of the teacher takes on particular significance. Admittedly, listening is work, and listening to someone with a "foreign" accent can contribute to a level of stress or tension, as well as problems. Understandably, individuals will seek to avoid the additional or extra work unless they understand that work and differences are inherent to all encounters. In this regard then, students will undertake to make each encounter a new learning experience.

In the case of one student, a "one-on-one" experience with me three weeks into the course gave her an opportunity to see past my colour. In a conversation I had with her at the end of the course, she pointed out that I said nothing "spectacular" to her. I was saying the same things I "had been saying in class," but in her words: "This time, however, I was talking with a person, not the black man or professor I had heard in class. . . . I started listening to him in class as a person. I had been concentrating on the strange sounds of his accent instead of what he was saying. After a while I got used to his accent and didn't think about it anymore."

Significantly, it was our "one-on-one" interaction — an interaction that took place away from the cultural milieu of the classroom, where peer sanctions help to maintain the established norms and practices — that enabled this student to put "our differences" into perspective. Is this a practice, then, that all teachers in my situation should follow? Surely, it will not work in all situations.

"This course will be right up his alley"

Like everyone else, on the basis of gender, race, ethnicity, disability, and other characteristics students often make stereotypical assumptions about professors' or teachers' qualifications or expertise and hence about what they will be teaching. For example, with reference to one of the courses I taught, one student pointed out: "I have never expected to be lectured in a course like this by a Black teacher. Thinking back, I guess that I took it for granted that a course dealing with Canadian culture will be taught by a person from the majority (white)."

But not everyone operates with the same stereotypes. While I am perceived by some as a person unlikely to be teaching about "Canadian culture," others believe that culture, race, and ethnicity are more likely to be topics of interest to a racial or ethnic minority or immigrant person. In one student's words: "The moment he walked into the classroom on the first day, his skin colour was predominant and I thought to myself, 'Oh, he's Black. This course will be right up his alley.'" No doubt such thinking is deeply rooted in our value system, nurtured as it is by schools, textbooks, media, family, and many other influences that portray certain kinds of people as having the expertise to address particular subjects.

For that reason I have often had to address the challenges posed by the stereotypes that present minorities as being limited in academic qualifications[3] and/or professional capacities and lacking in objectivity. On the question of objectivity, one student stated:

> I am now sure that if a white man had stood there and talked about immigration to Canada and how non-whites were discriminated against I would have taken it much differently. I found myself saying that both his writing and teaching were clearly taken from a black person's point of view and I wanted him to be more objective. Could this . . . really mean that I wanted him to be white? I'm not really sure.

In challenging these preconceived ideas, I note my qualifications and their relevance to my responsibility in teaching about culture, race and ethnic relations, inequality, racism, and discrimination, among other things. In addition I have had to assert the legitimacy of my interpretations or analyses of issues, and indicate that these are not merely based on personal or political interests but are also informed by theory — in the same way that any other explorations would be. Further, I suggest that the analyses or interpretations have legitimate standing in any academic discourse.

"My immediate reaction was to feel defensive about my WASP background"

The students' exploration of issues related to inequality based on social class, gender, ethnicity, and race is often accompanied by deeply felt emotions as they struggle to understand how the structures of our society have perpetuated and maintained inequalities, and how mechanisms such as classism, sexism, racism, and heterosexism have operated to maintain the status quo. Sometimes students claim that these issues as taught by a Black person contribute to their discomfort, fear, and defensiveness.

One student wrote: "Carl was the first black teacher I have ever had, which also made me slightly more uncomfortable. This discomfort, I believe, was more a fear of what to expect." Another wrote: "I looked around the classroom and saw a number of minority groups represented amongst us, including the teacher. My immediate reaction was to feel defensive about my WASP background." This indicates that as an educator, not only am I responsible for organizing and structuring courses that challenge students intellectually, but I am also expected to anticipate and be sensitive to their feelings. While sensitivity is a critical requirement for all teachers, this prerequisite becomes more significant in this case because my race is factored into both the course content and my interactions with students. In other words, my body is read as course content, curriculum, and text. In following this pattern, students tend to take no responsibility for their part in the pedagogical approach, learning process, interactions, outcomes, and consequences.

Typically, teachers will challenge students to critically assess a situation or seek alternative explanations for social issues. In some cases, my challenges are seen as a deliberate attempt to "bring out individuals' prejudices," or as inappropriate and/or reflective of my militancy or oversensitivity to issues of prejudice or racism. Some students even go further to suggest that I "have a chip on my shoulder" and I am "taking out my anger on them" because of my "experience with racism." Once, after a student became angry and walked out of class, he sent me a note:

"I found that while being in your course (not your fault) my prejudices have become stronger because I don't like breaking people down to a race or culture, skin colour or language, I accept people for who they are if they're an asshole so be it. . . . P.S. as a child did some one ever persecute you, you seem touchy."

There is no question that this student, like everyone else, breaks "people down into race, skin colour" and other characteristics. Indeed, in our interactions with people we are constantly making assumptions about their backgrounds, experiences, and personality (are they "nice" people?) in our attempt to make sense of all the information being communicated to us. To make sense of people we code the information using age, gender, race, ethnicity, hair colour, and other characteristics, as well as our prior knowledge and experiences. Nevertheless, social etiquette warns us against "making judgements." It seems therefore that we can categorize individuals in our thoughts, but we must not articulate it or admit that we do so — and instead say to ourselves, "I accept people for who they are."

For my students I was breaking this rule of etiquette — in other words, violating the cultural norm. I was making explicit something that is practised, and I dared to bring it into the educational process. Contrary to the students' claim, it was not that the course brought out their prejudices or made their prejudices stronger; it was their resistance to making explicit the prejudices that inform their assumptions and practices. Their comments and behaviour indicate their resistance to engaging in activities that would have them take responsibility for their prejudices. Hence they pass that responsibility on to me for "doing this to them," and in the process question why I am not like the rest of the population — "as a child did some one ever persecute you, you seem touchy." Clearly, an assumption related to my background was being made about me.

Further, as part of their resistance, some students claim that I am "intimidating" or I make them "angry." One student commented: "The first day I entered your class I had a really open mind. . . . When I left the class, though, I was feeling really angry. In fact, when I went home that night I told my parents that I had a prejudiced Black teacher." This comment is consistent with many others that make an association between my race, gender, and the conceptualization and analytical work in which we are engaged. As we've seen, one student questioned how she would have responded if I had been a white man talking about immigration and discrimination against minorities. Certainly, she would have reacted differently. With few exceptions, a white male teacher (the female teacher would probably draw a different reaction) would not be considered as subjectively teaching from a white perspective or viewpoint. As a number of scholars have pointed out, whites tend to think of themselves as neutral, normative, average, and objective (McIntosh 1995; Ng 1993; Phoenix 1997; Roman 1993, 1997; Sleeter 1993).

Thus students will regard any readings and assignments (and by extension the teacher who assigns them) that require them to critically reflect or re-examine their long-held world views — views legitimated by years of education, teachers, media, significant others — as being biased, prejudiced, and misleading. Ironically, they do not think of what they might have learned otherwise as being from a "white point of view." For, after all, it is difficult for them to begin to believe that their education has been one-sided and limited.

Evidently, I bring to my teaching a framework and knowledge informed by my education in sociology, my scholarship, my experience as a Black Caribbean immigrant student, and now a professor and researcher; and there is no escaping how this framework and 159 knowledge inform my analysis, interpretation, and understanding of events, situations, practices, and interactions. But I do not think that this inherent bias should deter me, or any other teacher, from engaging students in critical analyses, even though students might use the claim of bias to challenge my credibility as a teacher and the legitimacy of my analyses or discourse. I interpret students' challenges as part of their resistance to what I try to communicate. At the same time I think it is important for me to challenge students to examine their "own lenses" — the ones they use to identify what I say as bias.

My experience has shown that when students are unwilling to accept other or alternative explanations — why working-class people, women, or racial minorities, for instance, are justified in challenging the social and economic system that has disadvantaged them — they identify what I say as bias. Further, it seems to me that the reason for their suggestions of bias springs from *who* presents the information rather than from the course content itself or from the students' unwillingness and/or fear of confronting issues. So I tend not to engage in discussions that attempt to dispel the idea that I am biased. For I believe that through critical education students will come to understand that there is a relationship between attitudes held, socialization, race, gender, and social class; and that educational processes necessarily involve our intellect, biology, and emotions.

Furthermore, teaching is not done merely to confirm the status quo, but rather to enable us to take agency and challenge ourselves so that we empower ourselves and become critical participants in our educational processes and in society as a whole. If students become uncomfortable or angry as they learn about the mechanisms in society that have privileged and/or disadvantaged them, and about their role in promoting and maintaining this situation, this may well be the important starting point of a critical and necessary self-reflective journey.

"I felt a sense of pride and belonging because . . . the person in charge was just like me"

Evidently, my experiences with racial minority students, and their experiences with me, were different. For some Black students (often a small proportion of the class members), I was their first Black teacher, and like their white peers they felt "uneasy and unsure of how to react" towards me; others felt positive and comfortable, and some made public "their differences" in relation to my background. Clearly, there was much more to the dynamics of our relationships. Some reported that they felt a responsibility to ensure that they did not make fools of themselves, because with a Black teacher they are "noticed more." Correspondingly, they expected that my behaviour would not embarrass them. For this reason they scrutinized my colour and accent, even my clothes. In the words of one student:

"Our teacher walked in dressed very casually. He is also what you call a typical looking black man, with a short haircut and dark brown skin. To top it all off, he spoke with an accent. I could understand, but I wasn't so sure that everybody else did."

Other Black students felt that my being Black was in their "favour" — it helped them to feel validated. One said: "I suppose I felt a sense of pride and belonging because for once the person in charge was just like me — a minority. I felt like I had something over my classmates." I would often find these students to be supportive, co-operative, and committed to the educational process. For instance, in situations where I would be characterized as prejudiced and biased, racial minority students would be unequivocal in their disagreement with their (often white) peers. Black students, in particular, were most emphatic in suggesting that their peers' positions were based on ignorance, resistance, and racism. One of them said:

> I realized that our class was only acting the way they were because of their ignorance and the colour of Carl's skin. I know if it was a white teacher who was saying the same things, their reactions would have been much different. With [my teacher], it seemed that they didn't want to learn or believe that what he was saying was really true. Many people imply that he was being prejudiced and only cared about what was happening with blacks and nobody else. . . . No matter what Carl said they always had something to say trying to make it look like what he was saying was all because he was black.

But it seems that in return for these students' support and co-operation I was expected to show preferential treatment or "go easy on them." As one student said, "I actually thought that maybe I'd get special treatment because Carl is black." However, fortunately for me, some students appropriately reasoned that since the majority of students are white and the majority of teachers are predominantly white, white students should not expect to be treated differently because of the colour of the teacher. "They couldn't possibly expect preference. After all, there are too many of them for special treatment."

One area of ongoing concern, and one that causes much tension and conflict, involves grades. In attempts to prove my bias, students would refer to grades. Those who received low grades would look for reasons, and it was often convenient to blame me — my prejudice, bias, subjectivity, lack of clarity.[4] If Black students were in the class, evidence of my bias would be that I graded Black students "easier," and some students would make comparisons between the grades received by white and Black members of the class. One Black student reported that he felt such comparisons were unfair:

> After our group received a good mark, the class turned around and said it was due to . . . favouritism for our group because there were two black people within our group. Boy, did that ever make me mad! I felt that I worked very hard for what I had accomplished. I took the extra time to talk to our teacher like he was any other teacher to find out what was really expected of us in the assignment.

This is not to suggest that Black students do not do the same and claim racism when white students get better grades than they do. But generally, where grades are concerned Black students are very much aware of the peer group dynamics when the teacher is Black. They claim that they have to work hard to satisfy the "high expectations of the teacher" (who some suggest has similar expectations as their parents), and to prove to their peers that they deserve the grades they receive. This issue of grades sometimes produces pressures that many Black students want to avoid.

Also, some Black students are "looking for a break" from the white teachers and the educational system from which they have felt alienated. But Black teachers are not uncritically accepted as the alternative. We are scrutinized, tested, and evaluated for the extent to which we "ignore" or "affirm" Black students or "take the place of the colonizer." Sometimes I might be one of the few teachers who point out weaknesses to these students or from whom they receive low grades (especially if they have been "succeeding" with white teachers all along), and they perceive me as imposing "harsher standards" and having "unreasonable expectations of Black students." Moreover, they see me as "carrying on where white teachers have left off" — "the continuation of colonization but a different overseer."

Having to negotiate issues related to grades, assuming expectations on the part of Black teachers, feeling uneasy about their "first" experience with a Black teacher, and contending with the perceived prejudices and racism of their white peers: all of these experiences contribute to a difficult educational situation.[5] All of them can lead to ambivalent and antagonistic relationships between the Black teacher and Black students as students grapple with maintaining a friendly but distant relationship. Writing about his experience dealing with this contradictory and contested terrain of being a Black teacher of Black students in a majority white institution, Cecil Foster, in his book *A Place Called Heaven: The Meaning of Being Black in Canada* (1996), discusses in detail a situation that arose in his journalism class with a Black student named Cheryl. He suggests that from very early in their meeting, "Cheryl and I were on a collision course." Although Cheryl's lack of punctuality and poor class attendance had contributed to the difficulties in their relationship, Foster posits:

> It might have been her attitude that turned me off from the outset. Or, it might have been the fact that she is black, and I expected more and better of her. I expected that, being black, she would not simply presume that I would pass her just because we had the same colour of skin. To the contrary, I demanded more than just coasting if college life was supposed to be preparing her for the realities of life outside the classroom. . . . There would be no coddling on my part. This would be a good dose of tough love from one black to another. (Foster 1996: 118-19)

Fortunately, this situation with Cheryl turned out positively after Cheryl's mother and Foster were able to have a talk and iron out the difficulties. But it highlights how Black teachers' experiences with Black students are often no less fraught with tension and difficulties than they are with white students.

So while I welcome the opportunity to be a part of the educational process of Black students, I am conscious that I do so within the context of their experiences with racism, stereotyping, and discrimination, and within an educational system from which they feel alienated. Consequently, I cannot expect to be accepted as a teacher without questions being raised, and without ambivalence, tensions, and conflicts, because Black students too have internalized the white cultural values of their schooling or have become quite cynical about the capacity of anyone working within the system to change their situation or the system. Further, I cannot assume that these students will be unquestioning or uncritical allies just because I share with them the same history and many of the same racial experiences. For these reasons, I must be prepared to deal with the ambivalence, expectations, conditional support, and doubts. Given all these issues, it can be expected that our relationships will often be filled with tensions and conflicts.

"What if he had been white?"

The issues raised here are certainly not unique to me. Many racial and ethnic minority people, women, and people with disabilities have related similar experiences as teachers (see Mukherjee's article here; Essed 2000; Foster 1996; Graveline 1998; Iseke-Barnes 2000; J. James 1993; Karamcheti 1995; Ng 1994; Srivastava 1997; Williams 1991). In some avenues, experiences like these are considered to be part of the "minority experience." Accordingly, as a minority teacher, I must give consideration to how my race, tone of voice, eye contact, smile (or lack thereof), the way in which and when I introduce certain topics, and what I say have an impact on my interaction with students. I have to be selective in the comments I respond to and the challenges I take up. And while I have always welcomed students' challenges, even those that boldly express their displeasure and anger, I am well aware of their disruptive effects on the teaching and learning process and must be ready to address the consequences. Nevertheless, I find it appropriate to enable all voices to speak during classes, for this is what active engagement is all about.

Further, I see the challenges that I receive from students as a reminder of the paradox or precariousness of my role as a teacher. On the one hand, I have authority vested in me by the position I hold; at the same time, this authority is mediated by my colour. This mixed role reflects the extent to which my authority is situational at best and circumscribed by my minority status in this society. Thus, when students ask, "Where are you from?" or "What do you want?" or comment on my accent or teaching style, they are providing subtle reminders that I am a member of a minority and that they are thereby asserting their position in relation to me.

In writing of this paradox of power, which she experiences as a Black law professor, Patricia Williams (1991: 95-96) points out: "I am expected to woo students even as I try to fend them off; I am supposed to control them even as I am supposed to manipulate them into loving me. Still I am aware of the paradox of my power over these students. I am aware of my role, my place in an institution that is larger than myself, whose power I wield even as I am powerless, whose shield of respectability shelters me even as I am disrespected."

By factoring my race into our interactions, and claiming that their inexperience with Black teachers is responsible for some of the problems they experience with me, students (both white and Black) absolve themselves of their role and responsibility in the educational process. Their strategy is to avoid the confrontation with self, and to delay the pain of knowing that they must change. Hence, to protect themselves and to evade the immediate need to confront their expectations and question what they have all along accepted as truths, knowledge, objectivity, morality, and neutrality, they see the problem as resting with me, their teacher, not within themselves or societal structures and ideology. Indeed, this is an excellent example of a case in which societal, institutional, and individual aspects of racism play themselves out.

Still, amid all the anxieties, frustrations, denial, anger, surprises, cynicism, and hostility, by the end of a course some students do critically reflect on what they have learned and admit to the role that race has played in their perception of and reactions to me. As one student asserted: "I was mistaken and thought that Carl, himself, was prejudiced terribly against whites. What if he had been white? Would I have had these same feelings of aggression towards him?" Another student wrote:

> As I sit and write this assignment one revelation hit me that I did not think of before. The uptight feelings I had in the class, although brought out because of the topics, were affected by the instructor. It has nothing to do with his capabilities as a teacher but rather the colour of his skin. This may sound racist but let me finish. In the eighteen years I have been in school, I have never had a Black teacher, or one of any minority. To have a Black teacher teaching race relations and the class discussing agendas that hit close to home, surely affected the way I perceived my environment.

It is inspiring to know that eventually some students will come to recognize their role in the learning process, and admit to what they have learned. The positive responses to the learning experience provide a needed and necessary support that helps put into perspective the negative comments that tend to be received in course evaluations at the end of the semester. Here I am taking for granted that course evaluations are often uncritically assessed by some teaching colleagues and administrators, with little consideration given to course content, students' profile and experiences, and of course the background of the teacher.

In the end, receiving the comment "I've never had a Black teacher before" is understandable because, according to Statistics Canada's 1996 census figures, only about 300,000 Black or African Canadians live in Ontario, making up about 3 per cent of the province's population. (Some people, particularly Black community members, suggest that this is a conservative estimate.) This relatively small number means that many students do not have the opportunity to experience

165

learning with Black teachers. The numbers in turn relate to discriminatory immigration policies that have limited the ability of African peoples to come to Canada, and to the structural inequalities and discriminatory practices that account for Black people's lack of access to teaching opportunities. Unfortunately, students do not usually encounter this important information, largely because it is part of a subject matter that is not critically explored in their education.

As for me, being referred to as a "Black teacher" does matter. I am a teacher who happens to be Black, and this identity informs my position in society and how I see the world. My race operates as a significant social force, profoundly influencing my interactions with students from the very first day I walk into the classroom. Given the way in which society has constructed the perception of Blacks, students enter the classroom with stereotypes that mediate my qualifications, potential, and expectations as a teacher. As an African Canadian, which is how I identify myself ethnically, I am aware that the role that my skin colour plays in my interactions with students cannot go unnoticed. Undoubtedly, as anti-essentialists would argue, my identity is not fixed, but naming identity can open up dialogue and provide insights into self in relation to context and social encounters (see James 2000; also Bramble 2000; Martin 1994). Furthermore, I recognize "the undiminished power of racism and its effect on black people who continue to comprehend their lives through what it does to them" (Gilroy 1993: 102). Finally, while being Black cannot be regarded as something that is incidental to being a teacher, it should not be the most significant factor that is used to judge me, categorize me, or deny me the privileges that accrue to other educators.

Notes

1 I use the terms minority, as opposed to people of colour or racialized or minoritized students, and "visible" minority to convey the hegemonic relationship of these ethno-racial group members to the social and political structures of power in our society.

2 In this revised version of the article first published in *Talking about Difference* (1994), I am taking the opportunity of revisiting my ideas and interpretations of the students' comments that I advanced in that earlier piece and of offering additional and, in some cases, different interpretations in light of additional information and new perspectives. Another version of this essay appeared as "The Paradox of Power and Privilege: Race, Gender and Occupational Position," *Canadian Woman Studies Journal*, vol. 14, no. 2 (Spring 1994), pp.47-51.

3 At times students have insinuated that I might be an "equity hire" since I was a member of one of the employment equity/affirmative action target groups. But while it was never explicitly suggested that I had benefited

directly from an equity program, most often, and particularly when I was teaching aspiring police officers, it was what I "symbolically" represented — the group of minority people, that is to say, "young Black men," who were perceived to be robbing them of their chances to fulfil the careers to which they aspired. In this regard, I was the recipient of some students' frustrations and anger because they saw me as being biased and as defending the programs. They always seemed to know some "unqualified" Black person who had obtained a job at the expense of a white person. Many students saw this as injustice, and would contend that they "should not have to pay for past practices." In reflecting on these discussions, one student said, "Some anger was most likely directed towards the instructor not as an individual but as one representing all the frustrations and individuals that may pose a threat to our advancement to a career."

4 A lack of clarity on my part was something that many students would claim to be the reason for them not doing well on assignments. Obviously, sometimes this problem has to do with them not wanting to take responsibility for the work that they must put in. This latter point is sometimes expressed in their statement "What do you want?" — indicating that I am asking for things that are unique to me.

5 Sometimes students express their dissatisfaction with such an educational context or resentment towards Black teachers in statements like "I do not like Black teachers" or "I prefer white teachers."

WHITE TEACHER, BLACK LITERATURE

●●●●●●●●●●●●●●●●●●●●●●●

LESLIE SANDERS

When I agreed to write an article for this collection, I thought it would be a relatively easy and interesting task. As a white person engaged in research and teaching in the field of African American literature for almost twenty-five years, I have frequently had to reflect upon my position. But writing this essay hasn't come easily at all. Early drafts sounded like manifestos or apologies. Some things I really wanted to say felt personal and private; other ideas, when put in writing, seemed pretentious. Contemporary identity politics, both in theory and in practice, now complicate how I might want to describe my position, which some formulations of Afrocentricity assert is untenable, in any event. So why and how did I become a scholar and teacher of "African American literature"? And why am I still doing it?

My reasons are, at root, intensely personal, but so too is any scholarship. I think people usually choose fields that provide them with a way of articulating their most basic questions about life. Lost in all the complex issues that could be discussed is the obvious idea that we study in order to *learn from*.

This process of learning from is complex. We have increasingly come to understand that all knowledge is constructed from particular points of view, and relies on particular assumptions. As we study we are also making knowledge because we make connections, see significance, and interpret — always from particular points of view, both individual and cultural. The history of the field of African American literature is a good example of how problematic this process can be. White scholars of Black culture have often represented the academy at its most imperialist. For example, in the early 1960s, the U.S. sociologist Daniel Moynihan pronounced the African American family dysfunctional. His "expertise" determined conventional wisdom and government policy for the next generation, to the extreme detriment of those whom the policies purported to help. The belief that the scholar is an "authority," capable of ascertaining truth, is extremely dangerous.

White scholars in African American studies can, however, undermine conventional views of academic authority, simply by refusing to claim that authority. We can, instead, be students, seeking to learn rather than to pronounce, sharing what we discover, testing its usefulness by constant dialogue with those for whom our findings, and their own, are more personal and critical. I think I do fully understand how problematic my being in the field is for others, how my position carries meanings that I may not intend, but for which I must still take responsibility. Yet although I must always give thought to what I am doing, I do not think that my presence and my work are intrinsically wrong or offensive.

It took a while for me to understand why this field engages me so completely. African American culture permeated the postwar Long Island, New York, world that I grew up in, but I knew little about Black people and had little contact with them. I spent most of my school years in Catholic schools, and very few African Americans on Long Island were Catholic. School desegregation, the Montgomery bus boycott, and the early days of the civil rights movement were events I knew about, although they did not impinge upon my reality except as news reports. In 1962 I began university in Toronto and spent summers waitressing in a Long Island resort area. In retrospect, I was surprisingly uninvolved in protests about either civil rights or the war in Vietnam, the two upheavals that profoundly altered my generation and the United States as well.

My lack of engagement was not for want of political consciousness. In grammar school I already recognized that home lessons differed from school lessons. Memorably, in grade five, after a nun's paean to Joseph McCarthy, I said that my mother didn't like him at all. My mother's terrified response when I told her of the incident silenced me until high school. There, however, along with a very small band of "radicals" in the Catholic girls' school I attended, I spent my entire time, it seemed, arguing with the extraordinarily right-wing faculty, and also with my classmates. There was little in the society I knew that I could support, and so neither Vietnam nor the civil rights movement presented epiphanies. The first seemed simply as horrible and unjust as any war; the second was, equally simply, only right and inevitable. Again in retrospect, during my undergraduate years, personal problems and the continual need to earn money to stay in school took my energies.

In 1968, M.A. in hand, wanting to teach but back waitressing, I was invited to work at Southern University in Baton Rouge, Louisiana, a public university that is still among the largest of the "historically Black" universities in the United States. The job was in a special federal program for the "educationally disadvantaged," situated in fourteen Black post-secondary institutions. It also entailed attending eight-week summer conferences in which the faculty developed curriculum, as well as several mid-term conferences to evaluate our progress and frequent external evaluations of our teaching. Each program had an equal number of "in-house" and imported faculty. Students in the program took our courses in first year and part of second year before integrating fully into the university.

I arrived halfway through a summer conference, barely knowing where Baton Rouge was and, as one of them wryly noted, hardly able to tell my new colleagues apart. And my life changed irrevocably. The program, which even over thirty years later remains the most exciting educational experiment I've ever encountered, embodied the critical pedagogy about which Paulo Freire had just begun to write. During the summer conferences the diverse and intense group of young Black militants, older Black scholars and preachers, young white radicals and intellectuals, and the occasional older, stolid, and traditional white faculty managed to reproduce and fight out every conceivable aspect of American race relations. The Black artists and historians whose work gave rise to the Black arts movement and to the field that had just claimed the name of Black studies came to the conferences to teach and inspire us. People were often very direct.

And so the two years I spent reading, talking, living, and teaching at Southern introduced me to a people and a culture from whom I've never stopped learning. When I returned to Toronto to do a Ph.D., I chose a dissertation topic, the development of Black theatre in America, which allowed me to consider what I had learned and to explore the things I wanted to know. One friend in particular, an African American woman from New Orleans whom I first met at Southern, was my real supervisor; our mutual boss at Southern used to tell us our stars were crossed: her M.A. had been on Bernard Malamud. But there is more to it than that.

In the United States much has changed in the racial politics of Black studies in the last three decades. Before the Black arts movement, Black and white scholars of Black literature made modest claims for a developing literature. There was little work done, and some of it, from white scholars in particular, was grounded in narrow and largely unexamined notions of "good art." Before long, young Black writers and scholars were seeking to develop ways of talking about Black literature that rendered such judgements moot; at the same time, of course, white scholars in the field were met with suspicion, if not direct hostility. At stake, of course, were issues of authority; a new generation of Black scholars and artists assumed the task of describing, critiquing, interpreting, and developing a literature. White folks not welcome.

So why did I stick around? I stayed because nothing else drew me in the same way. Looking back I realize that my immediate and powerful engagement with this literature had to do with my feeling that the work I encountered was constantly testifying to the truth, and with an immediacy, honesty, and concreteness that I had never experienced before. It consistently illuminated experience that, although not mine, clarified things I knew, or needed to know — things I needed to understand that the people I knew and the books that I read weren't talking about.

Being "different," an outsider, is an accustomed and even comfortable position for me, and so being on the margins of my field is not difficult. Single child of a single mother in a society that saw us both as tainted; Jewish, but raised from the age of seven as a Catholic yet taught never to deny my race; isolated because of the adamant but unnamed anti-Semitism in the Catholic world I inhabited; poor in the way I only recently came to recognize through friends; that is, in the way of the child of a bourgeois refugee who never gained her financial footing in the new society; raised socialist in a Republican, if not fascist community; a woman who knew from childhood that I had to make it on my own; reared by a mother whose hostility to feminism still confounds me: combatting the elusive was, for me, a fundamental way of life. None of these things was ever named for me, so concrete issues came as a relief. You're okay, but you're white. Yeah, I can dig that!!! Which is not to say that I didn't begin with a wellspring of racism of my own, only that it was (and still is) continually confronted in ways intense, unavoidable, and cleansing. It is to say that many people taught me, helped me, gave me love and support. Sounds corny, but it still is true.

I must ask my readers to consider: if I were writing about my experiences as a scholar of Spanish, Chinese, and Russian literature and culture, my gratitude for those who have helped me, and continue to help me, would seem perfectly normal. My appreciation of a literature, a language, an entire culture, a people, would be a matter of proclivity. No one would question my presence in the field, nor my presence in the classroom. The meanings attached to my presence in this field are not the same, however. The politics of race relations and racism, of scholarship that has defined entire peoples into speechlessness and their cultural productions into exotic objects of curiosity, mark my presence in the field, dog my footsteps, gloss my words. Professors profess expertise; scholars aspire to the definitive articulation of their objects of scrutiny. White person (woman, American) tells people (white people, Black people) what Black people mean.

My meaning is more problematic in Canada, where there are so few academics of African Canadian/American/Caribbean origin, than it is in the United States, where the majority of academics now engaged in the study of African American literature are Black, and where African American academics are, at last and to a large measure, the arbiters of what constitutes good scholarship in the field. In Canada, few academics concentrate on the work of African Canadian/American/Caribbean writers. Only a very small proportion of these academics are "people of colour." Even fewer have pursued African American literature/culture in particular. Can I make a constructive contribution in Canada (to whom and to what, this sentence does not easily finish)?

Certainly there is one way in which I cannot contribute and that is as an "authority" on anything at all. I do not mean, by this, to say that I know nothing: I would be lacking in self-respect if I claimed ignorance of what I am learning and have learned. I also believe myself able to create conditions in which people can, if they wish to do so in a class I teach, learn from and about African American people and their culture. Claiming authority, however, suggests one has the right to create, to define, and to defend against counterclaims what will, even what ought to, constitute knowledge about a subject. In the context of the liberal arts, in particular, authority also suggests the right to speak for those about whom one claims, "I know." That is not an authority I can ever claim.

In my practices as a teacher in this field, I try to make clear to students that I can only act as a resource for them, offering what I know as only one of the many resources available to them in their own process of knowledge-making. I find that Black students and white alike are astounded at what their schooling to date has hidden from them. They are amazed at the material that is available, material I make them seek out with massive bibliography and other assignments. In other words, my goal is that they leave my courses with the sense that they have only scratched the surface, and that the entire field is there for them to pursue and advance in their own fashion. It is painful to see the tremendous hurt that the Black students feel when they realize how cheated they have been. I see my role as trying to create an environment in which they can transform this pain into the energy to take charge of this process of knowledge-making.

I look forward to a time when there will be, in Canada, the kind of academic community now emerging in the United States, filled with people who can legitimately claim authority, and whose work will challenge and enrich us all. Encouraging students, changing curriculum, and altering hiring practices are contributions I can make towards this goal. Yet I am also concerned that a kind of institutionalized "intellectual multiculturalism" will surface, without effecting the radical change necessary in the composition of the academic community. This version of multiculturalism confines people to studying their own lives, and sees them as suspect when they pursue and speak about issues other than their "own." It is, in a way, but not entirely, the flip side of what renders me problematic as a white scholar of African American culture. Fields such as African American literature are in themselves massive and complex. They also fundamentally alter what scholars now call "dominant narratives," and if these remain unchanged, we are not much further ahead. This knowledge is critical to us all, not just to those for whom it is of particular interest and relevance, be they teachers or students.

What is at stake is power: who gets to say what about whom, and who gets to decide what is true. It seems to me that only in a truly diverse academic community can these problems be resolved. In the meantime, the problem isn't resolved simply by insisting that, for example, only Black people should teach Black studies. Certainly the opportunity to pursue the field should exist even when no Black teachers are available.

Getting where we need to go is not easy. These days I sometimes wonder how I will feel if what I hope for becomes true: that way before I am ready to retire, my students will be ready to replace me. It will be a joyous day, certainly, and it will also be hard. I really love my work. Perhaps they will invite me to give a guest lecture . . . maybe even two.   173

Afterthoughts

Asked by the editors to revise my piece, I find no changes I want to make. I discover, however, that thinking about it makes me restless, and as I read through the whole collection for inspiration I feel uneasy, even impatient.

I wonder about the intransigence of racism, and about the fear of difference, about dominance and whether it is ever relinquished voluntarily, about the pain and anger in almost all the voices contained here, about the extreme difficulty of having to negotiate everything through race and gender and ethnicity. I feel caught in a double bind: I recognize that new readers may be joining this conversation for the first time and "need to hear it." But I also want to move on, deeper into these troubling issues, and I wonder how we get to the next stage.

For example, on reading Carl James's "I've Never Had a Black Teacher Before," I am reminded of the Black Power advocates during the U.S. civil rights movement telling their white companions in voter registration drives in the South to go to work in their own communities, to talk about racism and oppression to white folks, and to leave the black folks to them. If I speak with a class about racism, am I relying on white privilege and authority to "teach that lesson"? If so, what a conundrum. I rely on that which I decry to teach about it. How do we bring about the change that vests Carl and me with equal authority?

If we switch the topic to gender, what happens? But maybe the problem here is less one of race than of ideas of "objectivity" and a belief that I can only have knowledge of something in which I am not personally invested. What if, in the classroom, we challenge *that* idea rather than only the ones that arise from racism? Another conundrum: authority in the classroom is not typically a concept on which enlightened educators dwell. Yet that is what is at stake. The students who resist probably have never been in a position in which a person of colour had authority and power over them. Which issues should be directly addressed?

To me, these issues are an extension of things I tried to address in my article. Having offered to be displaced by my students, I also chafe under my promise. Why is it that virtually all the students in my courses on African Canadian and African American culture are Black? Twenty years ago that was not so. Has a result of anti-racist education been the solidification of a belief that Black studies are only important for Black students, and that their purpose is to raise self-esteem, not to increase our understanding of the world in which all of us live?

In my article I question why my interest in the field (that is, my work as a scholar and teacher) is different from someone else's interest in French, Spanish, or Russian culture. Why is it, in an age in which popular culture is so completely influenced by the various Black cultures of the African diaspora, that learning in relation to those cultures is so completely absent from our schools? Why is the learning confined to Black History Month? Are we any further ahead in terms of reformulating what kinds of knowing counts?

Conversely, I also ask, do I — why do I — have to have an ethnic/racial community through which to mediate my living? Is it possible, one generation beyond migration, or having left a faith and become an unbeliever, to have an ambivalent relationship to the being of my ancestry without betraying it? What is the language in which we can be humans to each other, now that we see how utterly the language of liberal democracy has failed in this regard?

* * *

I recall being at a conference, over ten years ago now, where a discussion that began as a debate about gender and voice in the classroom expanded to one about race, class, and sexuality and the question of marginality. It soon became clear that no one in the room was willing to claim the centre. What would claiming it mean?

These days I tell my students that in their essays they "are not allowed to say" that "society" does this or that, believes this or that. I want them to be more thoughtful about attributing responsibility. If we aren't part of the solution, we are part of the problem — I do believe that. However, I don't think we can be responsible for history; we can only be responsible to each other in the present and for our own living. I recall a class in which one of the very few white students, for a very long time, questioned and resisted contemplating the existence of racism and its effects. Finally she disclosed — in journals — a painful personal history more immediate to her than the oppression of others. Yet she had chosen the course. Once she realized that her resistance expressed her sense that her own suffering was unacknowledged, she could put aside her own issues and open herself to the course material and discussions.

Privilege is difficult to acknowledge for those who have it, and easy to resent for those who do not. Privilege is also specific; it accrues from whiteness, or from class, or from heterosexuality, for example, yet the label is totalizing. Acknowledging the ways in which we are privileged, and not, is a valuable exercise. However, it seems to me that in the absence of a powerful ethics and personal generosity, few will relinquish privilege, and few who are denied it will cease resenting it. Can guilt produce change? Are guilt and responsibility the same thing?

Responsibility is continual; it is expressed in what we buy, in where we shop, in what causes we choose to support, in what we say or do not say to friends and acquaintances, in whether we ensure a diversity of voices on parent and civic councils, and so on. Supposing, for example, everyone chose to boycott a newspaper that published a racist column, or a radio station with a racist broadcaster? Finally, we don't take guilt into the polling station; we take responsibility.

The power of the articles in this book comes from their grounding in individual experience. As a result, however, no matter how nuanced and insightful, at root each article implies either "I should have done this" or "This should not have happened to me." Called into account are both individual and systemic racism. Less articulated are the questions of where individual responsibility for systemic racism lies, and conversely how individual actions can create social change. We seem to lack ways of talking about the connections between individual efforts and systemic issues — a problem that has been particularly noticeable since the so-called triumph of capitalism, with its ethics of the marketplace, which are neither egalitarian nor humane.

Put positively, the key question is: how can people learn to take pleasure in difference and to experience diversity rather than sameness as the basis of humanity? This is by no means a new question, but it does need to be asked anew in the conversation in which this book engages.

Whiteness in White Academia

••••••••••••••••••••••••

Luis M. Aguiar

A friend often reminds me that the Portuguese people are one of the few minority groups to become "Black" through immigration. Historically, Portugal has been a "white" imperialist power that colonized and spread "whiteness" throughout a sizable chunk of the world (De Figueiredo 1975; Raby 1988).[1] Immigration to Canada, however, made the Portuguese "Black."

Compelling data support this view. The Portuguese are segmented into specific job ghettos, residential neighbourhoods, perform poorly in school, are subjected to streaming, criminalized by the media, and possess an "exotic" culture of food, customs, and traditions. With the exception of the work ethic, which the Portuguese are assumed to have in abundance, they share these "characteristics" with Blacks in Canada. The Portuguese Interagency Network (PIN), an umbrella organization for Portuguese community agencies in Toronto, went so far as to argue, before the New Democratic government of Ontario, for the community's "blackness." PIN's goal was to have the community designated as one of the "historically disadvantaged" groups in the province so that it could benefit from new employment equity legislation (interview with Ana Costa, Oct. 20, 1997; PIN 1993). The government rejected this position.

Is it an exaggeration, however, to suggest that the Portuguese have become Black as a result of immigration? Is it not the case that immigration makes most immigrants Black? Perhaps, but unlike most other immigrant groups the Portuguese were once "white," imperialists, and colonizers. This is not so for the Irish or the Jews who immigrated to the "New World." For them the opposite was true — they became "white" via immigration (Ignatieff 1995; Brodkin 1998; Jackson 1998, 1995). Hence, the Portuguese have endured both economic marginalization and "racial" demotion due to immigration.

This brief article is not the place to explore these points in greater detail, though I will consider the Portuguese "racial" status throughout these pages. Are the Portuguese Black, or have they, like the Irish, Jews, and other "white-skinned" Europeans, undergone a racial transition to whiteness? The Portuguese too (though few by comparison), have their lawyers, bank managers, municipal and provincial politicians, and even a few cultural performers in mainstream white media and the arts (Silva Magazine 1996/1997). And so, perhaps, rather than being a matter of Black or white, the Portuguese experience in Canada is of "racial middleness." Karen Brodkin (1998: 1-2) writes, in the case of Jews in the United States, that racial middleness is their "experience of marginality vis-a-vis whiteness, and an experience of whiteness and belonging vis-a-vis blackness." But racial middleness implies a neutrality and safeguarding of identity unencumbered by whiteness or blackness. Is this possible in a culture in which power lies in whiteness, and in which ethnic minorities have little access to cultural outlets (James 1999; Li 1994; Tator, Henry, and Mattis 1998)? In a discussion of Spanish-speaking peoples' identity in the United States, Neil Foley (in Davis 1999) suggests that "to identify oneself today as 'Hispanic' is partially to acknowledge one's ethnic heritage without surrendering one's 'whiteness.'" The Portuguese are not nearly as well integrated into the socio-economic and political mainstream as Jews are in the United States and Canada, nor have they arrived at the same self-analysis as Hispanics in the United States.

Here I will comment on these issues by discussing my own background and educational training in white academia. I recognize the limitations of, and my trepidations concerning, this approach. It is only one person's account and nevertheless runs the risk of being appropriated by reactionaries bent on highlighting my "immigrant work ethic" and/or trajectory as a "self-made" man. I vehemently object to this type of interpretation, because I believe that I have achieved educational success in spite of the system rather than because of it.

I borrow the concept of "Black" from the work of A. Sivanandan (1990, 1982) to capture my experiences in white academia and comment on the Portuguese in Canada. Sivanandan argues that Black serves as a "political colour" to unite non-white minorities in England and elsewhere for the purpose of resisting racism, discrimination, exploitation, and imperialism, and for mobilizing to achieve political change. The idea of blackness is a powerful metaphor that can be used in the struggle against racial divisions erected by bourgeois economic and political forces. But visible minority writers in England have recently criticized the use of Black as a political colour. They argue that the concept fails to appreciate, for instance, the unique identity, specific experiences, and political struggles of, in particular, South Asians in England (see Werbner and Modood 1997; but also Asian Dub Foundation 2000). Other critics reject the conceptualization because it evokes a binary reading of social relations, leading to misinterpretations of contemporary racial identities in the West (Torres, Miron, and Onda 1999: 1-16). Irrespective of these critiques, the concept retains a political edge necessary for identifying issues of power, domination, and resistance in our society. For this reason I accept its continuing significance under the contemporary political structures of capitalism (*Race & Class* 1999).

White or whiteness is the racial identity I assign to the dominant class in Canadian society and its culture and institutions. There is a large body of literature on whiteness, both for and against it (Creese 1999). Ruth Frankenberg (1993a: 1) defines whiteness as (1) a "location of structural advantage," (2) a "standpoint" from which white people understand the world and their position in it, and (3) "a set of cultural practices that are usually unmarked and unnamed." Many immigrant communities recognize the advantages of whiteness and seek to transform themselves by distancing themselves from those who are Black and marginalized by the discourses and institutions of whiteness. In addition, whiteness entails the power to regulate and reproduce itself in various institutional contexts. Hence, I use it to capture the cultures of place and institutions through which my trajectory has taken me, from an immigrant kid growing up in Anglo Montreal to a doctoral degree at York University in Toronto.

A key question guides my reflections on this trajectory: if the Portuguese are Black and education is recognized to be the most direct route to whiteness, and since I have climbed that hierarchy to its highest level, what impact has it had on me? This article describes my navigation of white academia, beginning with my immigrant roots.

Immigrating

I was born in a small village on the Island of São Miguel in the Azores to a "homemaker" and a day labourer who intermittently found work as a handyman in the field orchards of the richest local landowning family. My father is illiterate and only learned to sign his name in order to emigrate. My mother never finished third grade. She was pulled from school to help her mother raise eleven children. My brother stopped school at grade four; my sister went only two grades further than he did. After a few years as a day labourer like my father, my brother found work as an apprentice mechanic. My sister returned to school upon our settlement in Montreal in 1975. She is the only other person in our family to have a high-school leaving certificate. Had I remained in São Miguel, I too would have had a short educational career since, under the Portuguese dictator Salazar (De Figueiredo 1997), schooling on the island for the working class was not encouraged. But if you were bright and disciplined, or able to convince school administrators and the local priest that you were genuinely interested in the priesthood, you were taken to a boarding school in one of the larger towns to pursue your educational training. Students were allowed a home visit every weekend, provided they did not "misbehave." The few girls who were from poor backgrounds and continued on in school were verbally harassed with appellations of "class traitors" or *putas* (sluts) by the local community. Boys pursuing higher learning were "sexually suspect" and "unmanly" because they preferred mental to manual labour (Willis 1977). My father often reminds me of yet another discourse regarding education and working-class students. He would tell me not to study too hard because it will "drive you insane." He never had a shortage of names of acquaintances to serve up as examples of men (never women) who became insane as a result of too much reading and studying. I do not believe that bourgeois students suffered the same attacks on their masculinity from within their class.

At age eleven I immigrated to Montreal with my sister and mother (my brother joined us two years later). At fifty-eight years old, my father had immigrated three years earlier after securing a visitor's visa (with the help of a distant cousin living in Montreal), and "going underground" to earn his landed immigrant status. My father first rented a room and later, when the rest of us arrived, a whole house on the corner of St. Dominique and Duluth in the heart of the Portuguese community in Montreal. That was my first house in Montreal. I do not recall my own initial reactions to this house, but I do remember my mother saying how frightening it was to have an old oil furnace in our corridor and furnace pipes running above our heads from one end of the house to the other. She also remarked that this feature would make it difficult to render the house aesthetically pleasing. My sister resumed school and grew to adulthood in the community. She would often complain about the smell of her clothes as a result of my mother's cooking. Henceforth, fish and *chouriço* (Portuguese sausage), two staples in our diet, became less and less common on our dinner table. The furniture my father had purchased (with the help of another cousin)[2] before we arrived was also not to my mother's taste, though there was little she could do given the debt incurred at the local Portuguese-owned furniture store. I lived with my parents in various houses in the Portuguese neighbourhood until 1987, when I married and left for Hamilton, Ontario. My parents still rent in the neighbourhood.

From eleven to fifteen years old I was a lonely hermit locked in the house, stepping out only to attend school. Friends were non-existent, but sweets, chips, ice cream, pop, and televisions were abundant — with TV especially available for the first time in my life and obsessively consumed. Not surprisingly, I ballooned to a fat young teenager who frequently stood in front of my bedroom mirror punching my young, fat, and developing body. In school I attended the "dummy" class to learn English with other recent immigrants. This schooling did not work well, because we spoke Portuguese amongst ourselves, thereby delaying our acquisition of English. Some of us also resented being held back when we had already learned many of the regular subjects (particularly mathematics) in Portugal.

Navigating white spaces

I attended primary and secondary school in the Portuguese community in Montreal, steps from McGill University. Most of my student cohort were Portuguese, but collectively (and subconsciously), we undertook a path towards burying (or was it suppressing?) the "old" Portuguese identity and heritage for a rebirth in a new identity via the consumption of whiteness and the defence of the "white way of life" of English-Quebeckers against the growing nationalistic identity of the Québécois (*Globe and Mail* 1976: A1). Portuguese was the domestic language, spoken only with our parents. As I grew older, I withdrew more and more from the community, as did my friends. Many of them lost their ability to speak Portuguese. Those who could still speak Portuguese, like me, did so largely because their parents never learned to speak either of the two official languages. I (and my

181

friends) continued to withdraw from community events, parties, celebrations, and relations in the Portuguese community. As I see it today, the community could not accommodate the needs of most adolescents because its structures were set up to ease the settlement process of the older and recently arrived immigrants in the community. In carrying out this vital activity, the changing needs and challenges faced by teenagers went largely unattended. As a result, there were few community forces to hold at bay an encroaching white culture. Even Portuguese girls were uninteresting to us; they had been supplanted by our desires for the whiteness of white girls.

My friends and I did learn some French in the classroom, but spoke it only when coaxed to — usually in the workplace when doing part-time work. For the most part, the Québécois world of Montreal remained mysteriously foreign to us. I attended English schools, movie theatres, dance clubs, restaurants, and shopping malls, and watched English-language (often U.S.) television shows and events. I travelled in white spaces and white culture. At the same time, Québécois culture was parochial, provincial, invisible. In many ways it was similar to the Azorean experience we were trying so hard to leave behind (Barbosa 1978; De Melo 1991). The majority of Portuguese immigrants to Canada are from the Azores, and within that home community the Azorean culture, language, and history take second place to that practised by immigrants from mainland Portugal. There are tensions within the community between the two groups, and many of the Azorean resent the denigration of their heritage by people from the mainland. The mainlanders claim that Azoreans are uncultured and unable to speak proper Portuguese. Some of this experience relates closely to the experiences of the Québécois in English Montreal.

I absorbed whiteness by distancing myself from my own culture as well as by establishing a relationship with the Québécois — a culture I had much more in common with.[3] Azorean immigrants in Montreal had endured generations of political and cultural control from successive governments in mainland Portugal in cahoots with the local island bourgeoisie. The Azoreans felt and lived as second-class citizens in their own territory. And similar to the Québécois experience, the Azores bred its own revolutionary and nationalistic identity pushing for independence from Portugal.

But at least at first none of these seemingly common historical experiences came to bear on me, my friends, or our parents. Instead, we turned to whiteness and an English Canadian identity, even if it meant adopting a politics and agenda that were not our own. Unlike the Irish who came to United States, however, the white Portuguese benefited little from their whiteness (Li 1988). Still, we were convinced of the rewards of assimilation, and the advantages of being white in Montreal. If only we learned the English language and culture, consumed the white landscape of the city, and, perhaps most important, "defended" the Anglos against the "menacing" and increasingly militant Québécois, we could gain entry into Anglo Montreal. Or so we thought.

But how did "whiteness" become normalized for me in Montreal? Or did it? Certainly, going to an English and Catholic school system was an important part of assimilating and suppressing my identity and heritage. Learning English in school not only led to exposure to a discriminatory historical record and narrative favouring English-Quebeckers, but also to the inculcation of Anglo-Saxon desires and politics. The Anglos were the framers of "the nation," and the English culture shaped its identity. The Québécois history and culture were rarely presented to us, and when they were they played a supportive role to English agency and vision. But learning English had other long-lasting consequences. Via English I entered the English-speaking geography of the city. St. Laurent Street divides Montreal between east and west. West of St. Laurent lay the English-speaking world and all things "desired" — the shops and clothes, the landscape, the movie theatres, the universities, the culture of the city, the women. Going east was rarely contemplated. The Québécois part of the city was "imagined differently." That side of the city was conceived of as being "socially liberal." It was in that space that pleasure was located. We imagined illicit drugs to be easily available and accessible. We saw the prostitutes patrolling St. Catherine Street East, the strip joints and adult movie theatres in abundance (with their laxness in monitoring age requirements), the women overtly flirtatious. It was on this side that a friend and I, at age fifteen, would pay three dollars to watch four hours of B-movies so that we would catch the third feature — an adult movie. It was also on St. Catherine, east of St. Denis, that my underage friends and I roamed the laneways poking our heads in the back doors, key holes, or other crevices to get a glimpse of the exotic dancers in the bars.

During those years I fantasized about inventing a new name (identity) for myself.[4] Though Luis is a common Portuguese male name, it was too foreign-sounding to allow me to suppress my ethnicity. It thereby inhibited my goal of passing for white. I repeatedly embarrassed myself whenever I had to introduce myself in different milieus. In my fantasies I would assume the identity of a Leslie or Larry or

Lawrence or sometimes Lloyd. Though I liked the sound of Lloyd, I was bemused by a name beginning with double consonants. Eventually I settled for Lee. In my mind a white name would ease my transition into the mainstream, because by that time my language skills had improved and I had no clear accent. I was also white-skinned. Moreover, Lee was the name of the star of the *Six Million Dollar Man* television series, which ran on ABC television from 1974 to 1978. For a young boy in his adolescent years, assuming the name of a superhero such as the six-million-dollar man was an appealing fantasy.

I never did formally change my name to Lee, but as part of a school gang I was baptized with the nickname of Playboy — a more appealing name because of its sexual connotations, and especially since it did not immediately label me as an ethnic minority. Even today many of my high-school friends do not know my real name.

I did not achieve particularly good grades in high school or college, though I did well in history. After high school I applied to CEGEP and was accepted by Dawson College. That college had a reputation as an institution overrun with ethnic and racial minority students from working- and lower-middle-class backgrounds, also as a place where students delayed the inevitable — a degreeless exit into the secondary labour market. Whereas the other English-language colleges — Vanier and Champlain — catered to, trained, and developed the minds of students from middle-class backgrounds (many from ethnic minority families) for entry into a university, Dawson produced semi-skilled workers for the "peripheral" economy. It is true that Dawson surpassed the other two colleges in media and computer training, but it lagged far behind in disciplines geared to further academic education. I, an immigrant from a working-class background, with social sciences as my choice of stream, was clearly misguided for success in the labour market. If you attended Dawson College (especially in the social science stream), it was practically a fait accompli that you could not go on to attend McGill, one of the universities of the elite. Predictably, I was refused admission to McGill and instead attended Concordia University, which had a reputation not unlike that of Dawson College. For instance, when I attended Concordia in the mid-1980s, rumour had it that McGill students carried a button that read: "If you can't go to university . . . go to Concordia."

At the same time as I entered college, I met a young woman, and we dated for six years before marrying.[5] I love my wife, but when I think about my trajectory of negotiating whiteness during those times, I wonder to what extent I subconsciously bestowed my love on her because she carries whiteness. Though from a white working-

184

class background, she was part of the mainstream culture and had the confidence to move about the city and take on the institutions of the state when needed. I, on the other hand, avoided confrontations with authority out of fear of embarrassing myself via my second-language status and as a way of avoiding being reminded that I was an "immigrant." As a result, I regularly coaxed her to deal with the state and other authorities on my behalf. (Perhaps she too, subconsciously, was attracted to the exotic foreigner I seemed to represent.) As I think more about this issue, I realize that it would have been unexpected of me to marry anybody but a white woman. After all, growing up in Montreal meant assimilating into whiteness, which, of course, included a white wife. Alice attended my high school and lived in the Portuguese neighbourhood to boot. Often, however, I was reminded of my blackness by her father, who referred to me as "the greaser," a racist term originally used by Americans to refer to Mexicans immigrating — legally or otherwise — into the United States (Ortega 1984). Of the half-a-dozen high-school friends I keep in touch with, only one married a Portuguese woman. (It is difficult for me to say what happened to the Portuguese girls I grew up with. I have lost contact with them and am therefore unable to determine if whiteness mattered for them as much as it did for me.)

Navigating white academia

Once, when asked about his political activism, Pierre Bourdieu said he did not engage in conventional political activism but instead sought to apply his analytical skills to the academy in order to understand how it forms intellectuals (Bourdieu and Eagleton 1992). His focus was on how institutional practices in the university transformed those (including himself) who did intellectual work in it. Bourdieu pointed out the class dynamics of the university and its power in transforming working-class students into "organic intellectuals" of the established order. He did not, however, appear to recognize the dynamics of whiteness — and that, along with the class and "racial" dynamics of academia, is what I want to look at here. Furthermore, I want to follow Bourdieu's lead and examine how my trajectory has been shaped by the university as a disciplining institution with regulatory mechanisms for self-reproduction via its "inmates."

There is little doubt that university has changed me. I speak, write, and function in a milieu largely manufactured by the legitimate status that the university holds in our society. My stint in the university has therefore afforded me a legitimacy of my own. For example, I can speak confidently and assertively and can claim an expertise as a result of my university training. But the university is not just about gaining professional legitimacy. It is also about navigating a foreign culture, a culture of whiteness.

Historically, of course, the university has been a white institution with clear preferences and a privileging of a specific race (white) and gender (male). Still today the university's legitimacy is accepted with little reflection on the class and racial biases that the institution expresses. So much of academia operates on an implicit level. Participants simply expect to insert themselves in the existing system and to know, or learn, the rules of conduct and expectations associated with the university as a place of study (or work). This "normalizing" process is largely unidentified and goes unchallenged. Professors are usually from the higher classes and have succeeded in organizing the university in their image, which makes for a "normal" culture for them. In other words, the cultural capital circulating in the university corresponds to the cultural expectations and makeup of the middle-class and bourgeois students entering the university.

The expectation of a familiar milieu is tremendously advantageous to students from these class backgrounds, especially for those entering graduate school. In most cases graduate students find bourgeois speech, dress, gait, body language, and colour that reflect their own backgrounds. In other words, what they find at the university is nothing out of the ordinary, for them. The regulatory mechanisms of the university as an institution have precisely been created to seem normal to them. This normalness is so omnipresent that it is difficult to detect, and so it often proceeds unchallenged and unchanged. Its powerful effect relies precisely on achieving this status of invisibility.

This experience of normality is not the case for students who come from ethnic, minority, working-class backgrounds. They do not possess inside information about what a university is, how it functions, and, more important, how the student can manipulate the institution. But their uneasiness in academia often affords them a disruptive and interrogative edge on the representation and reproduction of whiteness, an edge that escapes most white students. In the case of Himani Bannerji (1995), this edge rested in the violence of a colonial legacy being reproduced before her eyes in the context of university graduate studies. Or, as in my case, it came in the institution's lack of ethnic and racial inclusion, and an inability to reflect back to me familiar contexts and representations. The points of reference in the studied literatures ignored the European periphery (including Portugal), and instead stressed the histories, political economies, politics, and intellectual contributions of people in the United Kingdom, Germany, Sweden, and to a lesser extent France.

Rightfully so, critics pointed out the Eurocentrism of this literature and its discriminating view of the world. As a student of Portuguese background, I came to know more about England, Australia, Germany, Sweden, and France than about Portugal and the Azores. Over time I grew impatient with the whiteness of this literature, but impotent to do much given the pervasiveness of the practice. Had I been given a choice, I would have preferred to study the Portuguese political economy — including immigration waves — in my formal training. Surely, the prevailing representation has more to do with power and control of systems of knowledge in the English-speaking world than with assumptions about the intellectual barrenness of the rest of the world.

Building an academic career

The concept of "career" is a central part of academic life. People build their careers, change their careers, and sometimes destroy their careers by some scandal or dishonest undertaking. In addition people participate in shaping (or not) the careers of others. Most students know the importance of a career and the need to train for it. In graduate school students spend most of their time "building" their careers. They take courses with specific outlines and deadlines and receive official grades that are recorded in their files in the department and the school of graduate studies. They teach courses under the supervision of faculty members, write scholarship applications with the support of a faculty member, and undergo a long period of mentoring and disciplining within the department and faculty. With many students in a department at the same time, it behooves each of them to make him/herself visible. Visibility counts when it comes to all the intangibles available in a university — for example, excellent letters of recommendations, invitations to conferences and special events and to publish, and, in some cases, offers of course directorships.

But career has a class component that is often ignored. It is a foreign concept to working-class students of immigrant backgrounds. For me, the cultural capital that would communicate the importance of career was never part of my upbringing. As I grew up, my parents spoke of jobs — how to find and keep them. My father would usually go to the *canto* and wait there to be approached by a landowner, or his helping hand, to discuss the work, wages, and period of employment. *"O canto"* was the visual expression of the labour market where we lived: in a specific area of the town men advertised their willingness to work (simply by being there), and employers sought out labour power to hire. According to my father and my brother (who experienced it as a teenager for a couple of years), they had to get to the *canto* at the break of dawn in order to be able, just possibly, to select which employer to leave with. Sometimes they were lucky and were employed by the same landowners for consecutive weeks. In such cases the family was assured a steady income. More commonly, however, the men had to make daily trips to the *canto* in search of work.

I believe my father or mother never did mention the concept of career to me. The foreign nature of this concept was compounded in the new country as Portuguese immigrants joined the secondary labour market. In Montreal my father got work as a dishwasher, first at Dorval Airport and later in the Meridien Hotel, with no mention of a "career." It was not until I was in university that I learned that *carreira* was the Portuguese equivalent.

This lack of awareness of the culture of academia was itself compounded by the relationships developed in graduate school. At York University, experiences of being the "other," in terms of both class and ethnicity, persisted even though I had already survived McMaster University. Indeed, my class, ethnic position, and lack of knowledge about academia exacerbated my sense of dislocation. As a result I withdrew from the department, rarely communicating with anyone other than my course colleagues. I particularly disliked the pretentious relationships developed between students and some faculty members. Often I was uncomfortable with many of my classmates and their class origins and the gap between our experiences.

York University did have other students with immigrant origins, but they tended to be from bourgeois backgrounds and possessed the cultural (as well as social and financial) capital and class arrogance to persevere and do well in graduate school despite experiences of racism (Tomic and Trumper 1992). Some graduate classes were painful and intimidating. I sat through them witnessing which student would next seek to upstage the one who had just spoken. Here too, the immigrant working-class student is at a disadvantage because not everyone is equally prepared to participate in the discussion. This format silences many working-class students of immigrant background, but rarely is this recognized by bourgeois students and faculty members, who have grown up with the cultural capital of academia and thus fail to recognize its construction and reproduction via institutional and individual practices.

For these reasons I never felt at ease or secure in my sense of belonging to the sociology department at York University. In retrospect, I can see it was my self-imposed peripheralization within the department and the university that allowed me to succeed. I created my own space outside the department and most other university activities. In so doing I was able to distance myself from the climate of the department and at the same time carry on with my work at my own pace, and according to my own perception of what university education should be.

The imposter syndrome — disarming the Black student

Most working-class students in graduate training or academic posts worry about feelings of dislocation regarding their academic and cultural milieu. Their uneasiness stems from the foreignness of the culture, climate, and milieu within which they study and work. These feelings are frequently captured in the concept of the "imposter syndrome." That is, having no prior inside knowledge of academia, and navigating their way in uncharted waters, working-class students and academics of immigrant origin fear being "discovered." They fear being exposed as outsiders in a privileged and exclusive milieu in which they are not quite sure of the rules and practices of belonging.

I have not escaped this syndrome, and I often ask myself why and how I have gotten here. That question is usually followed by another set of queries. Given that I am in the university, does it mean that the system (of mobility, and merit, for instance) works? Am I an example of the system "working for anybody"? Can one discredit a system that has benefited a working-class student from an immigrant background, enabled someone with no family history of higher education to climb to the highest level of formal education? Other important feelings also emerge to take over my psyche. I experience numerous bouts of confidence and wonder when I will finally be denounced as an imposter and revealed to be incompetent and incapable of thinking in a scholarly fashion. These feelings repeat themselves perpetually, as does the need to "prove" over and over that I belong in academia.

My experience of graduate studies at York University was that everyone, regardless of class and gender, appropriated the metaphor of the imposter's syndrome for themselves to capture their feelings of anxiety. On occasion I have even heard professors claim that during their graduate school days, and sometimes even later in their professional lives, they too felt the shadow of the imposter on their back. I am suspicious of the widespread appropriation of this metaphor to capture seemingly everybody's experiences in graduate school,   189 including students of bourgeois background. I think these feelings of empathy by white bourgeois students disarm the Black working-class student because they homogenize all experiences, thereby co-opting the specificity of the experiences and feelings of students from Black backgrounds.[6] Again, many things taken for granted by bourgeois students, such as the idea of a career, are simply not so for working-class students from immigrant backgrounds, and less so for Black students. The attempt to empathize with Black students is a means of generalizing an experience that serves to devalue the experiences proper of Black students (cf. Haas and Shaffir 1991).

Academia was a foreign place for me in many practical ways. For example, the "ideal type" graduate student experience was far from my everyday world. I, and most working-class students from ethnic minority backgrounds, had to earn a living while going to school full-time. We had little possibility of getting government loans, largely because we were afraid of debt and, unlike students from upper-class backgrounds, did not assume that a job awaited us immediately after graduation. My parents, struggling themselves to make ends meet, were not financially able to support my education. And the less I needed from my parents the better, since I already felt responsible for their inability to buy a house or car because I was not providing an income to the household, which is a given for kids from working-class families of immigrant background.

Conclusion

Now, as a full-time contract faculty member in the sociology department at Okanagan University College in Kelowna, B.C., I find that an academic career no longer seems an outlandish proposition. What does seem outrageous and unexpected to me at this point would be a failure to achieve an academic post in Canada or the United States. This attitude vis-à-vis the academic labour market is recent, and it has developed in a cultural milieu foreign to me, my family, and even my "white" wife. Perhaps it too indicates a certain arrogance on my part as a result of educational formation in white academia.

I am aware of the ambiguities of my thoughts here. It is not clear to me if I can find anything conclusive in this discussion. It is still not clear to me why and how I have achieved academically. I had no fertile background of social, cultural, or financial capital readily available to me for the purpose of my educational training. I was also relatively late in pondering graduate school as a goal. I did not have key teachers or memorable events that transformed me into an academic protegé. Moreover, my parents were too busy making ends meet to offer moral support or advice on my educational climb. How could they? The system was alien to them as well. Today I still feel terribly guilty because of my selfish educational pursuits that deprived my parents from owning a home or car or having some higher level of comfort in their retirement years. My parents have never complained about my lack of financial contribution to the family, but my sense is that they are extremely disappointed at not achieving the immigrant dream of owning their own home. To my mind, only immigrant students of working-class background feel this heavy load of class guilt.

During the interview for the job I now hold, the chair of the department asked me how I had planned for my education. My response to her was that this idea of "planning" was a bourgeois concept. I (and my family) did not plan for my educational ascent, because for us it was a foreign concept to believe that making a living meant a university education. Hard work, ethnic affiliation, and family support would make for a successful life in Canada. I do not mean to suggest that Portuguese working-class people do not plan, because they certainly do so in many ways — for their houses, mortgages, kids' weddings, and work, for instance. What I am suggesting is that, for us, education was overtaken by more pressing class concerns having to do with the basics of survival.

Acknowledgements

Thanks to Carl James, Paty Tomic, Alice Reynolds, and Ricardo Trumper for their help and encouragement in the writing of this article.

Notes

1 In 1976 Grace Anderson and David Higgs (1976) published the first significant study mapping the experience of Portuguese people in Canada. They spend their first chapter arguing that the Portuguese might have been the first West European "explorers" in Canada. If this was indeed the case, then the Portuguese have the dubious distinction of initiating the genocidal campaigns against the proper inhabitants of the "New World." This was, in other words, not atypical of what they did elsewhere.

2 This was the same cousin who wrote my father's letters to my mother — since he could not write them himself — and read my mother's replies. As a kid in Portugal, I remember my mother being endlessly frustrated by her inability to communicate clearly and straightforwardly with my father as a result of the intermediary role my cousin played. This role of pseudo-correspondent is no doubt a significant one in immigrant communities. As far

as I know, no academic research has been done on those who provided this "service" for their illiterate ethnic compatriots.

3 While attending Dawson College, I read Pierre Vallières (1971) and Léandre Bergeron (1971). These political manifestos were key texts in the early stages of Quebec nationalism. I too felt their power and understood their struggles.

4 In fact, I had already been given a new name when matriculating for school. From birth, my full name is Luis Leonardo Marques Correia Aguiar. It follows the Portuguese cultural practice of name-giving, which includes the surnames of both sides of grandparents as well as the name of your godfather when baptized. The Canadian state, however, rejected this practice and shortened my name to two. From 1975 to 1980, I became known as Luis Silva. "Silva" was one of my grandmothers' names, which my sister has and I don't. Due to a bureaucratic error, she was Mariana Silva and I was Luis Silva. In 1980 I changed my last name to Aguiar. More recently I have added two middle names — Leonardo and Marques.

5 Recently Alice told me that her father did not want her to date Black or Portuguese men. According to her father, Portuguese husbands beat their wives. When this advice did not work, and she continued to date me, her father changed tactics, often reminding her — and occasionally in front of me — to "play the field."

6 Again, I'm conscious of the problematic use of this concept to capture my "white" ethnic immigrant experience. And in no way do I want to imply that Black students' experiences can be considered as being the same as mine. However, I have not yet found a more appropriate and powerful concept to capture my experiences in academe.

Learning from Discomfort: A Letter to My Daughters

••••••••••••••••••••

Barb Thomas

Dear Karen and Janette:

A few weeks ago, Janny, we had a conversation at a friend's cottage —
two of us well over forty, three of you twenty and under, all of us
white. You were talking about the huge chasms between kids with different racial identities in high school — how you felt unwelcome
when you went to the Afro-Can club and you never went back; how
old friends from as far back as daycare got pressured by their peers to
avoid you as a friend because you were white; how you experienced
the different clubs in the school as being divisive and exclusive. Your
stepsister got angry with me when I started to talk about the reasons
why these clubs might be a place of relief and comfort for kids who
experience racism in the school and society. She said I was always
"sympathizing with the Black kids," but what about a white kid's
feelings of being excluded and laughed at by a group of Black kids? I
said that both kinds of pain could be happening at the same time, and
that it wasn't necessary to deny Black kids' realities in order to pay
attention to the feelings of exclusion she as an individual might feel.
And this is, of course, not simple, because she, as a Jew, also experiences a form of racism in anti-Semitism.

I've been thinking about the many times we've talked about these   193 questions, trying to hold different truths in our hands at the same time without smashing the ones we don't like. And this cottage conversation has some of that same spirit. But it also has some echoes — uncomfortable for me — of the louder, more strident pronouncements out there in the streets, organizations, and newspapers about "white people's pain," in particular "white women being silenced."

It is important to acknowledge and address your own hurt; and there are different kinds of hurts, different scales of hurt and wounds. There are also different kinds of power to ignore others' wounds, or get your hurt recognized. We've got some names for those huge wounds — words like racism, sexism, imperialism, poverty. These wounds are not accidental — they are done to some people by other people. And the damage has been, and continues to be, massive.

Right now there is an enormous denial of the big wounds, in particular of racism, by the people who are not on the receiving end. You'll hear such people say they're tired of "hearing about racism," or "listening to women griping" or reading newspaper stories about child poverty. "What about my job, my problems, my freedom of speech?" They'll talk about something called "political correctness," which is a label slapped on anyone who feels and expresses revulsion against the big wounds. They'll rail about "angry women of colour who hurt my feelings when they said I was racist."

As white people, we have the immediate luxury of saying these kinds of things and actually getting listened to. But I don't think we have the long-term luxury, not if we want things to be any different for your children. When people who are not the targets of racism get that uncomfortable and angry, and are that determined to trivialize enormous social problems, you can bet there's something substantial to look at and change. And when people can't see what's right around them, there's some effort being exerted not to see.

I didn't always think or feel this way. In fact, you've witnessed some of my awkward, stumbling journey thus far, often to your embarrassment and inconvenience. However, the times I've learned the most have been when I managed to stay with my moments of discomfort and learn from them. And I'm distinguishing here between the constant discomfort zone where I live as a woman in which sexism is directed at me, and the less pressured unease I feel as a white person where I am not the target of racism. It's this second type of discomfort I want to explore from my own experiences. And you'll decide, as you always do, what is useful to you. I'll organize these moments around four of the questions you have put to me from time to time.

You asked me what, in my growing up, affected my learning about the world

My parents — your grandparents — and the communities from which we came, gave me both the nourishment to be critical, and the reasons not to be. You know that we emigrated from England after the war, when I was two, and my sister three months. My dad is English. You know that my mother was born in Canada; her grandparents on her mother's side emigrated from Scotland; her family on her dad's side descended from United Empire Loyalists. This ancestry was unremarkable in downtown Ottawa of the fifties and sixties, and unremarked. I didn't ask about it; I was "normal"; I didn't have to think about it. I only discovered this much later, when I heard other children, who had to know so much more about their histories in order to survive here, talk about their families. It was then that I realized my ignorance.

What I knew was that my sister and I were deeply loved, and that my parents deeply loved each other. This I learned, quite early, not to take for granted. This knowledge both helped and hindered me in my later rebellion against them.

Indeed, your grandparents were both very present in my life as a child. Dad's office was at home, and his and my mother's preoccupations were transparent, part of our everyday lives. My parents' travel and their opinions on international events had a profound effect on the questions I asked or didn't ask, and on my views on the world.

I was the child to whom Dad showed his stamp collection, and to whom he explained, with the help of a map, how the world was organized. From his point of view, the most significant part was the British Empire. Your grandfather had been a British officer with the Gurkhas in India from 1936 to 1945. We had many photograph albums of him in India and Burma. His own father had owned a colonial outfitting business, equipping English people "going to the colonies." There were photographs of my dad on horseback, or being served tea. The people in the foreground of all these photographs were white. Sometimes, in the background, there were Indian people, serving and carrying. (These are later reflections on something I took for granted at the time.) When I was a child, I loved these photographs of my dad in earlier moments in his life.

I first heard of Aden (which became Southern Yemen and is now the Republic of Yemen), Antigua, Australia, Bahamas, Barbados (where we were later to live), Bechuanaland (now Botswana), Bermuda, British Guiana (now Guyana), British Honduras (now Belize), Ceylon (now Sri Lanka), right through the alphabet to the Turks and

Caicos Islands and Zanzibar (now part of Tanzania) from the meticulously groomed stamp collection that my father helped me to continue. Together we would send for the prettiest ones (which always came from places other than England or Canada), or the special commemorative ones. In his book, these included the Bahamas 1942 stamps celebrating "450 years after the landfall of Columbus"; or the gorgeous 1906 Barbados stamp commemorating the "tercentenary of annexation" (I had no idea what this meant); or the 1939 royal visit to Canada. The same king or queen's head appeared on stamps from all these countries. We were all — including Canada — part of the "family of the Empire."

I felt these connections with "another home" at Christmas time particularly. In late October, we would pack up an enormous cheddar cheese, a big fruitcake, and other goodies to send to my aunt and cousin in England. And we would await the package of hand-knitted sweaters and books that would arrive every year. The books were Enid Blyton adventure books, or *Girls' Annuals* in which comics and stories were set around the world. Young white people (although I didn't see them as white then; they were just people) my age strode across countries, solving mysteries in jungles and deserts. They seemed to do so with resolve, cunning, and more compassion than their "enemies" — usually the people who lived there — appeared to deserve.

On Christmas Day we would count down to 10:00 a.m. for the Queen's message — a voice struggling through underwater cables and transmission problems; a voice heavy with responsibility, overseeing the Empire, urging compassion, harmony, enrichment together; a voice calming in its assurance that things would get done. There must have been messages before 1952 when she abruptly became Queen, but I don't remember them. I do remember the death of King George, and trying to imagine what a king really did. My parents were of the opinion that he was a "good king," whatever that meant, and that this was a very sad occasion indeed. And so the Queen's coronation was a grave and dignified event — a young woman assuming "enormous responsibilities." In order to help me imagine what these might be, I was equipped with lots of books about the Royals — the Queen and Princess Margaret as young girls, their education, their travels, their horses, their parents, lots of people in carriages. I was taught respect for the monarchy and a sense of being part of a benevolent "Commonwealth" where people treated each other decently and responsibly, but where sometimes things went amok. I never questioned that the words "empire" and "commonwealth" could be used interchangeably.

And then there was the BBC at 8:00 every morning — that garbled, pebbles-in-the-mouth voice crackling through the sea waves — pronouncing on Ceylon, Tanganyika (now Tanzania), Malaya (part of what is now Malaysia), the Mau Mau Rebellion, and India. My father and mother had a sustained and intense interest in international news, and always tried to develop my own curiosity in "world events." But as a child I never made the connections between these countries and their struggles and my life in Ottawa.

I think I had more daily experience of, but no words for, class differences. There were the "kids from Heron Park" who invariably became the "tech kids" at our high school. We were exhorted to be friendly, but to stay away from these kids. I had a friend, Sandy Olsenberg, who got talked about differently than anyone else. I was aware of differences between us, but didn't grasp their significance. Her parents listened to Johnny Cash; her dad was often unemployed; they moved a lot; she got to eat more junk food than I did; Sandy had lots of responsibility; she looked anxious much of the time. I once brought home a boyfriend from university who named himself as a working-class kid. My parents were concerned about "important differences between us." It appeared we were not working-class. However, at the same time my father would get angry with me for using words and references designed to make my father himself feel stupid. He would warn me about the social folly of "my pseudo-intellectualism" — quite rightly I now think — but also because he shared the anxiety that many self-taught people have that they will appear unlearned to those with a few more years of school. I was the first in our family to go to university.

Unlike your experience in Toronto, my Ottawa childhood was filled with the static noise of worlds outside my neighbourhood and, at the same time, devoid of real, daily contact with the people in those worlds. But that doesn't mean there was no contact. I think it was my fifth birthday party. My parents borrowed the movie *Little Black Sambo* from the library along with a projector and screen and set it up in a neighbour's house. I remember this movie vividly. I felt wonder, curiosity, derision, anxiety. Were there creatures in the world like this? Were there really jungles? Is this who lived here? Why were children my age having to deal with tigers? Was this a human child? There was nothing and no one to help me answer these questions.

There was no respectful, authentic representation of African peoples, Native peoples, Asian peoples. Most white children like myself, growing up in Canada in the fifties, "met" the other four-fifths of the world through comics; through movies such as Walt Disney's *Song of*   197 *the South* (see Alice Walker's essay on how this movie hurt her and other people in her community); through radio programs such as *Amos 'n' Andy* (now satirized, sort of, in the movie *Amos and Andrew*); through the countless westerns on radio and TV, such as *The Lone Ranger*; through missionaries at church; through the limited range of people authoring the school textbooks and novels; through the narrow world view of teachers; and through the garbled voice of the BBC. Almost without exception, these versions of the rest of the planet were written and directed by white people.

This "absent presence" or "present absence" of four-fifths of the world characterized what "contact" I had with people who *did* live in Ottawa and environs at the time. When we went for picnics with my grandparents to see the site of my grandfather's family farm that is now buried by the St. Lawrence Seaway, we did not talk about the Aboriginal peoples who lived there before the Loyalists, or whose land may have been taken to give to the Loyalists. It was not in the school books, and it was not part of my family's consciousness at that time, either. It was only much later, in the summer of 1993, that my mother recollected why her father's family never relied on store-bought drugs. She was reminiscing that her father and aunt always looked for boneset and other plants good for stomach ache. She told us that when her father's family migrated to Canada as Loyalists, they learned about the healing properties of local plants "from Indian people who lived here."

In Ottawa I was more specifically aware that French people and Jewish people "were not like us." French people were "poor and less educated"; Jewish families "had lots of money." Face-to-face contact was sporadic, guarded, unequal, and just enough to reinforce these powerful stereotypes. Certainly, nobody named social class, ethnocentrism, or racism as factors affecting people's lives, or shaping what we learned to see and hear, and not to see and hear.

In these years of my youth, I was self-absorbed and protected from trouble in ways that neither of my parents had been. I had the choice to stay unconnected to the larger world I inhabited. At Queen's University I remained unaware of even the mild political activity on that campus. There was evidence of people's pain, oppression, and resistance all around me. Their muzzled voices were present in the events that one *could see*, like the civil rights marches on television, or the sustained and vicious forms of contempt expressed towards Aboriginal peoples; and in the things that one couldn't see, such as the exclusion of most people who weren't white from the university; the all-white teaching staff; the total European focus of all studies; the strange silence, even during those civil rights days, concerning race and racism in Canada. I walked around as though vaccinated from the disturbance that these real people and these real struggles might make in my life. This kind of blinkering and ignorance, this distortion of the world, is one of the chief effects of a racist environment on white people.

And yet, I must have been exerting some effort to not see/hear what was around me, because I had some indefinable unease, some snuffling sense that there was more to the picture, some curiosity and some fear about how it was with other people, whomever they were.

I'm reminded, as I read the above again, that I have really only begun to answer the question June Jordan poses: "What took you so long?" In her essay "On Listening, A Good Way to Hear," she challenges a white American activist to explain what took him so long to "very very very very slowly realize that something is hideously wrong."

You asked me what I learned when we lived in the Caribbean

I had to leave Canada and live and work in Barbados for two years to see what Ms. Jordan was talking about. It was there that things came unravelled — quickly, it seems now — but in identifiable stages. Barbados was one of the places behind the beautiful stamps; a place that had celebrated a "tercentenary of annexation," a part of the "family of the Empire."

I was twenty-four, your father was twenty-five, and you were two, Karen. I remember sitting on a bus to Speightstown in the first week we were there. I was looking at the skin on my arm and thinking, "I'm white. What took me so long to name this?" This sounds so elementary now. It wasn't to me then. I remember thinking that "white" was less my physical colour (indeed, I was a violent pink) than it was my "social" colour, if you know what I mean. It had everything to do with the mixture of deference, resentment, and polite distance that I felt from so many people — the effort people had to exert to see beyond my whiteness to whatever qualities they might find attractive in me. This awareness emerged in little lurches. I'm sure I whined, initially, about people not seeing the "real me."

And I was learning, through Caribbean writers, that the Empire was not a happy family. I read about Europeans exterminating Arawak and Carib peoples to clear land for European plantations; Europeans capturing African peoples to provide a pliant labour force; Black and indigenous people resisting this sustained brutality against them; the legacy of this history economically, socially, psychologically; and the current, continued struggles of Caribbean nations to forge authentic, new, democratic paths for themselves.

My learning was stimulated by more than books. I could see the effects of colonialism in every aspect of daily life. Observations, and frequent conversations with friends, neighbourhood children, and students, many of whom you met, Karen, raised whole new questions for me. There was one exchange in particular where fifteen-year-old Anthony Griffiths told me that he really liked me because I was white. I was startled and hurt. Didn't he like me "because of me"? I racked my brains for a question that would explain this to him, and settled on, "How would you feel if I told you that I liked you because you were Black?" He replied in a deeply wounded voice, "I'd think you wanted me for a puppy dog." I looked at him helplessly. He was not talking about individual hurt caused by a comment; he was talking about what white people could do to him and other Black people. I realized, then, I had no notion of the scale of damage that had been done to him. The effects of racism on me were not "equivalent" to the effects on him. And, whether I liked it or not, I could not filter out my whiteness from Anthony's responses to me. Anthony Griffiths helped me to begin to analyse power, in particular, the power behind the exercise of racism. In the world as it is, Anthony Griffiths can hurt my feelings, but he has none of the social power, none of the weight of history that would help him, through the exercise of racism, to reduce my circumstances, my life chances, my sense of myself.

These everyday moments forced me to examine what "white" represented, what white people had done, and were continuing to do to Black people in Barbados. And from Barbados, I had to think about the rest of the Caribbean, and the United States, and Africa, and other parts of the world, and eventually, Canada. What had taken me so long? I was furious at the information I had been denied, and ashamed of my own collusion in the situation.

At the same time I was reflecting on my situation as a woman and developing questions about feminism. I was young, married, with a small child — you, Karen. A white American anthropologist was also living in Barbados at the time. She was there with her child — defiantly not married — investigating why Barbadian women would not participate consistently in the birth control schemes that proliferated there. She would express exasperation with the women who were my neighbours. She saw them as taking abuse from their men, getting pregnant when it wasn't necessary, and not fighting for their rights. She saw part of her job, in addition to her research, as "promoting feminism." It seemed there were certain ways you showed that you were a feminist. It seemed that neither myself nor my neighbours were feminists. It was in Barbados that I learned something else that now seems obvious — that women's struggles are shaped by race and class. I had struggled to prove that I could both have children and go out and work. Some of my neighbours would have loved such a choice. They were fighting to put food on the table for their children. For them, working outside the home was a given. Women carried loads of sugar cane and food on their heads for miles. This was every-day life since slavery. They took care of middle-class (usually white or light-skinned) women's children to the detriment of their own. Many of my neighbours did not see birth control as some kind of liberation; some of the birth control experiments made women sick and unable to have children; in the absence of old age pensions, children were their security. And women looked out for each other's children, including you, Karen, in ways I had never seen in Canada. I had to ask myself whether Canada was as child-loving as I had thought; I was forced to broaden my understanding of women's rights; I had to question a feminism that only acknowledged some women and some rights.

Some of these issues were only half-formed insights and questions when we returned to Canada in 1972. But the two years in Barbados made everything different. Toni Morrison, in her book of essays called *Playing in the Dark: Whiteness and the Literary Imagination*, has a wonderful passage that, for me, names this shift in my vision:

> It is as if I had been looking at a fishbowl — the glide and flick of the golden scales, the green tip, the bolt of white careening back from the gills; the castles at the bottom, surrounded by pebbles and tiny, intricate fronds of green; the barely disturbed water, the flecks of waste and food, the tranquil bubbles traveling to the surface — and suddenly I saw the bowl, the structure that transparently (and invisibly) permits the ordered life it contains to exist in the larger world.

Having seen "the bowl," I now had a responsibility to chip away and widen the cracks in it. And the biggest cracks came, I discovered, from people who were outside the bowl, who were organizing to make a different structure that would meaningfully include them.

You'll hear that not much was going on in the seventies or even the eighties, but this is someone's wishful thinking. Over the next years I learned a great deal from efforts to organize non-profit daycare, to get our voices heard as parents in schools, to support farm workers 201 and domestic workers in their organizing, to build community and coalition, to expose racism, and get new policies and practices in public institutions. When I came back from Barbados, I "discovered" — I guess a bit like Columbus — what had been happening for some time. Native peoples, lesbians, women, poor people, artists, workers, South Asian people, and others had formed organizations, were talking back, and were making a difference.

For a number of years after Barbados, I was furious with my father and ashamed of my family's participation in this Empire — this "fishbowl." My father and I had fruitless fights in which I disparaged him cruelly for the criminal activities of the British, for what he had done in India, for American imperialism. We managed to hurt each other a great deal, I think, before we made peace with each other's lives. I know that is part of what has taken so long. Another writer, Minnie Bruce Pratt, says a helpful thing for me:

> When we discover truths about our home culture, we may fear we are losing our self; our self-respect, our self-importance. But when we begin to act on our new knowledge, when we begin to cross our "first people boundaries," and ally ourselves publicly with "the others," then we may fear that we will lose the people who are our family, our kind, be rejected by "our own kind."

I both feared and wanted this as a way of distancing myself from my own shame at not seeing, earlier, what was all around me. But my parents never let this happen. You'll remember the painful time in 1983 when I was working in Grenada and the U.S. marines invaded. There was a handful of us who came back to Canada choked with rage, and incredulous at the lies that were passing for news. We spoke about what we had seen, and we went on a cross-country tour to make sure that other people heard about it, too. My parents found it really difficult to believe that the Americans would have deliberately done something that wasn't for the protection of all of us. However, whether or not they agreed with our analysis of what the Americans were actually doing there, they did believe that the Americans had contributed to my immediate physical danger. They collected all the news clippings, and soon after our return went to a party with the clippings, as usual, tucked in my mother's purse. They were assailed by criticism from old friends, angry that I was misleading people and that I was saying all these "Communist things." Your grandparents tried to defend me by accurately quoting from the clippings, and they were supported by another friend who loudly and contemptuously dismissed the entire gathering. Shortly after this, my parents attended a little photographic exhibit on Grenada, entitled "A Small Revolution" — wonderful photographs documenting the extraordinary achievements of Grenada from 1979 to 1983 — the real reason for the invasion. They gave me a poster of this exhibit for Christmas. I was more moved by the love in this gift than anything they have ever given me. And I stopped arguing with them.

You asked me how the two of you helped me learn

You were constantly brushing me up, uncomfortably, with my ignorance, and my unfamiliarity with the world. I'm grinning as I remember you, Karen, on the back steps, your two-year-old fist clutching the hair of your friend, her fingers stroking yours, both of you quite entranced with each other. And when she pushed her finger into your arm it left a white mark momentarily. Why was that? Why didn't her brown skin do that? Why did the water leave your hair all lank and plastered against your head? It didn't do that to Sophie's. And while I rushed around trying to find out about melanin and skin colour, you'd come up with some harder question. Why was Sophie's mother upset because we gave Sophie a Black doll? Why, when you wore clothes that a relative had outgrown, did Sophie's mother throw your perfectly fine, outgrown clothes back on our doorstep calling them "dumps?"

And just when I thought I was on the right track, a reaction from one of you would shake things up again. How was I to comfort you, Janny, when you were five years old, and we had just read the book and sung the song the "Drinking Gourd"? You began to sob that you were frightened that they would come and catch your friend, Fran. I tried, awkwardly, to explain that slavery was over, but that its legacy was not. And I also fully realized something, at that moment, that I had only partially grasped before. You needed to know more about how Black people had fought back, and continued to do so. We read Harriet Tubman; we talked about South Africa. And you needed to know that some white people resisted being caught into a set of oppressive relations with their Black neighbours.

And when you were seven, Karen, there was the day I heard you calling, taunting, "nigger, nigger," to your friend, Connie, next door. Before I reached the back door, I realized that my rage was also about my failure, and would not help Connie or you. And so we talked about that word, about where it came from. And we went to talk to Connie and Connie's mother. I'm not sure whether your friendship survived that day. But it was an important jolt to my liberalism. It was not enough to have a variety of books, exposure to different music, or to live in a cosmopolitan neighbourhood. Contact between people was still not equal. There were weapons you had in a fight with Connie, that she didn't have against you, and you had, at seven, learned to use them, as I had at seven. Resisting white supremacy required an everyday, active set of interventions. There was no such thing as "non-racism," only "anti-racism." This was a very important lesson for me, and one that directly influenced my increasing focus on anti-racism work in my job at the Cross Cultural Communications Centre.

Indeed, at ten years old, Janny, you already grasped that inaction about racism by adults had left kids on their own to fight it. Do you remember sitting at the dining-room table eating supper — you, your friend Fran, and I? You were congratulating Fran on the damage she had inflicted on the eye of one of your classmates, Louis. Fran nodded. I, of course, asked what happened. Fran responded economically that Louis had called her "nigger" and she had punched him out. I asked, in my law-and-order way, if there hadn't been some teachers around who could have helped. You two looked knowingly at each other, and Fran began explaining — slowly and carefully, because clearly I wasn't too swift — that if teachers did hear that word, they always found something else to do, or pretended they didn't hear. If you reported the incident to a teacher or principal, they either asked you what you had done to provoke it, or they punished you for being a tattle-tale. "So," concluded Fran, slowing down to let me get the point, "if you're going to get punished anyway, you might as well have the satisfaction of punching the guy out." I had no response to this inescapable logic. This was just another incident in the daily series of child-wise nudges that shook up my comfortable edges. What took me so long, anyway?

Meanwhile, you were making your own paths. I still remember your march home from a grade nine science class, Karen. You asked whether the Board of Education had a policy that could stop teachers from being racist. It seemed that your science teacher had slipped into the classroom at a raucous moment. Everyone was acting up, but he had swooped down on your classmate, Bao, and sneered, "What's the matter with you? Your kind are well-behaved and quiet, so what's your problem?" In the uneasy silence that followed, no one had spoken up — for Bao, or for themselves. You returned to school the next day, having read the Board's race relations policy. And you went to the science teacher at break and told him that you now knew there was a policy that said he couldn't say the things he had said to Bao; and that your parents knew what you were doing; and that if he ever did that again, you would report him. In mentioning that your parents knew about this, you were demonstrating your growing strategic sense that when you speak up you risk punishment, and where possible, you need to protect yourself.

Always, the two of you have challenged me to "make the way by walking." You never allowed me to hoist some politically cleansed flag, and hitch myself to it. Daily living is so much more messy, and if you're paying any attention at all, that living is constantly throwing up new questions. After watching the movie *Jungle Fever*, Janny, you and I spent three hours analysing the powerful scene in the middle where a group of Black women talk about their experiences with Black men, and with white women. They don't mince words. You felt uncomfortable and accused. You had already seen the movie once with a male friend who was Black, and the two of you had struggled for adequate words to talk about questions of sexism, racism, and sexuality without hurting each other.

And there was the youth meeting at a local high school that you attended with a friend, Karen; you were one of the few white people there. You wondered whether you were intruding; you tried to watch alertly for signs that your presence might be inappropriate and hoped you'd be able to read the cues. There is a politic to respecting people's need for caucusing and organizing, while at the same time continuing to learn and do your share of the work to make things better. It's important to keep wrestling with that balance and not give up trying because you're afraid you'll get it wrong. There are other questions. What am I responsible for? What will others hold me responsible for, whether it's fair or not? How do I claim the parts of culture(s) that help me be whole, while at the same time opposing those many aspects that oppress, divide, and diminish? How do I both protect myself against malicious and small-minded attack, and leave myself open to continued challenge? These questions take me to the final part of this letter to you.

You asked me what role(s) white people have in fighting racism

In a certain way, this entire letter is an attempt to answer that question. I can't speak for anyone else, but the efforts I feel best about are those that don't, in themselves, reproduce racism, that build coalition, that acknowledge leadership from activists who experience racism, that ensure that I speak from where I am, and that I move things forward and not back. This is everyday work; I haven't found this easy. I know you two haven't either.

There's a prevalent notion around that white people can choose to fight racism, or not, and people of colour don't have this choice. Let's start with the first part of this statement. It's true that white people are not the targets of racism; and that indeed, many whites have benefited, and continue to benefit, from dominating and excluding others. Many white people not only do not acknowledge racism as a system of domination, but also choose to do nothing about it if they do. "Having a choice" makes us suspect, because we might pack up anytime the going gets tough. History is littered with examples of people from the power group taking their ball and going home when they're "misunderstood," when they're accused, when the consequences are distasteful, when people "aren't grateful" for their efforts.

We'd better be clear about the reasons we fight racism and other big wrongs. This is where I have come to at this point in my life; I fight racism because I can't be with myself in the world without trying to do so. I fight racism, as I fight other forms of domination, because it has killed millions of people; because it has totally messed up relations between people(s) on this planet; because it forces me into oppressive relations that I reject with other people(s); because it lies about who is in the world and who has made what happen; because it has limited what I have been able to see and know; because it diminishes the friendship and community that I seek, with others, to build; and because I learned through the two of you that inaction is complicity. When I'm clear about that place in myself, I can, as bell hooks says in her book *Black Looks*, "be capable, via *my* political choices, of working on behalf of the oppressed." But I can't work on behalf of anyone else until I know where I am.

And what about the second part of this statement of who has choice about fighting racism? People of colour and Aboriginal persons do not have a choice about being the targets of white domination. However, each person makes decisions about what their stance towards this will be. Not all persons of colour or Aboriginal persons fight racism, any more than all women fight sexism. Certainly there are different consequences and risks for people of colour who fight racism than there are for whites. In your classrooms and workplaces, you will sometimes hear people of colour deny racism, and its effects on themselves and others, just as you'll hear women trivialize sexism. And you will hear white people welcome these pronouncements. In these situations, you will have to speak from your own rejection of racism, and not what you think or hope others will say.

As you already know, there are consequences to speaking and acting against injustice, just as — I believe — there are consequences to not doing so. For people of colour daring to name and challenge racism in a workplace, reprisals are often swift and brutal, crude as well as subtle. Colleagues shun you, talk about you behind your back, suggest that you're crazy and too angry to have any perspective; information about new training, developmental assignments, promotions, and new job postings reaches you later than anyone else; decisions affecting you are made at meetings where you are absent; job vacancies you apply for which were previously permanent become temporary; hiring selection teams ask questions about your personal life and views. And on it goes. I personally witnessed all of the above and more in the government workplace where I just finished a contract. These stories are not peculiar to this workplace. It is a serious decision for a person of colour or an Aboriginal person to confront racism — in the workplace or in the streets. It's a serious decision for anyone who's the target of those big forms of oppression to fight back. In lots of places, including Canada, people have been killed for doing so.

Are there consequences for white people fighting racism? Yes, but they're usually of an entirely different order. In my last job, my contract was not renewed. Management didn't like being reminded and challenged about acting on their stated commitment to fighting racism. But this happens less to people who are not at the receiving end of the hurt that you're fighting — men fighting sexism, for example, or straight people insisting on rights for gay people. Indeed, white people challenging racism are often met with an admiration and surprise that can be seductive. "What got you into this anti-racism thing?" I've been asked with interest by people of different racial backgrounds. This applauding of white people's anti-racism efforts is not confined to individual interactions. "Association with anti-racism work" can actually help white people get promotions and jobs, if they are careful, tactical, and "not too noisy." In an anti-racism pilot school project on which I worked a few years ago, several of the white teachers included their participation in the project on their resumés, and in many cases this "experience" assisted them in securing a vice-principalship or consultant's job in a Board of Education anxious to appear anti-racist. Contributions to this project produced none of the same benefits for Black and East Asian teachers whose efforts were critical to the work. You will encounter this in your work as a teacher, Karen. There is — still — a prevalent notion amongst white people that Aboriginal persons and persons of colour should be challenging racism; and that therefore their efforts and the risks that they take are unremarkable. Co-existing with this fiction is the puzzling view that Aboriginal persons and persons of colour cannot be "objective" when

it comes to racism, are likely to overreact and get angry, and are therefore highly suspect when it comes to fighting racism. The corollary to
all of this is that white people are best placed to get paid to do anti-
racism work, and they are more likely to get recognition for their
work. This is, in fact, a microcosm of how racism works. These are
some of the ways in which racism can co-opt anti-racism efforts, and
any white people who do anti-racism work.

Needless to say, this situation has justifiably ticked many people
right off. In this climate and these circumstances you need to pay
attention that when you talk back to racism, you aren't benefiting at
other people's expense. Indeed, there are jobs you may have to let
pass, or opportunities that are exciting to you that someone else
would really do better. This is not about condescending to someone,
or pushing someone forward "just because she's Black." This is about
making sure that the old affirmative action for white people isn't still
in operation, with you as a key beneficiary; it's about really trying to
get the work done with all the wits, skills, and different kinds of
knowledge we can assemble.

And you'd better not expect people to be grateful for your efforts.
In fact, the more you work on trying to make things right, the more
mistakes you'll have the chance to make, and the more you'll get criticized from different people. Sometimes their criticism will be useful
and, even if it is hard to listen to, supportive of you and of more effective work. You're lucky when you get that kind of challenge. But
sometimes people will try to tear you down, and erode even useful
work. Watch out for that; distinguish between the two.

Sometimes you will feel shame at being white; you will feel uneasy
about being middle-class and without disability. It's not easy to
embrace who you are, to find models you are proud to claim, and, at
the same time, to continue resisting the most abusive aspects of the
culture of which we are a part. However, in the long run shame
doesn't do you or anyone else any good. Shame is immobilizing
unless you use it as information to move on and to change things.
Part of being in the power group — whether you like it or not — is
being the target of anger when people start to analyse how they are
being mistreated by "your" group of people, and to demand that
things change. As white women, we live with oppression as part of
the "oppressor" group and as part of the "oppressed" group. These are
different places to be, and we occupy them at the same time. There
are different challenges to being a socially responsible person with
these simultaneous identities.

There are moments when you can become just another white person, even to people who love you, know you, want you in their lives. (You know yourselves, that there are times when our anger at men's violence against women, and men's power to avoid changing anything, can extend to all men — our fathers and other loved males. And sometimes, intimate men *do* collude in our oppression. Sometimes we *do* collude, as white people, in the oppression of people we love.)

Do you get the picture? It's what you know already; life is a messy, challenging business. Mostly, you walk one day at a time, clucking over mistakes, and being prepared to make some new ones, trying to leave your little corner of the world in slightly better shape than you found it.

If you take nothing else from all these words, take these five ideas and use them in your own ways. First, remember that *you are not responsible for wrongs committed before you were born, but you can't escape the legacy of those wrongs.* You need to understand some history in order to understand your current position in the world and other people's perceptions of you. *And you are responsible for what you do now.* In this regard, *there's no such thing as "doing nothing."* You two and others have taught me that. Even indecision, or unconsciousness, results in some action or inaction that has consequences for you and other people. The question is whether you're going to take responsibility for it.

Second — in whatever situations you experience it — try to *use discomfort to pose new questions to yourself, and to seek new insights.* I'm not talking here about an informed fear of physical danger or attack from other people; I'm speaking of the discomfort resulting from avoidance, silence, or the challenge posed by people seeking justice for themselves. Try to ask, even when it's inconvenient, "What and who is missing from this picture? Who else should be saying something about this? What's behind what's going on here?" (This last question could be about what's going on inside yourself, as well as an event in the world.)

Third, *distinguish between, on the one hand, hurt feelings that a person with privilege might feel at being excluded, and on the other, the sustained, systemic, and pervasive damage inflicted on all parts of the self, by the big wounds* — racism, sexism, class, imperialism, ageism, heterosexism, oppression of people with disabilities. As white people, and as women, you will experience both. There is a backlash against people who are organizing against these big wrongs. Part of that backlash trivializes the damage of these injustices and inflates the personal feelings of those people who are being challenged to change.

Fourth, *value your own experiences as sources of learning and wisdom about yourself and the larger society*, even if those stories are painful. The tensions in our personal lives, whether they are economic, social, and/or in our psyches, mirror in some way the tensions and contradictions in the larger world. This is not the same thing as thinking that your experience is everyone else's experience. My stories here are about some moments when I managed to be more "accurate about myself and to force my mind into a constantly expanding apprehension of my political and moral situation." (These are not my words; they're June Jordan's, but I like them as one descriptor of what I'm trying to do, what I've seen both of you try to do.)

And finally, *make the most of who you are without damaging other people with less social power than yourself*. This means being self-aware, and self-critical. It means using what you know and acknowledging and being curious about what you don't know. It means living as truthfully and as consciously as possible with all your social identities as young, white, middle-class women, but not being reduced by them. It means not being apologetic for who you are, but being responsible for what you do.

As Bernice Johnson Reagon (of the singing group Sweet Honey in the Rock) says, "Most of the things you do, if you do them right, are for people who live long after you are long forgotten. That will only happen if you give it away. Whatever it is that you know, give it away." And that is what I'm trying to do here. To put it mildly, you haven't always warmly welcomed the knowledge I wanted to give to you at different moments in your lives. But I feel some urgency now about what I've tried to say in this letter. Please take these thoughts with you as you decide how you will travel these roads.

Loving you in all the ways I know,
Your mother

P.S. Some writing by women that might interest you.

This is a very short, selective list of writings by women that I've found helpful over the years. I haven't included novels or poetry. All of these materials, in some way, explore the issue of identity(ies), finding voice, fighting back.

Anzaldua, Gloria. *Borderlands/La Frontera: The New Mestiza*. San Francisco: Aunt Lute Books, 1987.

Luanne Armstrong. "Being White." *Tessera*, vol. 12 (Summer 1992).

Bannerji, Himani, Linda Carty, Kari Dehli, Susan Heald, Kate

McKenna. *Unsettling Relations: The University as a Site of Feminist Struggles*. Toronto: Women's Press, 1991.

Barndt, Deborah. "Putting Ourselves into the Picture: Recovering History through Images and Stories." Unpublished Notes for Talk to Critical Pedagogy Series. Toronto: Ontario Institute for Studies in Education (OISE), Feb. 17, 1993.

hooks, bell. *Black Looks: Race and Representation*. Toronto: Between the Lines, 1992.

Jordan, June. *Moving towards Home: Political Essays*. London: Virago Press, 1989. (Two essays I quote from this book are "On Listening: A Good Way to Hear" and "Thinking about My Poetry.")

Joseph, Gloria I. and Jill Lewis. *Common Differences: Conflicts in Black and White Feminist Perspectives*. Boston: South End Press, 1981.

Lorde, Audre. *Sister Outsider: Essays and Speeches*. Trumansburg, N.Y.: The Crossing Press, 1984.

McIntosh, Peggy. "White Privilege: Unpacking the Invisible Knapsack." *Peace and Freedom*, July/August 1989.

Morrison, Toni. *Playing in the Dark: Whiteness and the Literary Imagination*. Cambridge, Mass.: Harvard University Press, 1992. (The essay I quote from is "Black Matters.")

Page, Joanne, ed. *Arguments with the World: Essays by Bronwen Wallace*. Kingston: Quarry Press, 1992.

Pratt, Minnie Bruce. "Identity: Skin Blood Heart." In *Rebellion: Essays 1980-1991*. Ithaca, N.Y.: Firebrand Books, 1991.

Razack, Sherene. "Storytelling for Social Change." In *Returning the Gaze: Essays on Racism, Feminism and Politics*. Toronto: Sister Vision Press, 1993.

Reagon, Bernice Johnson. "Coalition Politics: Turning the Century." In *Home Girls: A Black Feminist Anthology*, ed. Barbara Smith. New York: Kitchen Table/Women of Colour Press, 1983.

Rich, Adrienne. "Notes toward a Politics of Location (1984)." In *Blood, Bread and Poetry*. New York: W.W. Norton & Co., 1986.

Scheier, Libby, Sarah Sheard, and Eleanor Wachtel, eds. *Language in Her Eye: Writing and Gender: Views by Canadian Women Writing in English*. Toronto: Coach House Press, 1990.

Walker, Alice. *Living by the Word*. San Diego: Harcourt, Brace, Jovanvitch, 1988. (The essay I mention is "Dummy in the Window.")

Willamson, Janice. "Jeanette Armstrong: What I Intended Was to Connect and It's Happened." *Tessera*, vol. 12 (Summer 1992).

THE "RACE CONSCIOUSNESS" OF A SOUTH ASIAN (CANADIAN, OF COURSE) FEMALE ACADEMIC

••••••••••••••••••••••••••

ARUN MUKHERJEE

Some time ago, as I was walking to my class on the university campus, a South Asian male, probably in his mid-thirties, asked me for
directions to a building. He had chosen me for his informant, I
thought, because of our common past: we both could tell by looking
at each other that we were South Asians. Anyway, he looked lost and
I was only too happy to instruct him. Now, such a nondescript
encounter would surely have faded from my memory except for this
man's next question: "So what courses are you taking?" Why, I asked
myself, had this man decided that I could only be a student, despite
my very grey head of hair? The answer I gave myself was painful to
articulate and is painful to write about: he could not imagine a South
Asian woman in the role of an academic because they were such a rar-
ity on Canadian campuses.

After this internal debate I told my compatriot, "I teach here."
There was surprise and contrition writ large on his face as we parted
after he had said his "Oh, I see." And as for me, I pondered the complexities of my answer for the next few minutes. Although the man's
facial expression had changed from registering a desire for familiarity

to a combination of awe and admiration, I felt that his admiration would soon disappear if he were to know that I only taught as a part-timer, liable to be hired and fired at the whim of the people who made those decisions.

I still have to pinch myself to remember that my fortunes have changed since then. Now that I am in a full-time tenure-stream position I cannot help but connect my personal fortune with that of non-white Canadians in general. For I am fully aware that my present success is the outcome of not just my "merit" — that hallowed principle so often invoked by those who claim employment equity will flood our institutions with "inferior" appointees — but of the anti-racist struggles waged across Canada by communities that have borne the brunt of racism in Canada.

My active involvement in this ongoing struggle and my memory of the past struggles are the factors that constitute my race consciousness. Some celebrity academics put the word race in quotation marks because there is no such thing in biology as race. We all share the same blood types and the same gene pool. They warn us about essentialisms if we talk about race: things like Black people having rhythm in their blood and Asians being good at math.

My race consciousness, my awareness of being non-white in a white country, is certainly not essentialist. I am conscious of being non-white, of being South Asian (I cannot call myself Indian in Canada, although that is what I really am), of being "Paki," to the same extent that white Canadians are not conscious of their whiteness. They would rather be "just Canadians."

But being "just Canadian" is a privilege only white people enjoy in this country. It is we non-whites who are seen as deviants from the norm. So we are tagged with identity cards, some worn proudly, others with resentment. I can't, of course, speak for all non-white Canadians — we even disagree with the words that are used to mark our difference. Some find "non-white" totally unpalatable because it is rooted in negation; some love to use the term "people of colour" while others hate it because, in their minds, it obliterates our heterogeneity; some have no problem with "visible minority," they say, because one should call a spade a spade, whereas others find it a term imposed by a racist state. But I am always conscious of my being non-white and how that fact determines my total life experience. I doubt that I will ever become "just Canadian," whatever that means.

As to the negative qualifier in "non-white," I have absolutely no problems with that. After all, terms such as "non-violence," "non-cooperation," and "civil disobedience" also use negation. Moreover, 213 "non-white" is only one aspect of my multiple identities, for I am also a woman of colour, a Third Worlder, a South Asian, an East Indian, an Indian, a Punjabi, and a Mukherjee (my patronymic caste marker). What term I use to describe myself and my subject matter depends on whom I am speaking to and what I am talking about. (Some white academics have told me that I cannot be a Third Worlder and a South Asian at the same time. One has gone so far as to write that since I have a comfortable tenure-stream job, I cannot claim a Third World identity. If I were to use an analogy, this kind of thinking suggests to me that one ceases being a sister or a daughter if one becomes a wife or a mother.) I use the term "non-white" in order to talk about the binary relationship of power in which "white" is the dominant term because there is no denying that we live in a racist world order.

Being non-white in an academic setting means, or has meant thus far (I am banking a whole lot on employment equity) being the single non-white, male or female, at departmental meetings or social get-togethers or conferences. It has meant a tremendous loneliness of spirit because white colleagues don't seem to notice anything abnormal in a meeting room or a plenary at a conference where only a handful (or less) of non-white people are present. (I deliberately use the words "white colleagues" because the non-whites present at such gatherings always talk to each other about the "absence" of people of colour.)

My having entered through the gates that have long been locked to people who have dark skins, then, becomes an existential and intellectual problem for me. How have I managed to get in, I ask myself, when so many of my non-white contemporaries with academic ambitions did not make it? And now that I am here, what do I intend to do?

First of all, I intend to survive. I am here because I knew how to dissemble, to give them what they wanted so that they would give me my degree. That meant never reading a book by a non-white writer as part of the curriculum during my entire education in English literature, both in Canada and India. I try to look back on those days of my studenthood and reconstruct what I thought about the absence of non-white authors in the curriculum. I think again and again of the all-white American Literature courses that I was taught, both in India and Canada, and my unproblematic acceptance of their normalcy.

I realize now the power of the teacher as authority figure. My teachers made the racist, exclusionary curriculum normal for me. They made it normal by convincing me that the curriculum was composed of the "best" works ever written by "man." And whatever did not make it in the canon was not excluded because of racism or sexism but because of objective criteria that measure excellence. Not that I, or my classmates, ever asked any questions about why so and so was not on the book list. Messages about exclusion and inclusion, however, were embedded in the discourse of critical theory that we got in the class and in the books we were asked to read.

Racism has a long reach, and my soul trembles to think of how much I imbibed unconsciously. For example, during all of my twenty-five years of living in India, I never knew that the United States (Canada was not part of my curriculum at all) also had people of colours other than white. No one — that is, my parents, teachers, media — ever told me of the existence of these non-white Americans. The pictures in the papers and magazines were always of white Americans, and the books in my curriculum were the same. Here I can't resist a story Marie Marule, a Native woman from Alberta, told me. When she told people in Zimbabwe (then Rhodesia) that she was a Native Canadian, that is, "Red Indian," they responded, "But you are extinct!" Well, that was the silent message my anthologies of American literature gave me too. And it was reinforced by the white visiting professors of American literature and white Peace Corps volunteers.

As a non-white female academic I intend to make sure that my students will not go away with such unconscious racism unchallenged. Even when I have had no control on the design and content of the courses, I have told my students what I thought of the materials I had been assigned to teach. I began a course I taught on "American Literature" as a part-timer by telling my students who was not on it: Native writers, African American writers, and women writers, both white and non-white. And I made the absence of these writers on the prescribed curriculum a constant presence by invoking them as we read the sanctioned writers. (Two of the eventual course evaluations said the course had too much about racism and not enough about "technique.")

I have had to resort to similar strategies when faced with "Women's Studies" courses that did not include a word about the histories and texts of non-white women. I have told my students to be wary of accepting the experience of white women as the "universal" experience of all women. I have told them that I cannot rejoice with the celebratory histories of Canadian women that present white women getting the vote as "women get the vote," ignoring how Canadians of Native, Chinese, Japanese, and South Asian ancestries, both male and female, had to wait another forty years to enjoy voting rights. I have told them about the racism of such prominent feminist

215

foremothers as Charlotte Perkins Gilman and Nellie McClung, whose racism is the reason I can't feel as enthusiastic about Persons' Day as some white feminists. Such questioning of the curriculum leads my students to think about the enveloping cloud of racism in which we live as a society. It makes them suspicious of the curriculum that their society, in the shape of their schools, universities, and teachers, imparts to them.

Sometime during the course of teaching, the question of whether any of my students had non-white teachers before taking my course always crops up. The number of students who say yes to this question has been infinitesimally small thus far. That question leads us into another: who controls knowledge and how do they define it? We talk about the Eurocentric nature of the Canadian university and how few and far between are the courses offered on non-European (read non-white) cultures. We talk about whether it is possible to read texts by non-white writers, both male and female, in the framework of aesthetic theories developed in Euro-America.

I am delighted to see that the work we do in my classes also rubs off on the other work my students do. For instance, while reading Attia Hosain's *Sunlight on a Broken Column*, we noticed that the plot treated the servants in the household as characters in their own right. We went on to discuss such classics as Jane Austen's *Pride and Prejudice*, where large dinners are eaten in feudal homes with not a servant in sight — as though the dinner had cooked and served itself. We also discussed Virginia Woolf's *To the Lighthouse*, where servants can appear only off stage and not as part of the plot.

The South Asian text, thus, helps my students envision other ways of writing, other ways of creating and responding to art, and other ways of living. It takes them away from the "universalist" aesthetic norms that theorize on the basis of hand-picked "great" works of Euro-America, albeit with my theoretical help. It is not the text itself that can help them reach across the cultural barriers, for texts can be completely misread. (As Chinua Achebe tells us, a letter from a New York high-school student who had just read his classic text *Things Fall Apart* thanked him profusely for writing such an informative book on the superstitions and customs of an African tribe.) So it is my responsibility to challenge my students, both through my teaching and my research, to stop applying "Western" norms and "Western" values as though they were true for all times and all places. Because when one does that, one does not really encounter the complexity of cultural diversity across our planet, but only stares at oneself in the mirror. My goal as a teacher and a researcher has been to challenge this Western narcissism, this fake universalism that is really Euro-American ethnocentrism talking about itself in the vocabulary of "the human condition" at the same time as it denies the humanity of others.

I am, thus, always conscious of the "difference" that my being South Asian in a white Canada continuously produces, both inside me and outside of me. I am conscious that until 1947, the year of India's independence, the doors of Canada were closed to me. I cannot forget that Canada's racist immigration laws pertaining to South Asians were repealed only after the Indian prime minister, Jawaharlal Nehru, personally asked the Canadian government to get rid of them if they wanted a friendly relationship with India. I cannot forget the *Komagata Maru* incident, when Canada quarantined four hundred South Asians on this ship for two months, denied them food and water rations and a fair judicial process, and finally sent them back, some to their deaths at British hands. I cannot forget this incident, even though I did not read about it in Canada's history books.

I won't forget these facts, and other such facts pertaining to Native Canadians, Chinese Canadians, African Canadians, and Japanese Canadians, until I begin to see real changes happen. I won't forget them until I see Canadian schools teach about all Canadians, something they didn't do in my son's case. I won't forget them until I see Canadian universities open their doors to all Canadians and teach and produce research about all Canadians.

It is funny how some things stick in one's mind while so much else disappears with the flow of time. In the mid-1960s, soon after my arrival in Canada as a student, I was asked to visit an elementary school. The children I spoke to were grade four and five students, no older than ten or eleven years. One of the very first things they asked me was why India didn't solve its food problem by eating all the cows that wandered everywhere in the country. I must say that I was absolutely stunned by the question and how it was phrased. It assumed that Indians were so foolish that they could not see a solution to their problems that was staring them right in their faces. It showed a total disregard of the economy and culture of the country that they knew nothing about, and it showed an arrogance about their own intellectual superiority. For instance, it would not occur to these children, and their teachers, that the cows may not be "wandering" but "foraging." And that, of course, changes the whole picture. (For those wanting to know more about India's cow-based economy, I recommend Marvin Harris's *Cows, Pigs, Wars and Witches: The Riddles of Cultures.* Harris shows that in India a living cow is far more valuable economically than a dead cow.)

217

I learned more about this arrogance when I read Ontario's secondary school textbooks to find out how they represented my part of the world. They told the students about the customs and superstitions of the Indian people and blamed these for India's poverty. I learned that it was the idea of rebirth, as propounded in the *Gita*, that kept India from making progress. I also learned about the wonderful things the British did for my country. My rebuttal of these representations in *East Indians: Myths and Reality* was the beginning of my struggle as an anti-racist scholar.

I continue to teach and research in an academic environment that retains much of the arrogance displayed by the children in the school I visited. Its cultural and curricular practices militate against assigning more than a marginal space to non-Western, non-white cultures and societies. Such a skewered power relation with the dominant system makes me aware that I cannot do the "disinterested," "objective" research that those in power loudly proclaim as proper "academic" research. I must fight politically and in solidarity with other anti-racist struggles to bring about admission equity, curriculum equity, and employment equity on Canadian campuses. I hope my teaching, research, and political action will help to bring the day closer when universities will consider all cultures as equal and valuable and all human beings as equal and valuable.

There's a White Man in My Bed:
Scenes from an Interracial Marriage

•••••••••••••••••••••••••••••••

Pui Yee Beryl Tsang

Sunday I woke to discover a white man in my bed. Once I got over the initial shock, I took a closer look and realized that the stranger sleeping in my bed really wasn't a stranger at all. He was my husband of seven years. Why had it taken me all this time to realize he was white? Was it nearsightedness, the desire not to see his colour, or just plain colour-blindness? Why did this realization hit me at this precise moment? Was it that this awareness would somehow change the nature of our relationship, hurt or even end our relationship? He — the white man in my bed — kept sleeping through my minor brainstorm. Once, I mused, I would never have paid serious attention to any of these questions; they were too deep and profound for me to ponder. On that Sunday morning, however, they seemed so pressing that I had to take the time to reflect on them.

As I threw the covers off and opened my eyes to the bright sunlight filling our bedroom, I started thinking about my realizations. In the process I couldn't help but notice the whiteness of the white man in my bed. His skin was more than just white; it also had a translucent quality. Just beneath the surface of his skin I could see the blue

219

traces of his veins, the purple fibres of his muscles, and the delicate red etchings of his blood vessels. Lying next to him, I could see how truly yellow my skin is, with a deep opaque richness that hides everything beneath its surface.

White skin, I thought, is different in other ways. Sunlight scorches it faster and with more vengeance than it does other skins. Illness is more easily revealed in it than with other skins. It is even injured more easily and takes longer to heal than other skins. I looked at my arm, where there were scratches from our cat; they are no longer visible. I looked at the white man's skin; the scratches from our cat were still there, even though we received them at the same time. What is it about white skin that puts me on edge? How did these feelings arise in me?

Then I remembered . . .

The night before, the white man and I had gone for drinks and dinner at the home of a distinguished Canadian poet who was also white. Most distinguished Canadian "anythings," I have come to understand, are usually white. I didn't want to go, I didn't have to go, but I went to show the white man that I supported him. After all, he had spent nearly every weekend of the last month going to rallies, marches, and conferences for yellow, red, brown, and black people.

"These people," he told me, "are very important. They can help me publish more poetry and reach wider audiences with my existing work." "I'm not sure I'm going to like them," I confessed. "It's going to be okay," he reassured me. "Just be yourself."

"That's what I'm afraid of," I commented to myself.

It began auspiciously enough. There was the mandatory ritual of "Welcome to my home. Let me take your coat." Then it moved onto the obligatory "What would you like to drink?" More people arrived and the usual "Hi, I'm so-and-so, I write such-and-such. I've recently been published in XYZ journal" took place. Things were going relatively well. They were actually not bad company. They were witty, erudite, and undeniably brilliant. Their white skin, however, reflected the light in such a way that it cast an uncomfortable feeling on me.

We were having a good time discussing our various travels around the world, the weather, and the quirks of our respective cats. (It is a stereotype to say that poets are fond of cats, but many are.) Then conversation moved on to the Ontario minister of culture's new initiative to fund artists, filmmakers, and writers who have been traditionally excluded from participating in the cultural life of the province. The new measures that he enacted were meant to benefit Aboriginals, francophones, immigrants, and visible minorities. Everyone in the room, with the exception of me, was white. Everyone in the room, with the exception of me and my husband, disagreed with the objectives of the new programs.

They didn't like them because it meant that the Ministry of Culture would stop funding existing writers, most of whom were white, and start funding other writers, most of whom were non-white. But the white men and women in the room were not willing to own up to this. Instead, they claimed that Aboriginal, francophone, immigrant, and visible minority writers did not produce quality work. The whole notion of granting people money to write about their experiences as "minorities" in this country was a bogus one. "If these people were any good they could get money and get published," the white men and women said.

I challenged these people on their notion of what was quality. "How do you define quality?" I asked. "Does it have to follow European or North American notions of what is considered good?" They looked offended and asked me what I meant by that. I could feel my yellow skin grow more yellow and bristle, but I remained unrepentant.

"What I am suggesting," I patiently explained, "is that the writers' community in Canada excludes non-white people. It was initially created for white men and changed to include white women. It judges the quality of literature in terms of white European or North American literary traditions. When it does embrace non-European or non-North American cultures, it does so by appropriation. Look at how writers like Robert Kroetsch steal Aboriginal legends to add spirituality to their books. Your organizations don't recognize the existence of racism and how it shapes the experiences of non-white writers. You invalidate non-white writing because it focuses less on the intellectual European tradition and more on personal experiences, which most non-white literary traditions — Aboriginals, African, Asian, and Caribbean writing — value. When we confront you about your exclusionary actions and your subtle but vindictive racism, you use elaborate, theoretically constructed arguments to show that racism really doesn't exist; it is merely a figment of our imagination. So what are we supposed to do if we can't convince you that racism exists? Suffer in silence? Support your appropriation of our cultures in the hopes that we will gain a foothold in the literary community through your exploitation of our traditions? Throw off our conventions and traditions and embrace yours? What the minister of culture is trying to do is make room for us in the art, filmmaking, and writing communities, and I think it's about time room was made. This country has never been entirely white but its culture always has been. It cannot remain that way. It is becoming more and more non-white by the day, and it is important that we recognize and accept this fact. If not, we will face race and ethnic war."

I took a deep breath and sat back to see their reaction. In challenging them I was only being myself, a yellow woman. My points were grudgingly acknowledged by some, but were ignored by others who went on talking about how culture in Ontario is going to the dogs. (Are the dogs us, the non-whites?)

I AM FURIOUS. This kind of reaction is typical. I have learned, as an anti-racist educator, that it is meant to invalidate and segregate the non-white minority from the white majority. What they didn't know was that I wasn't going to let them get away with it. Whether they wanted to or not I was going to make them admit and confront their racism.

I spoke up and said, "This is silencing and I will not tolerate it. What I said must be addressed in your community. You must think about it."

The responses ranged from "I don't know what to say — you're right — but I don't know how to change them," to "It's certainly interesting but you really don't know anything about the writers' community," to "Look, I've had a bad day and I really don't care to get involved in your petty problems about white people." These people were in no mood to talk about racism and I knew it. It was time to stop.

The distinguished Canadian poet, though, thought that it was time to put me in my place. "I don't see," he said angrily, "what gives you the right to come here and call us all racists."

"I didn't come here to call you racists," I replied. "But when racism comes up, I call people on it. To tell the truth, though, I did expect you to be racists, given your reputations for consistently slagging non-white writers."

"Why did you bother coming, then? You had a choice not to come," was the nasty rejoinder.

"That's like saying that because I'm yellow I should stay in Yellertown." I bit off each word. "You're all racists. I'm leaving." Tears flooded my eyes as I left. Damn it! Why did I let him get the best of me?

As I walked out the door, I realized there was a presence behind me. It was a white man. The white man I came with. Then I felt sorry. I wasn't sorry for standing up for myself, but I was sorry for him, sorry that I might have damaged his career as a writer. These people were important, influential, significant. They could have helped him with his writing career. With their sponsorship — why did I have to ruin it for him?

Something moved.

The white man woke to find me watching him and thinking. Pulling the covers closer and squinting his blue eyes against the sunlight, he grinned and said, "It's early, go back to sleep." He reached for me and pulled me close. He was no longer a white man. He had become my husband again. Being so close to him revealed the contrasts in our skin even more, and the memory of the previous evening began staining my mind with worry.

"We need to talk," I said.

"Okay," he muttered.

"It's about last night. I'm sorry I ruined your chances to get more writing published, but I was right, they were racists," I explained.

"It's okay, you were right, they were wrong. Can I go back to sleep?" he groaned. He dozed off, but his arms were still around me, trying to pacify me. I didn't feel like going back to sleep. I struggled free and heard my skin separate from his as I rolled away. I got out of bed. I glanced at him as I left the room. Even sleeping, his white body exudes a strength that is foreign to me. As I walked down the hall to the bathroom, I pondered the source of his strength.

I know where my own power came from. It developed through a combination of experience and education. New things lived and new things learned have all helped me to form my character and outlook. They made me aware of who I am, and I am a survivor. I have survived the racial inequities of this society. I have survived them with my dignity intact and I have survived them with the desire to eliminate all forms of social injustice. His strength, though, does not come from survival. It was not acquired through knowledge or reflection, but through something deeper, something that suggested a sense of self that comes from a sense of belonging.

I turned on the shower. Stepping into the steamy spray, I soaped myself. The bar of soap was blue, the lather white, but it should really be green since my skin is yellow, and blue and yellow make green. The lather, however, remained white. As I watched, the white bubbles slipped from my breast, making my body seem white. I wondered if it is the whiteness of his skin that gives him the sense of belonging he possesses. Could his white skin be a protective shield that, despite its frailties, allows him to exist safely and comfortably in the white world? Most likely. No one questions his right to be there. He can make what he wants out of his life. He can become a writer and   223 people can admire his brilliance or condemn his impracticality. He can pursue a professional career and people can applaud his ambition or criticize his desire for respectability. He can tune out of society altogether, and people can think he's enlightened or view him as "out to lunch." No one, though, will say that all white people are like that because he's like that. He is never asked to prove his worth as a human being to anyone. The only person he has to satisfy is himself. He is secure and happy with the world.

For me the standards are different. My skin, in spite of its resiliency, is a target, drawing attention and arrows of scorn from others. People question my right to be here. I cannot do what I want. I have to agree with the existing order or else others will assume that people like me are lazy. I must become a professional or else others will conclude that people like me are stupid. I need to work hard or else others will think that people like me are useless. Everything I do has a bearing not only on me, but also on other yellow people. I am constantly asked to prove myself. I am unsure about myself and my place in the world.

Steaming water continues to spray from the silver shower head. . . .

I pour the pink shampoo out of its equally pink bottle and lather my hair. The bubbles are also white; they should be a deep burgundy because pink and black make burgundy, but they remain white. There seems to be no way of getting around the whiteness of the world. The world is white, through and through. White men and women created the world in their image to nourish, perpetuate, and sustain themselves. The institutions they developed only made room for them, for them and no others. Those who controlled these institutions, as I witnessed the previous evening, were intensely protective of them. They had to be defended at all costs. After all, they were proof to white men and women of their power.

As I was thinking about these things, my husband came into the bathroom. He stepped into the shower as I was rinsing off, the white soap suds sliding off my body and down the drain. I made space for him, but he said there was enough. As he soaped himself, the white lather disappeared against the white of his skin.

"I'm sorry about last night," I said, "but I couldn't stand by and let them oppress me."

"It's okay," he answered, "they were wrong. Do you think that white people have a monopoly on being right?"

"But you're white," I remarked.

224   "Yeah, but I'm not that kind of white person."

"What kind of white person is that?" I asked.

"The kind that thinks only white people and white culture matter."

"What's it like to be white?"

He stopped washing and replied, "Embarrassing, guilty. Not very good sometimes."

"Why?" I wanted to know.

"Because you have power," he answered, "a lot of power and sometimes you don't want it. After all, you didn't ask for it. It's part of your birthright. But what the hell does that mean? Does it mean you have the right to treat 'coloured folks' like shit?" He kept on washing as I stepped out of the shower to dry off, running the yellow towel over my yellow skin, refreshing it.

All through the day I watched him as he ate, puttered, and worked. His white skin reflected light and cast an uncomfortable feeling on me. Short, fast flashes of the previous evening's events streaked through my mind all day.

When we married, I knew that racial differences would emerge some day. I just didn't expect them to erupt in such an "us-shaking" manner, forcing me to confront the difficulties of an interracial marriage.

I was worried that my belief in a racially equitable society, which was based on my experiences as a non-white minority, had cost him his dream of being a writer and would mar our relationship forever. I didn't want him resenting me for spoiling his golden opportunity. I might have swallowed the other writers' racism, if only to support him, but I could not do that and still live with myself. I know that he supported my actions and my motivations, but my uncertainty of his sincerity jabbed at me all day long. I kept asking myself what was going to happen to us.

I tried to think about times in our relationship when the question of race came up between us, but I could think of none. When we are by ourselves we think we are the only two people in the world. There is no racial dynamic, just the silly giddiness of loving each other. We can afford to be colour-blind, to ignore our differences and even make jokes about them. Once we get out into the real world, though, it is hard for us to be equal. He will always be treated one way, based on his colour, and I another, based on mine. His colour allows him to be accepted everywhere, mine only in some places. My marriage to him will grant me grudging acceptance in some places, but I will always resent the fact that this "privilege" is not accessible to everyone. Does he really understand the complexities that being married to a non-   225 white woman can bring? Can our relationship survive the social pressures of an inherently racist society?

I'm not sure, but as I catch him looking at me, I am reminded of the things that we have been working for. He knows that the power and privilege he possesses are often unearned and must be relinquished if there is to be racial equality. This he does without hesitation. When confronted with a racist situation, he usually speaks up. (The only time he doesn't is when I am there to beat him to the proverbial punch.) Yet when he is confronted with the choices of joining the white establishment to do something he really wants to do or of denouncing it as racist, is it fair for me to insist that he take the moral high ground? Am I the one who is putting pressure on him or is he making his own decisions about what is right or wrong? Would he be anti-racist without me?

Questions flash in my mind in a brilliant kaleidoscope of colour. The pastel shades of the answers elude me. Only the colours remain.

Later that evening we watched a movie on TV, cats sleeping on our laps, a bowl of over-buttered popcorn between us. It looked like a scene from *House Beautiful*. The only difference was that such magazines show only couples who are white, not couples who are white and yellow. My husband had chosen the movie; it was about a Chinese American family trying to make it in 1949 New York. It was touching, poignant, all those words that describe good G-rated movies. This particular film made me laugh and cry at the same time. It uses every Hollywood cliché to depict people about whom Hollywood would never even think of making a film.

I looked over at my husband. He smiled. He knows me well. He understands how important it is for me to watch films like these, because they give me a sense of identity. The movie made me forget my bitter thoughts, and for the moment I felt as if we were the only two people in the world.

My doubts about our relationship returned later that evening. We were in bed. I was trying to sleep but my husband's white skin glowed dimly in the dark and made me think about our racial differences again. The white man had returned to my bed, and I didn't know what to do with him. Tired, I tried another solution to my problem.

"I love you," I said.

"I love you too," he said.

"Is my being yellow a problem for you?" I ask.

"No, not really. Is my being white?" he asks.

"Yeah, sort of," I reply.

"Oh, how?"

"I don't know," I said. (I did know.)

"So what's the problem?" he asks.

"It sometimes creates conflicts for me. Like last night. I wonder — marriage is hard enough. I don't know if the added pressure of racial difference is worth it for us," I said.

"It'll be okay. Let's take it one day at a time, alright?" he replied.

He becomes my husband again. The questions of interracial marriage still wander in my mind, but I will think of them on another day.

PART V
CONFRONTING STEREOTYPES AND RACISM

"I Didn't Know You Were Jewish"... and Other Things Not to Say When You Find Out

Ivan Kalmar

Imagine that you and I have been acquainted with each other for some time. And now you learn that I have written this article. You are surprised, and you say: *I didn't know you were Jewish!* Really? How touching. What would you have done if you had known? More important still, what are you going to do now that you do know? Watch yourself when you feel like saying something anti-Semitic? Not criticize other Jews? Avoid speaking about the Middle East? Not tell Jew jokes? Hide your doubts about the Holocaust?

Perhaps you mean to compliment me. I am not loud and aggressive. I am not interested in "jewing" people I have financial dealings with. If you are politically conservative, you might mean that I am not a subversive pinko radical, or a big-city sexual and cultural pervert. If you are on the left, you might mean that I am not a Zionist Imperialist. In either case you mean, ultimately, that I am "Jewish but nice." But I don't need your compliment. To me, "Jewish" and "nice" are not opposites.

Notice: you did not simply ask me, "Are you Jewish?" I could take that; it is an ordinary question of personal information. You said, "I didn't know that . . . " and you said it because you don't speak to Jews the same way you speak to non-Jews. If you had known that I was Jewish, you would have treated me as a Jew, rather than as a human being.

Let us go through some other things you may have said instead. I know you do not feel that you are an anti-Semite. If you give some consideration to the issues to be raised, then you will not *appear* to be an anti-Semite to Jews like me, either. I cannot speak for all Jews, of course, but I do know that many would agree with me on much if not all of what I am going to say.

I don't care if a person is Jewish; to me all people are the same

Maybe you think if you had said this, I would have been happier. Sorry. Yes, there are many Jews who would enthusiastically accept being "just human beings" rather than "Jews." In my book, *The Trotskys, Freuds and Woody Allens: Portrait of a Culture*, I call such people EJI (pronounce it "edgy," an acronym for Embarrassed Jewish Individuals). Jean-Paul Sartre simply called them "inauthentic Jews," and pointed out that there were no human beings who were not also French, English, Black, white — and/or Jewish.

I am not an EJI. No, I don't want you to treat me as a Jew rather than as a human being, because that implies that a Jew is not fully human. But I also don't want you to treat me as if I were not a Jew. I want to be treated as a Jew *and* a human being. I would like you to understand that being Jewish is a normal thing for a normal human being to be. It is, unfortunately, true that some of us Jews do not understand the point either, but it does not excuse you from trying to be more sensitive to the legitimacy of human differences.

What's the JAP's idea of an ideal home?

"Six thousand square feet with no kitchen or bedroom." Very funny. So you find out I am Jewish and you tell a "Jewish" joke. Why not, you think, the Jews are so funny. In one episode of the BBC television series *Alexei Sayle's Stuff*, the board of directors of a corporation is meeting to welcome Mr. Gold, their new accountant. They are told by the very "Aryan" looking new arrival that, despite his name, he is not Jewish. Though this happens to be the truth, everyone takes it to be a funny Jewish joke. The distinguished directors break out in inextinguishable guffawing. From then on they greet everything the accountant says with wild laughter. "Jewish humour," the chief executive exclaims, "very funny . . . "

You want to please a Jew, you think, with a Jewish joke. And you choose a JAP joke. A JAP is, of course, a "Jewish American Princess." There is not a more vicious anti-female stereotype around. It is no compliment to Jewish men to have invented these vicious insults to Jewish women, who are portrayed as lazy, frigid, spoiled, and stupid. Indeed, the JAP is everything a woman means to a frustrated macho misogynist. I suspect the Jewish men who make up JAP jokes are unconsciously using a subtle and rather effective argument: "Look, our women are just as despicable as your women and in the same way; and we put them down just as much as you; therefore you, goyish macho chauvinists, and us Jewish macho chauvinists have much in common." It's like the old Jewish saying about Sammy Davis, the Black comedian who was Jewish: "Get *him*, he's both!" A Jewish woman is both: a Jew and a woman. But the Jewish teller of a JAP joke wants you to hate the woman, not the Jew.

When you, a non-Jew, tell it, a JAP joke becomes not just anti-female, but clearly anti-Jewish. For you are not laughing about your own women (which would certainly be bad enough) but about ours. You are contradicting the Jewish JAP joke teller's intent. You laugh not only at women, but also at Jews.

It is not in good taste for a non-Jew to tell any joke whose butt is a Jew. Some fat people and bald people like to joke about their physical characteristics. They hope that way to preempt any aggression or derision on your part. It is often for the same reason that Jewish jokers tell a joke that puts down the Jews: a "Jew joke." (Anti-Semites love to use the adjective "Jew" rather than "Jewish": Jew woman, Jew doctor, Jew boy.) Would you tell a fat joke to a fat person? Why then would you tell a Jew joke to a Jew?

You meant to be friendly by telling the kind of joke you feel you hear Jews themselves saying. But you ended up merely sounding inconsiderate again: to Jews, and, if it was a JAP joke you told, to women.

My mom's such a Jewish mother

For decades American Jewish comic performers have won great fame putting down their mothers. Telling their inanities in the first person, they have convinced the public, Jewish and Gentile, to think that Jewish mothers are nagging, guilt-inducing monsters. I cannot really blame you for picking up a stereotype that is aggressively marketed by

Jewish entertainers. By telling me that your mother is a Jewish mother, you wanted to say that we have much in common. But I hate the "Jewish mother" stereotype, another misogynous insult dressed in Jewish garb.

That mothering can be smothering is well known from all cultures. Just like the JAP concentrates the hostility of all misogynists against wives, girlfriends, and daughters, so the "Jewish mother" is the anchor for all anti-mother resentment, felt just as much by Jews as by Gentiles. Indeed, "Jewish mother" has become a normal English expression for a passive-aggressive, guilt-inducing female progenitor. But please. Some Jewish mothers are "Jewish mothers," just as some non-Jewish mothers are. I don't know if the percentage of "Jewish mothers" is higher among the Jews, but I doubt it. Even if it is, could you please not generalize? My mother is not a "Jewish mother" and I'd like you to leave her out of this.

What about the Palestinians?

Now I feel you are not even trying to be nice. Your expectation is that your question might irritate me. It does, but not for the reason you think: not because I hate Arabs, or because I oppose the Palestinians' legitimate rights.

Of course, I have views on the Arab-Israeli conflict. And, of course, as a Jew I am ultimately on the side of Israel, the Jewish state. I am emotionally bound to Israel, a realization of a dream that my ancestors have held for centuries. Moreover, Israel seems proof to me, like to most Jews, that another Holocaust would not be possible. This time we know how to use arms. If, God forbid, we have to go again, we will not go without a fight and we will not go without taking our enemies with us.

I also do happen to believe in the rights of the Palestinian people: rights to self-determination, and possibly a right to a state of their own, as long as its aim is not to take our state away from us. I deeply regret and am ashamed of the human rights abuses committed by the Israelis.

But I do not want to talk about this with you, because your question, coming on the heels of my revelation that I am a Jew, makes me fear that to you "Jew" recalls "abusive Israeli occupier" (that is, Zionist Imperialist). If so, chances are you know little of the complexities of the Middle East; little of the large and widespread opposition, not only among world Jewry but also among Israeli Jews, to the Israeli army's practices; and little of the abuse committed by Palestinian

233

terrorists, not only against Jews but also against fellow-Palestinians as well.

When you know me better, I will be ready to discuss this issue with you. But not unless you accept the following disclaimer: I hereby declare that any resemblance between me and the prime minister of Israel is purely coincidental.

We all believe in one God

OK. This time you truly mean well. You want to show me that you and I are both God's children. True, those of us who are religious, Jews, Christians, and Muslims, believe in one God. Yet I don't think it is true that we believe in the *same* God. Now I know that many rabbis would contradict me on this. But they just want to be nice, whereas I want to be frank.

Our God does not have three persons like the Christian God: the Father, the Son, and the Holy Ghost. He did not become incarnate in Jesus. He has no human form at all; indeed, nowadays it bothers many of us a lot that we refer to him with the masculine pronoun, as if He were a man.

We associate God with the history of our people. We thank God for taking us out of slavery in Egypt, and have trouble not blaming Him for allowing the Holocaust to happen. He speaks to us immediately, without the mediation of a Jesus and his family, or of saints (though some North African Jews do worship the memory of some sages as if they had been saints).

Our Gods are similar, but not the same. I would say the same to you if you were a Muslim, a Buddhist, or a follower of any other religion. I respect your tradition and I expect you to respect mine. But to equate all religions is not the same as to respect them. A religion for all people would have to be a new religion that means to replace all previous ones, and it is implied that this new religion would be more perfect than the old, "particularist" ones. Of necessity, religious universalists believe that their view of religion is better than that of the "particularists," and therefore create their own brand of religious one-upmanship. The universalists feel superior to the "particularists" just like the Christian missionaries felt superior to the pagans. (*Iglesia catolica*, after all, means "universal church.")

What, however, distinguishes our Jewish religion and has distinguished it since the Middle Ages is that we are proudly particularist. We do not think that our religion is better for everybody, just that it is better for us. We are more tolerant of other ways of thinking about religion than the "universalists." We wish to keep our religion and let everyone else keep theirs.

There can and ought to be a brotherhood of religions. But there is not and cannot be a universal religion, any more than there can be human beings who are not also French, English, Moroccan, etc. — or Jews.

Do you eat ham?

When you invite me for dinner and ask me if I eat ham, you mean to show your understanding of the fact that traditional Jews do not eat pork. You want to make something I will eat; I understand and appreciate your concern. You mean to be considerate.

But remember this. If it is true that those of us who are religious have a concept of God that is not the same as that held by non-Jews (although there is a great variation among us in terms of religious belief, just as there is among you), it is also true that many, perhaps most of us, have no concept of God at all. Quite a few Jews do not believe in God; I am still not sure if I do myself.

Those who are observant of the ancient behavioural code known as the *halakha* are a rather small minority. Even many of those who are affiliated with Orthodox synagogues don't really keep it. The Conservative, Reform, and Reconstructionist congregations, which comprise the great majority of synagogue members in North America, have all modified or at least reinterpreted the *halakha*.

"Eating kosher" is a practice prescribed by the *halakha*. It means much more than just not eating pork. For example, meat must not be mixed with milk. Also, nothing must be served on plates that were ever touched by non-kosher food, unless a special cleansing ritual is observed. This means, of course, that even if you don't serve ham, your kitchen is automatically disqualified. To put it simply, no strictly Orthodox Jew can eat with you unless you buy ready-made kosher food, or unless you serve only vegetables (which are always kosher) and you serve them on plates and with utensils that have never been used before. In practice, the problem can be solved by using paper plates and plastic utensils. But you're better off not inviting an Orthodox Jew for dinner at all. Think of coffee or a ball game instead.

However, the great majority of us are not Orthodox. Jewishness is a matter of much more than religion: a culture, an ethnic identity, a shared history, family memories. It is perceived by us as a sort of magical identity, which we do not understand ourselves. Even Freud, a master decipherer of the mind's subtleties, could not manage to spell out just what it was that made him Jewish. He was, he wrote,

> completely estranged from the religion of his fathers — as well as
> from every other religion — and [one] who cannot take a share in
> nationalist ideals, but who has yet never repudiated his people, who
> feels that he is in his essential nature a Jew and who has no desire
> to alter that nature. If the question were put to him: "Since you
> have abandoned all these common characteristics of your people,
> what is there left about you that is Jewish?" he would reply: "[What
> is left is] a very great deal; indeed, probably, my very essence."

Jewish identity consists of much more than Judaism. For many of us,
Judaism is not even a very important part of it at all.

At any rate, you can quite reliably tell an Orthodox male by the
skull cap on his head, although even some people with skull caps make
compromises like eating kosher at home but not outside (a fairly popular practice, though not officially approved by their rabbis, among Conservative Jews). Women are harder to pinpoint, although the most traditional wear wigs. If you don't see these outward markers of Ortho-
doxy, chances are you are dealing with someone who is not strictly traditional. You are probably dealing with a Jew who is quite comfortable
eating what you serve him or her. I certainly would be.

So when you ask me if I eat ham, I am not offended, but I feel a
bit taken aback. Perhaps a better way than asking me about ham
would be to just invite me. If I were Orthodox, I would tell you what
my religious practices require.

What do you think of Jesus?

And while we're dealing with religion, what about Jesus? Here and
there I meet a religious Christian who longs to find out how it is possible for me, a member of Jesus' people, to "reject Him." So I am
asked what I think about him (big "H" for Christians, small "he" for
us). The simple answer is that I don't. I don't think about Jesus.

I happen to be a devoted lover of Christian art and music. And I
often find images of Christ deeply moving, a genuine symbolic depic-
tion of the divine spirit. I am similarly touched when I see some
images of the Buddha or of Hindu gods. But Jesus is no more an issue
for me than Shiva is for you. I am not for or against Jesus, and I have
not rejected him. I have read the New Testament, and I find some of
it quite interesting, and other parts quite stirring. But I am a Jew, and
happy to be one. I am not asking you to be a Jew; please don't ask me
to be a Christian.

The problem is that if you are a Christian then Judaism *is* an issue for you. After all, Christianity started as a Jewish sect that opposed mainstream Judaism. (The early Christians' opposition centred mainly around Jesus: the Christians believed he was the Messiah, and the rest of us did not.) But Judaism did not start in opposition to Christianity. We have no beef with Christianity at all.

Medieval myths libelled us as desecrating the Host, for the primitive Christian's image of the Jew is that of a Christ-killer, whose religion is devoted to opposing the concept of Jesus as the Messiah. This attitude reads into Judaism much more preoccupation with Jesus than there ever has been.

But even sophisticated and enlightened Christians are puzzled that we don't accept Jesus as the Messiah. They want to know why. Indeed, Jewish-Christian dialogue groups often break down when the Christians bring up Jesus. Some Christians simply refuse to understand that the relationship between Jesus and Judaism is an issue for them, but not for us.

We are not "the people of the Old Testament." Our religion has evolved throughout the centuries, just like Christianity, though ours has done so without Jesus. When Christianity added the New Testament to the Old, we added the Talmud. I am told that there is one line in the Talmud about Jesus, though it is of no importance at all. Our religious texts, ancient, medieval, and modern, ignore Jesus almost totally. They say nothing important at all about him, pro or con.

We respect Christianity, like we respect all other religions. But Jesus is to us simply a foreign religious personage. Next time you want to ask me what I think about Jesus, ask yourself what you think of Krishna.

Merry Christmas and Happy Hanukkah

Now here is one that most other Jews not only appreciate, they are positively thrilled by it. When you say Merry Christmas and Happy Hanukkah, you are recognizing that not everyone is a Christian, you are noticing me as a Jew, and you wish me to share in the cheers of the holiday season. So why should I object?

I do not consider your greeting offensive, but I would like you to spend some time thinking about what it really means. You might then reconsider whether you want to wish me Merry Christmas and Happy Hanukkah next year again.

Let us start with the issue of Christmas. In public many Jews love 237 to praise Christmas to the hilt, to make absolutely sure that they do not appear "different." Only in private, among other Jews, do some of them admit that their enthusiasm may have been a bit of a show.

I am reminded of the merchant that I visited one December to arrange for a print to be framed. He had beautified, indeed overdecorated, his store with innumerable wreaths, pine-tree branches, and pendants for Christmas. He expressed his intense disappointment that it was too late for him to finish my order by the arrival of Yuletide. And he topped up the transaction by wishing a merry Christmas to me and mine. He appeared quite shaken when I revealed that I did not celebrate Christmas because I was Jewish. "So am I," the storekeeper replied dejectedly, and added — "I hate Christmas."

Talking about Christmas is one of the truly favourite devices by which Jewish speakers wish to bridge the gap between themselves and the Gentile audience. When the pioneer American Jewish cineaste George Cukor made his first movie, it was a tearjerker about a poor child at Yuletide. And not everyone remembers that the all-time hit "White Christmas" is a composition by Irving Berlin, who also created "Easter Parade" and "God Bless America." It is in the tradition of these great entertainers that the mainly Jewish army of Hollywood sitcom writers churns out, year in and year out, their obligatory sappy Christmas episodes.

Being nice about the Christmas spirit has a triple objective. First, it may steer attention from the fact that the speaker is not a Christian. Second, if it does not do so, the speaker will at least have made an appeal to the Christmas spirit of tolerance. And third, the speaker will have demonstrated a positive attitude to the one holiday that makes all Christians and Jews acutely aware of following different ceremonial traditions in the most intimate circle of their family.

But I hate Christmas. I hate Christmas because during the Christmas season I am put upon, time after time again, by well-meaning non-Jews to declare my difference from them. When I am wished a merry Christmas, what am I to do? If I return the greeting, my Jewish conscience accuses me of not having the *chutzpah* to say "I do not celebrate it." If I do say so, however, I get into an unwanted discussion, often with someone I do not really wish to chat with; or I might spoil the holiday mood for someone I do care for. I am also not a little upset by the arrogance of people who think it a matter of course that *everyone* celebrates Christmas. To hear them talk about it, Christmas is as naturally part of December as snow in Minnesota. I don't care if the Japanese or the Indians have bought the idea and, though not Christians, welcome Santa and erect Christmas trees. We don't have to.

I certainly do not hate Christmas for what it means to Christians. I like togetherness, I like peace on earth, and I like presents (so do the Jewish merchants in shopping malls). I just wish it wasn't rubbed in my face, when I am not part of it. For let's face it, the reason many of us Jews do not like Christmas is that we are jealous. Worse yet, we fear that our children will be jealous, that the presents their Gentile classmates receive will make them want to become Christians, like the natives who join the church because the missionaries give people bicycles.

So what do we do? We come up with a Jewish version of Christmas: Hanukkah. Hanukkah is probably traditionally the least significant of Jewish festivals. Unlike major holidays, for example, on Hanukkah it is permitted to work. Yet the majority of non-observant Jews, the EJI, who do not even know the dates of such major festivals as Sukkoth or Shavuoth, do not fail to observe Hanukkah. This is profoundly ironic. The events that Hanukkah celebrates are not even in the Hebrew Bible, but in the Greek-language Book of the Macabees. The "zealots" of Israel, armed Pharisee fundamentalists, rose against the Graeco-Syrian rulers of the land, who were amply assisted by "assimilated Jews." One of the things that most shocked the zealots were Jews who ran and exercised naked in Hellenic stadiums in the Holy Land. Hanukkah or Rededication commemorates the zealots' victory. This resulted in their recapture of the Temple, where they relit the "eternal flame." (The little consecrated oil they had for the purpose miraculously lasted eight days — hence the eight days of the festival.)

How much Hanukkah has become a Jewish Christmas is demonstrated by office workers who put up "Happy Hanukkah" signs next to "Merry Christmas." Once I was at my office when a non-Jewish employee was posting up a "Happy Hanukkah" sign as part of the "festive season" decorations. I politely reminded her that Hanukkah was already over. Since the holiday is observed according to the lunar Hebrew calendar, it does not always coincide with Christmas, and sometimes, as was the case then, comes much earlier. So what sense did it make to celebrate Hanukkah after Hanukkah has ended? My mild protest was not at all well received. It was hushed up almost as an indecent remark, not only by the Gentiles, but by the Jews as well.

As far as the kids are concerned, Hanukkah has allowed us not only to match the *goyim*, but to trump them. Non-Jewish children get presents on Christmas. But many Jewish children get one every night for the duration of the eight-day festival.

The farce of Hanukkah as a Christmas substitute was revealed a   239 few years ago, when an ultra-Orthodox group erected a twenty-eight-foot-high Hanukkah menorah in a strip of parkland near the municipal centre of Beverly Hills — and no Christmas tree. Four Jewish residents of the posh and very Jewish Southern California township protested. With the official support of the American Jewish Congress, they went to court to have the menorah removed. The resulting litigation lasted for years. There has never been such trouble in the thousands of places all over the United States where there was, along with the menorah, also a Christmas tree. What the neighbourhood EJI were up in arms about was, in the last analysis, not the menorah, but the lack of a Christmas tree next to it. The ultra-Orthodox had the guts to try to recapture Hanukkah as a Jewish holiday, rather than as a symbol of non-difference between Jew and non-Jew. Merry Christmas and Happy Hanukkah; we are just like you. You celebrate, we celebrate.

When you said "Merry Christmas and Happy Hanukkah," you did help me avoid the tensions of Christmas; you made sure I did not have to identify myself as "different" from you. But I would rather be uncomfortable than phony. As far as I am concerned, Merry Christmas posters will do just fine at the office, without Happy Hanukkah. It would be nice, though, if next fall, when we really celebrate a major holiday, someone put up a sign saying Happy Rosh Hashanah.

By now you might be feeling overwhelmed. "Is there nothing I can say to a Jew without being considered insensitive?" you might ask. Relax. If you take what I have just said into consideration, chances are you will no longer say things that offend me. But if you slip up, don't worry. I know you mean well. Remember, I am not only a Jew. I am also a human being, like you.

But You Are Different: In Conversation with a Friend

•••••••••••••••••••

Sabra Desai

Sabra: So, you think I'm not like the rest of them.

Alex: Yes, you are different. Well, you know what I mean.

Sabra: No, I don't. Tell me exactly what you do mean.

Alex: Well, when I see you, I don't see your colour. I don't see you as a South Asian. You're not like the rest of them. I'd like to think that I judge you through my own personal experiences with you. I don't judge you on the basis of your culture, colour, or class for that matter. I refuse to see you as being different. You're just another human being.

Sabra: First you tell me that I'm different, and then you say that you refuse to see me as being different. So, which is it? Let's try to unravel this.

Alex: Well, I meant that you're more like me, you know, like one of us.

Sabra: Oh, so, I'm more like you and less like, should I say it, "a real South Asian." You see, although you're not saying it, your statement reveals that you have some preconceived ideas of South Asians, the people that I'm supposed to be so unlike. This means that whatever your preconceived ideas are of

South Asians, they make South Asians less acceptable, less attractive, and less appealing to you than I. Well, this is not just stereotyping, it is racist stereotyping.

Alex: Well, just wait a minute, Sabra, you're accusing me of being a racist. You're taking my statement entirely out of context, and you know that isn't what I meant. I really don't appreciate the implication that I am being racist.

Sabra: Before we get to unravelling the implications of the statement "but you are different," let me ask: are you upset that I'm challenging your thinking? Would you feel better if I were grateful for being "accepted" by you and less analytical or critical of your reasons for doing so? I think that part of what might be upsetting you is that for all your willingness to "accept" me, you're not ready to accept me as a South Asian.

Alex: By saying that you are different, I assumed that the senseless stereotypes of South Asians do not apply to you. I thought you'd appreciate my comment, but you've surprised me. I thought that coming from a society where you were very much defined by race, you'd want people to ignore differences and treat you the same as everyone else.

Sabra: You obviously don't recall asking me this very question once before. You once told me that you thought that having come from a country as racist and as segregated as South Africa I would endorse the concept of "melting pot." To that I said: in spite of the fact that I left such a racist society, where race was all that mattered, in my mind to say that one's ethnicity or race does not matter is still racist.

So goes one of the many conversations I have had with Alex and a number of other friends. One tires of these exchanges after a while, for it seems that I can never be accepted as the person that I am, but only as what my friends have made me out to be. I at least expect my "differentness" to be acknowledged, although I really want it to be appreciated or, if they genuinely care, to be explored. I wish that Alex and company would recognize that I am a member of a marginalized minority group and that as "mainstreamers" they have a tendency to negate, romanticize, or stereotype our experiences and differentness. I am a South Asian human being, but there appears to be some difficulty or reluctance on their part to accept me as such, to try and understand what being South Asian is to me and then to try and come to grips with that reality rather than attempting to make themselves comfortable with some sanitized image.

242   I think that one may be "different" by degree within the context of

one's ethnocultural group but it is not possible to be different from something that, by definition, one is a part of. So, perhaps because I do not fit Alex's preconceived notion of what a South Asian should be, she doesn't think of me as one; she sees me as the preferred anomaly. My ethnicity, culture, and colour do not matter to her. She says that she sees me only as a human being. For me, the implication of this is that being a South Asian somehow devalues me and lessens my humanness. So, in order to relate to me she remakes me into her image; she whitens me so that I can be like her. In other words, she is suggesting that if I change the colour of my skin I could be just like her, that I grew up in South Africa, where every aspect of my life was mediated by the colour of my skin and my ethnicity. As a person classified Indian, and of course non-white, whether it was the privileges that were denied or the ones granted me by both statutory and informal laws, they were all arbitrarily applied to me because of my colour and ethnicity; nothing else mattered. For example, where I could go to school, where I could live, where I could receive medical services, or for that matter be hospitalized and what jobs I could aspire to were all dictated by the laws of the country. Where and with whom I could play were all largely predetermined for me because of my skin. What my white counterparts — yes, I dare say counterparts — could take for granted I could not. Where I could shop, whether I could try on the garment before buying it, and what restaurants I could eat at were all considerations to be taken seriously. In apartheid, pre-Mandela South Africa, one small infraction could mean that I was breaking the law.

All of this is part of me. It is central to who I am, even though I have now spent more than half my life here in Canada. I am a product of that social context; it is part of my cultural identity. Saying that I am different does not change the way in which my ethnicity and race are used to set me apart from whites. I say that because in my experience the labels of ethnicity are reserved to describe the "others," most often "minorities," who remain across the divide — the ones referred to as "them," "they," and "those people." We are different when some people want to exclude us on the grounds that we do not fit, we do not know the rules, we do not speak the language, or we are not desired as neighbours. Yet, paradoxically, some people perceive us to be the "same," particularly when we are to receive certain long overdue rights and privileges such as equal access to jobs, housing, culturally sensitive social services, education, and recognition of our heritage languages.

Recognizing my differences is in a way acknowledging the 243 irrefutable and undeniable power of racial construction and culture on all our lives. Therefore, words like "Black" and "white," referring to the race of a people, cannot be simply dismissed to suggest that one is colour-blind. The very act of not referring to my race or ethnicity, when it is central to the discussion or context, renders me invisible. The omission delivers a powerful message concerning what must be ignored — that is, colour, culture, and ethnicity.

In saying this, I can hear you ask the question, as several have so often asked, "But don't you think that this constant reference to skin colour or one's racial identity by minorities reinforces the racism in our society? It might, in fact, reinforce the existing stereotypes." To this I say: not recognizing that things such as gender, skin colour, race, and ethnicity mediate one's life chances in a society largely differentiated on the basis of these variables is like burying one's head in the sand. Any denial of the significance of race or skin colour implies that skin colour poses an insurmountable obstacle for white people when they interact or deal with people of colour.

Wishing that we lived in a colour-blind society is not necessarily a virtue. Colour-blindness, as I come across it, means a denial of the differentness in culture, identity, and experiences of those who are less valued in society. This denial reflects the tendency of the oppressor to minimize and deny the impact of the oppression. The oppressors can afford the enormous luxury of ignoring the formative and fundamental influences of social context and history on "other" people's lives while remaining keenly aware and protective of the benefits and privileges of these same influences on their lives and the lives of their descendants. An African Canadian friend of mine once said, "When you see me and do not see my colour, it is just as problematic as when you see me and all you see is my colour." Colour-blindness is an illusion in the minds of those Canadians who like to think that as a nation we are not racially hierarchical. Until very recently, despite the hundreds of years of domination, exploitation, and oppression of Aboriginal peoples, the prevailing idea concerning race and ethnic relations was that racism did not exist in Canada. It has been documented and ought to be obvious at this stage that social divisions based on colour and ethnicity are a fundamental characteristic of the political and socio-economic configuration of our country.

I am continually reminded of my "differentness" from mainstream society. I am variously referred to as an immigrant, visible minority, racial minority, "Paki," ethnic, coloured, and East Indian: loaded labels decided for, and applied to, South Asians in general. It is also mainly people like myself who get asked "Where are you from?"

or "What are you?" These questions always remind us of our status and the inherent "otherness" and inferiority associated with that status by mainstream society. The questions imply that members of the dominant group, the so-called "founding nation," do not have an ethnicity and/or that people like myself are not of this land.

This approach undoubtedly sets up the dynamic of "us" and "them," "ours" and "theirs," that operates between the so-called "old" and "new" immigrants. These relations are entrenched in a racist Anglo-centric nativism. The recognition of this dynamic helps us understand the notion of the immigrant as the "the other." Immigrants are always being reminded of their "otherness" in everyday interactions by being made to feel different, and by being made to feel conscious of their distinctiveness. Immigrants are made to feel outside the circle, outside the game, and always on the periphery and frequently excluded because we are different and distinct from the game- and rule-makers. At the same time, as immigrants we are aware of our "otherness" as being disturbing, annoying, and even frightening because of the preoccupation with the traditional (white and Anglo-Saxon) way of life of the country being under pressure and threatened.

Perhaps by challenging the connotations associated with ethnic and racial stereotypes, particularly negative ones, an individual like me forces "mainstreamers" to confront their stereotypic images and biased attitudes, at the same time creating for them a dissonance by presenting them with the dilemma of holding onto "old ways" in the face of refuting evidence. Stereotypes, as the "victims" know all too well, influence attitudes and actions towards the members of the disadvantaged group in very real ways. For example, in a society where negative social stereotypes and biases towards a particular group are prevalent, access for members of that group is restricted or even denied altogether. Stereotypes, therefore, serve a social, economic, and political purpose for oppressors. Some people cling to these stereotypes quite steadfastly because it is easier to discriminate against someone who is seen as being inferior, because by virtue of that inferiority the person is not deserving of equal rights and privileges.

When people say that I am different, they usually mean it as a compliment and fail to see the inherent racism in their flattery. An encounter with another friend, Jane, is a case in point. Jane describes herself as a feminist who understands the inherent inequalities in our society and the patriarchal system as well as the prevailing attitudes that maintain the status quo. Given her understanding and analysis, she sees herself as always standing up for the rights of minorities because she understands the issues. Some time ago, after we had gone

245

to an opera together, Jane remarked that at first she was not sure I would accept her invitation to go, but she now recognized that I was different. I said to her, "As a feminist, how would you feel if someone said to you, 'Oh, but you're different, you're not like the rest of those feminists.' " She replied that she would be offended. "It's a sexist remark. Feminists are not a homogeneous or monolithic group." This is precisely my point. Her statement indicates that differences are not to be found among the South Asian monolith; we are not heterogeneous like the majority group. Furthermore, in this context, I find the cliché "but you are different" particularly self-righteous and condescending. I thought, "What privilege, what power, what arrogance. She defines me, imposes her definition upon me and presumes that I am complimented by her statement."

In conversations like these I am usually told, "You make it all so serious. You should learn to relax, you take life too seriously. You must admit that things have improved a lot for racial minorities. Relax! Lighten up!" But I have to be serious. Life has made me acutely conscious of the inequities and indignities that people like myself have to endure and resist every day. Jefferson said, "The price of freedom is constant vigilance." How can I relax and lighten up when the situation demands that I maintain my vigilance? It is difficult to relax when you live on the margins or the periphery of society, the place where the dominant culture forces you to be.

Yes, we have made some progress, but both Blacks and whites have to be vigilant to maintain the gains we have made. This struggle is very much in evidence even with programs such as employment equity that were set up to break down barriers and make employment opportunities more accessible. Without getting into the assumptions surrounding employment equity and my understanding of it, I want to describe an incident that I think poignantly illustrates one of the paradoxes of life for racial minorities in racist societies.

About two years ago, at the end of a presentation on employment equity, a participant came up to me and said, "I'm not a racist, but I really think that women, minorities, and Aboriginals should not get a job just because of who they are. I think we should all be treated equally. If I came to your country, could I get a job regardless of my skills and qualifications?" I said, "Well, in Canada aren't we all entitled to a job?" To which he said, "That's not what I meant. I didn't mean Canada. I meant where you came from originally." And I said: "The truth of the matter is, in the country that I come from, you would enjoy more entitlements and privileges as a white visitor than I would as a native-born South African." He did not expect such a reply, and I hope that he has been cautioned against making inappropriate assumptions. I suspect that one such assumption was that I came from India and that, of course, with such a caste-based society behind me, how could I be so bold and impudent as to question the benevolence of my adopted country?

The second assumption is that employment equity means giving jobs to members of racial minorities and other groups of people who by definition are unskilled and/or unqualified; and in this way the overall standards of "our country" are being lowered by "those people." Thirdly comes the assumption that by treating everyone "equally," that is, by maintaining the status quo, we are being just and equitable; the assumption that this is, after all, a free and democratic country and under democracy people are supposed to be treated the same. The assumption fails to recognize that being treated the same does not mean being treated equitably.

The truth is, a large gap exists between the rhetoric of democratic equality and its day-to-day realization. It is just like saying, "Well, I am not prejudiced, children are children, I treat them all the same," which is not an uncommon attitude in social and psychological services as well as in education. This implied neutrality epitomizes the equality of treatment that is supposedly granted all citizens of a democratic country. Neutrality is supposed to mean equal opportunity because no one person gets preference over another; neutrality is supposedly the ultimate in equality. It suggests that we should be blind to colour, gender, and class, and what more could we want? Anything that goes contrary to this ideal is reverse discrimination. This approach represents a paradox for minorities. It suggests that when it is useful for members of mainstream society, those who are normally seen as different are conveniently perceived to be the same. I once heard someone comment that race and gender discrimination was the oldest and longest form of affirmative action going for white middle-class males.

I have another example to relate. Once, when I was receiving a job offer, a male acquaintance said to me, "Well, congratulations. I hear you're shortlisted. You stand a good chance. You have a lot going for you as a woman and a racial minority." I responded by saying: "What I am about to say is not from a position of arrogance but from a position of confidence. You have just rendered all my schooling, professional training, and ability to zero. You have devalued everything I have strived for and achieved through hard work and perseverance. I'd like to think that if I do join the group not only would I add some colour (smile, smile), but that I would bring a fresh and different perspective to the position I am hired for."

Sometimes I have challenged the implication that employment equity means taking jobs away from white middle-class males and giving them to unskilled minorities by asking, "Are you suggesting that I should not have been given an opportunity to have this job because I don't have the skills?" or "Are you suggesting that I don't have the skills to do this job because I'm a minority woman?" To this I usually get the reply, "But you are different, you are qualified, you can do the job." These kinds of seemingly complimentary remarks indicate the pervasiveness of what one might call "innocuous racism" — although in my mind there is no such thing as innocuous racism or being "a little racist." Racism is racism. I am South Asian and have no desire to separate myself or have others separate me from "my people" or from my group of ethno-racial identity.

So when I hear "but you are different," I think that I am being judged and evaluated in terms of how closely I reflect the generalized preconceptions of my ethnic group. The person, me, to whom these stereotypes are applied becomes the focus of a judgement, while the judge does not take a moment to think about how flawed her or his thinking may be. Perhaps, part of the problem is because those who make this statement are not aware of how their privilege and power as well as their location have brought them to their definition of difference. Moreover, this approach is uncritical, evaluative, and judgemental in that it implies that being different from one's ethnocultural group is somehow possible and desirable when in fact being different is also to be an anomaly or an aberration.

Implied in this statement is also the notion that difference means being deficient or being culturally deprived. This notion is underscored by the assumption that the standards of the dominant society — that is, white middle-class culture — represent the norms by which all other cultures should be measured. The notion takes for granted that deviations from the white middle-class norms mean cultural deficits. Therefore, the closer one is to those norms the smaller the deficit, and of course the further one is from the norms, the larger the deficit. In other words, one becomes whiter, "more normal," as one renounces one's culture.

The cliché "but you are different" is loaded with many racist assumptions. One assumption is that the minority person wants to be taken into the proverbial fold, to be an honorary member of the dominant group and be grateful as well as proud that she has made it: "I am one of them." Often the cliché seems to be proclaimed with a liberal self-confidence that makes the speakers totally oblivious to the condescending, patronizing, and moralistic implications of their statements. I often bristle as I listen to the self-righteous confidence with which people unconsciously exercise judgement over me. There is no sense of the flawed thinking, or any recognition of the prejudice and racism in their statements.

Nevertheless, I still find it useful to engage my friends in these discussions because by carrying on in an open and honest dialogue we are able to unravel our inextricably linked realities regardless of where race and cultural politics situate us. A line from a poem by Miguel Algarian sums up quite well what I think my friends and I should strive for in our conversations and interactions, indeed in our friendships: "When I see what you see, the distance between us disappears."

Ties That Bind and Ties That Blind: Race and Class Intersections in the Classroom

Paul Orlowski

Each September, on the first day of every school year, I am always filled with an intense curiosity, almost awe, as I watch the students casually walk into the East Vancouver classroom where I teach.

After all, the classrooms of my youth in the east end of Toronto — Scarborough to be more precise — were filled almost entirely by peers who came from a similar background. We certainly all had a similar skin colour. By contrast, the students I now see come from myriad cultural backgrounds, including First Nations, Latin American, Chinese, African Canadian, European, and Indian, both Hindu and Sikh. The majority of them are, like me, first-generation Canadians. Race relations have got to be a lot more interesting for these young people to experience and negotiate than they were for me. Given the homogeneity of the neighbourhoods and classrooms of my youth, I never even had the chance.

As a child growing up in the 1960s I lived under the delusion that racism was on the verge of being a thing of the past, that before too long it would be something discussed in historical terms only. To be sure, at times I was the recipient of an Anglo-Saxon peer yelling "You Pollack!" in the schoolyard, and some of my Italian friends were referred to in derogatory terms based on their ancestry. Yet no matter which European country we claimed as our heritage, we were all in the same classroom, learning the same curriculum, trying out for the same sports teams, listening to the same music. To me racism did not seem to be a part of the Canadian experience, because it didn't resemble anything like the racism of the American south, which we heard so much about at the time.

Now, after three more decades of life experience, I look back with embarrassment at my naiveté towards the ideology of racism and how it operates, how it always changes its form and level of intensity as societal conditions change. And there is no question that the racial and ethnic makeups of both Vancouver and Toronto have been drastically altered in recent years, as those cities have shifted from being centres of Western society into postmodern Meccas. At the same time the Canadian economy has also rapidly changed, mainly because of globalization, and mainly affecting the working class.

In the daily newspapers not a day goes by without at least one major article on race relations or racism in our society. Indeed, the largest of British Columbia's dailies, *The Vancouver Sun*, now has a section called "From the Ethnic Press" in its opinion pages. The effects of the global economy also receive close attention. In this regard, though, the media tend not to focus on the economy's deleterious effects on the lives of the working class. They prefer instead to praise those industries and persons who have been able to make lots of money through their own individual efforts.

On the issue of race, British Columbians have had to contend with several major media stories in recent years. The rise of the federal Reform Party, now the Canadian Alliance, coincided with accusations that it was harbouring a good number of racist bigots. At the same time the provincial NDP government found itself under media attack for its 1993 anti-hate laws, designed to make non-white people, including immigrants, feel more comfortable living in the province. In 1997 an NDP cabinet minister, Jenny Kwan, addressed the legislature in Cantonese, only to be heckled and ridiculed by a Liberal MLA of Dutch ancestry. The next year saw these two political parties fight a major public opinion war over the Nisga'a Treaty, which provided for the transfer of title to about 2,000 square kilometres of land in the northern part of the province, plus several hundreds of millions of dollars in government payouts. The treaty held the promise of

251

bringing First Nations people into mainstream British Columbian society.

Canada's westernmost province had entered Confederation in 1871 with the understanding that it did not have to negotiate treaties or recognize Aboriginal title to land, a position held by successive provincial governments until they were forced by the courts to drop it in 1990 (McKee 1996). Negotiating treaties with British Columbia's Aboriginal peoples became a priority of Mike Harcourt's NDP government after being elected in 1991. The incredible backlash against the Nisga'a Treaty demonstrated that a lot of people remained opposed to the shifting of the social location of Aboriginal people. This opposition remained in place despite the benefits to all British Columbians of settling treaties: huge cash flows would enter the province from Ottawa, and business would be more likely to invest in areas with the land question solved.

First Nations people are not the only ones to feel white resentment in British Columbia. No one in the province could ignore the negative hysteria surrounding the unsolicited arrival of four shiploads of poor Chinese people onto B.C. shores in August 1999.

So on the first day of every school year, as I watch a Chinese student follow a Vietnamese student through the doorway, a Hindu follow a Sikh, and an Aboriginal student walk in with a white classmate, I ask myself just how do I expect to negotiate the different social relations, the varying amounts of privilege and oppression that each of these students has experienced, mostly because of their racial or ethnic backgrounds. For me, it has been a challenging journey, as I attempt to learn how to let each student know they should feel proud of their cultural heritage at the same time as they should let each of their classmates feel proud of theirs, too. After all, simply to let people celebrate their differences from each other without looking at commonalities can be problematic, not only for the teacher, but also for society.

I have taught in B.C. high schools for well over a dozen years, with almost equal time spent in a blue-collar town and in an alternative program in a high school composed of mostly working-class students in Vancouver's polyethnic east end. During this time I have been privy to many conversations and episodes that speak to racist attitudes. Occasionally, these attitudes result in acts of physical violence, almost always away from the school site. These teaching experiences pushed me into researching the mechanisms and conditions in which racism is allowed to exist and even flourish.

It occurred to me that the students, who are from a variety of ethnic and racial backgrounds, have much more in common with each other than they have differences. I wondered about the effects that the highly touted global economy was having on their social relations. After all, their uncertain economic prospects differ a little from one ethnic group to the next, yet they often blame each other for what many of them perceive to be bleak times ahead. They seem to pay little or no mind, however, to those who do have some say in what is going on in the economy and social fabric of Canada and, in particular, Vancouver.

These thoughts crystallized for me one day when I saw, on an outside wall of an east-end store, some graffiti that read: "CLASS WAR! NOT RACE WAR!" This directive from the street led me to dig a little deeper into the social relations of the students in my classroom. More specifically, I wanted to see what kind of connections, if any, these young people made between race, racism, and their economic futures. To be sure, the focus of my teaching changed. My curiosity became so acute that I enrolled in an M.A. program at UBC so that I could research and better understand the processes governing the social relations of working-class adolescents. I decided to examine how youth from five different ethnic or racial backgrounds perceived racism and economic inequality, and gathered data through observations and individual and group interviews. The resulting ethnography, which fulfilled the thesis requirements, took eighteen months to complete, but I believe the insights and revelations I gained from it will help make me a better teacher and, for much longer, a better person.

The challenge for me as an anti-racist educator was made easier as soon as I realized that an awareness of social-class interests was the missing key among this student body. This idea profoundly shaped how I came to teach courses in social studies, psychology, cultural anthropology, and, later on, even First Nations studies. I felt that I had a better handle on how to lead the students to an understanding of how power works in our society, and of the hidden yet powerful structures of race, gender, and social class that influence their daily experiences and limit their future economic prospects.

Like most of the students in the program, both of my parents came from working-class families. Because my Irish mother and Polish father emigrated from England in 1956, I have some idea of the immigrant experience. For example, I understand the tensions many of my immigrant students have with their parents as they construct themselves in our Western postmodern society at the expense of traditional values. My siblings and I went through a similar process with our parents, particularly with our father. But today my own identity

253

has been constructed so thoroughly into that of a "Canadian" (without any hyphen) that my Korean, El Salvadorean, and Yugoslavian students, to name but a few, always expressed surprise when I told them that I could understand some of their frustrations because I was also the child of immigrants. They had a lot of difficulty, however, in recognizing me as an older version of themselves. To them I was an educated white middle-class male who, whether they could articulate it or not, had considerable privilege because I belonged to the dominant group in society.

So what had changed from the conditions of my own youth as compared to what these young people were experiencing? I had come to learn that people of Eastern European extraction were despised much less than they were a few decades earlier, following in the footsteps of both the Irish and the Italians. My own schooling had been laced with liberal concepts, including the idea of meritocracy, which theorized that people's individual success had everything to do with how hard they worked. I was taught that beneath the skin, everyone was equal. By corollary, school dropouts had no one to blame but themselves. I later found this "colour-blind" perspective I was raised in — that beneath our skins everyone is equal — to be "power-blind."

None of this explained, however, why the white working-class students had trouble identifying with me. The teachers in the all-white schools of my Toronto childhood had taught me that racism was something horrible. Yet most of the white adolescents in my classes seemed to exhibit a "white defensiveness" attitude. They appeared to believe that immigration policies, affirmative action programs, and Aboriginal land treaties were all part of one big plan destined to result in the inevitable: poverty for them. The times had changed. And I began to suspect that globalization and free-trade deals with countries that had lower labour standards were somehow implicated.

As many teachers can attest, simply to say that non-European people experience considerable racism from whites can unleash a strong negative reaction from the group that has been accused. "Chinese people think they are way better than us!" is a comment I have heard on several occasions. Discussions with students from all kinds of racial backgrounds, before, during, and after my thesis work, confirmed that to be even partially successful, anti-racist objectives were going to have to break through incredibly strong and complex obstacles. Just ask any Korean person who has lived in Japan, or a Vietnamese employee in a Chinese business. And what is the caste system of India if not a social hierarchy based on ethnicity, religion, and class? These relations are ancient, much older than any liberal or communist ideas about equality. Anti-racist educators today have to look at the historical issues brought to Canada from other parts of the world.

The teacher who claims that "everyone is equal" may get students to utter this same refrain in class, but many of them won't believe it because they come from homes and cultures that teach something completely different. In fact, it became clear to me that the home has a significant influence on a young person's formation of values. A teacher has to be especially careful, I came to realize, in presenting notions of privilege and oppression to young people. Yet any educator who wants to make our society more tolerant of differences must try to do so.

These differences between ethnic and racial groups have dominated the public discourse on Western culture in recent years. Yet, for the most part, visible and non-visible minorities have only been able to articulate their position through the lens of the corporate media. In British Columbia the Aboriginal land question becomes a frightening proposition for a non-Native who sees front-page headlines claiming "Indians want all of B.C." People of Asian descent who want to discuss Canadian immigration policy must wait until the media-induced hysteria around a few boatloads of Chinese migrants subsides. Interestingly, instead of being portrayed as victims of poverty they have been called immoral "queue-jumpers," a description that not only demonstrates that they cannot be trusted but also tarnishes the reputation of all the Canadians of Chinese descent. Furthermore, over the years many non-white, working-class youth have told me how disgusted they are with the Vancouver media's portrayal of them as thieves. That portrayal has an impact on their lives every time they enter a store or come into contact with the police.

In multicultural centres such as Vancouver every student's identity has been constructed out of race or ethnicity. All of the students I spoke with were very aware of their race. Any person who has spent even a little time in a Lower Mainland school in recent years has noticed the racial grouping phenomenon. A daughter of Chinese immigrants explains her own participation in this process: "When I started school I didn't know how to speak English. If I were to see a Chinese person, I might say a few words of Chinese to them, just to communicate. When I was in elementary school I always thought that Caucasian people were more outspoken while the Chinese people were really quiet. All of my friends were like me and we felt more comfortable around each other."

Members of all four of the non-European groups who participated   255 in my research — Vietnamese, First Nations, Indian, and Chinese — said they had learned cultural traditions from their elders at a young age. The situation for the white students, however, differed significantly: they did not recognize themselves as holding the traditional "teachings" of any European culture; nor did they even realize that they had a skin colour until they went to one of the large East Vancouver high schools. One adolescent girl described this epiphany: "I lived in Maple Ridge when I was in elementary school and there weren't any. It hadn't gotten out there yet. You know, like different races. But in grade eight I went to Waterford [Secondary in East Vancouver]. I noticed a huge change. Everyone I saw walking down the hall was, like, a lot of different races beside white . . . I was shocked!"

White culture becomes a hidden norm in our society, in a process that also tends to hide both its interests and privileges (Roman 1993: 71-74). As Vancouver inevitably becomes transformed into a postmodern metropolis, the interests and privileges of white culture seem to be successfully hidden from the consciousness of many white people themselves. In courses I have taught over the years, countless white students have expressed strong resentment about the perceived privileges of First Nations people and Asian immigrants. They believe those groups have been granted much more privilege than they themselves have. For them privilege consists of material conditions only, and they believe that their white skin has not entitled them to any extra benefits. It has, in their minds, acted as a detriment. This belief is the crux of the burgeoning attitude known as "white defensiveness," an attitude that is, sadly, fast becoming part of the white working-class identity, especially during this era of free-trade deals and globalization. The seeds for this superior attitude were planted during the era of empire building and colonization, and, sadly, the resulting growth has not withered during the recent decades of liberalism and multiculturalism. Many scholars have pointed out that, despite the end of the European empire, its legacy is still at the root of public school curricula (Willinsky 1998; Gikandi 1996).

At the same time, Asian adolescents have no trouble pointing out the dominance of a hidden white culture. I became more acutely aware of a somewhat invisible white hegemony after a Chinese student plainly stated: "It bugs me that Caucasian people think they are normal and everybody else is not. To them, everybody else is from some group like Chinese, or East Indian, or something else. But not Caucasians. I really don't like it. It bugs me!"

Don't mention to an Aboriginal youth that white people have less privilege than others. This idea is, understandably, very difficult for

First Nations people to accept. During a group discussion involving seven Aboriginal youth, a very articulate girl gave a moving and powerful testimony of her feelings towards the land and white people.

> Well, I know that many Native people are still angry with white people for what happened. I mean, who can blame them? But for me, I just feel we have to get on with it and make the best of it. I mean, forgive, maybe, but don't forget. It's too hard to forget. We Native people are not greedy people. We know it's not our land. We are just caretakers of the land. Lots of people from all over the world were going to eventually come here. I just wish it could have happened in a better way, you know. All of us wish that, right? [Many of the others say, "Yeah."] We can't change that. I think we're just . . . I just see us as very humble people.

One can only imagine the effect that words like these have on the listeners, especially if they happen to be a member of the race responsible for the oppression of Aboriginal people. Such testimonies from Aboriginal youth, almost all of whom came from poor families, helped to motivate me to work for Aboriginal rights, to educate others about the historical wrong that has taken place on this land. These students have made me extremely aware of my own ignorance about the colonial experience of Canada's First Nations at the hands of the Europeans. I must sadly confess that, as a child in Toronto, I didn't even know if there were any "Indians" still alive, let alone any who still practised traditional customs.

Today Aboriginal peoples make up 4 per cent of British Columbia's population. They have been represented in every classroom I have taught in. I have learned from these young people about the gaps in my own knowledge of Canadian history — a history I have since come to know has been laced with political and social strategies bent on breaking the Aboriginal spirit. The subsequent direction of my studies, whether in the formal academic setting or on my own time, led me to request and be granted permission to teach a relatively new curriculum in this province: First Nations Studies 12. It surprised me to learn that I was the first teacher to want to teach it in Vancouver, even though many Native people live in the city.

My experience so far teaching First Nations Studies 12 has motivated me more than ever before to "get it right" and talk about Canadian history from a non-Eurocentric, non-essentialist point of view. Bringing in Aboriginal elders as guest speakers and using resources by Aboriginal scholars have helped the pedagogical process become one of enlightenment for myself as well as for the students, about half of   257 whom are usually First Nations people. It is probably no coincidence that many of the Native students want to "hang out" with me during free time at school, nor is it unconnected that the appearance of FNS 12 at our school seemed to coincide with a noticeable rise in pride among our Aboriginal students.

Aboriginal students participating in the study have said that during their elementary school years they were made to feel inferior, even by some teachers, because of their ancestry. Many of them had enrolled in All-Native junior alternative programs for grades eight, nine, and ten, and during that period of their schooling they first began to feel pride in their heritage and become confident in who they were as individuals and as a people. A few students have told me that recent political events, such as the Nisga'a Treaty and Louis Riel's altered status from a traitor to a "Father of Confederation," have made it easier for them in mainstream society. I believe these observations are noteworthy for educators and curriculum specialists.

In British Columbia's Lower Mainland, a strong ethnic identity is crucial not only for protecting the traditional culture but also for protecting an individual. It is not uncommon to hear how a conflict between two students, usually male, from different races can quickly escalate into a dangerous situation in which peers from the two racial groups come to the aid of the original combatants in intimidating, threatening ways. Some Indian students of Hindu and Sikh extraction, recorded here with phony names, explained how this process works:

Baljinder: Say you start to feel threatened, you know. Like say an East Indian guy walking around is saying, "Look at all these Brown guys." So the white guys who hear this start to build up a whole crew so they don't have to feel scared. And it goes on from there.

Paul Orlowski (PO): Are you suggesting that fear is the underlying motivator that causes students to band together according to race?

Baljinder, Herb: Yeah.

Ronnie: Yeah, there's a colour thing. Like people trust their own kind more, to watch their back. I mean like, I got lots of friends from different races. I dunno like, I know my white friends would back me up. I dunno about some other guys. Like you know, other races. They just think of themselves as a little better than me.

Herb: It's like, you know, who do you think your real friends are? You usually think your own kind will back you up, no matter what.

Mandy: It does happen in high school. Like someone you don't even know, and say there's some trouble. Well, someone will back them up because that's their own race, even if they don't know them.

In the Psychology 11 course I teach, the curriculum has a component on gender. Because of exchanges such as this, I have focused on helping the students deconstruct violent forms of masculinity in the class. The crucial element, of course, is to help the male students see not only that it is beneficial for females that certain forms of masculinity be altered, and to illuminate how power works in our patriarchal, polyethnic, industrial society, but also that the males themselves will benefit.

There is no question that the manner in which working-class masculinity is socially constructed in the cultures that my students come from is a large factor in the escalation of simple conflicts between two males into racial "gang" fights. The scenario is a demonstration of the commonalities in the working class across racial lines, albeit a negative example. In terms of social theory, it is a classic example of a race/class/gender intersection, one that I feel teachers should help students deconstruct. This situation also demonstrates the complexities involved with the ideology of racism.

Almost all of the teenagers I have asked about racism believe it is on the rise, at least in British Columbia's Lower Mainland. For the most part, the main form of racism that they recognize is overt, such as name-calling (Elliott and Fleras 1993: 57-69). There were many exceptions, of course. A Chinese girl who had spent considerable time in California said that many Euro-Canadians practise a covert form of racism, or "polite" racism. Interestingly, she preferred the overt form that she found prevalent in the United States, because it was clear there where she stood. Every Aboriginal student I have ever engaged in these kinds of discussions understands the systemic racism that is informed by the institutional racist Canadian laws that historically forbade Native people from voting in elections, from owning businesses, and from participating in traditional ceremonies, and that forced their children to attend residential schools designed to break their culture. By comparison, none of the Asian students seem aware of the institutional racism against their races that ended only in 1948. This lack of awareness is undoubtedly related to their status as first-generation Canadians.

During my research into the ethnography, an interesting insight emerged from the data analysis: all of the supposed racist attitudes expressed by the students had an economic link. Nothing has had a more profound impact on how I address racial or ethnic relations in

259

the classroom than this insight. This is not to claim that if class concerns were to disappear, then racism would follow suit. Rather, it is to suggest that economic and political processes that work to further oppress Canada's working class will, in turn, contribute to the rise of racist attitudes. The relationships between groups of people often involve materialist aspirations and exploitation, relationships mediated by money, race and gender, and, of course, history. In other words, the ideology of racism works in very subtle ways to keep power where it is.

Again, though, social hierarchies based on ethnicity are not the exclusive property of Europeans. In Vancouver, Vietnamese students claim to experience negative attitudes from some Chinese people. These attitudes are based on preconceptions of wealth and have apparently come over from East Asia with the latest wave of immigration. An eighteen-year-old female student commented: "In my personal view, I think Vietnamese and Chinese are the same. But Chinese people think they are better than Vietnamese. . . . You can tell by the way they talk and their attitude towards us."

Over the years I have heard both Vietnamese and Chinese youth explain how their parents told them to keep away from Aboriginal people. On the surface, these suggestions would seem to reflect racist attitudes, albeit in a covert, or "polite" form — I have only heard one Aboriginal youth speak of an experience he had with discrimination from a Chinese classmate. A deeper analysis, however, points to Asian immigrants buying into the colonial attitudes of the dominant race towards Aboriginal people. The pejorative views that many East Asian immigrants hold towards Aboriginal people is based on a lack of historical understanding of Native/white relations. This problem speaks to the necessity of educators working to employ anti-racist strategies that address the historical colonial experience of Aboriginal people and the postcolonial aftermath they have had to endure.

First Nations people are not the only group considered inappropriate for friendship with Asian youth. Many students spoke of parental pressures not to befriend white peers. Consider this exchange among several Indian students:

Baljinder: I have a friend who has parents who won't let anyone who is not brown into his house. You have to be their culture. You have to be brown to be inside his house. They won't let any white guys in, that's for sure. So obviously, he's only going to start hanging out with only brown people, right. And I know a lot of people who are like that.

Herb: I can understand your friend's parents. Cuz like they probably see mostly white people smoking and drinking. They get this impression that white people are wild.

Baljinder: And they also know that a lot of white people stay out later. The kids go out and stay out late.

Mandy: Yeah, that's right. The parents see it like that. That white parents are less controlling and less strict than East Indian parents.

Herb: Cuz the whites know the culture. Like they know how it goes. I know like for my mom. She was raised in a family and her dad died young. She had to always help her mom. Like she was raised where she would do nothing, like not have any fun. She would be working hard all the time, her whole life. And like, you know, some white parents, they've had fun. They know how it is.

Mandy: That's not allowed in our culture.

Herb: Like my mom doesn't even know what happens to us out there in Canadian culture.

Ronnie: Same with my mom.

Mandy: My parents don't know either.

Herb: But we see it. Like, we understand the white culture. I know that the white guys I know, their parents used to party when they were younger. But then they settled down, have kids, and all that. So they don't freak out when they see their kids partyin'. They know they'll stop one day, too. It's just part of the culture. But my parents don't get it. They're from a totally different world.

Ronnie: And having fun is not part of that world.

Indian students see their parents as holding attitudes towards white people that could be considered racist. Once again, however, a closer look reveals something else at work: a parental concern for what they perceive to be in the best interests of their children. As I can attest from my own experience, immigrant parents expect their children to be law-abiding and to work hard and do well at school. Moreover, working-class immigrants do not have the money or, in most cases, the "right" skin colour to help their children get ahead in other ways. The way they see it, a good education is the best way for their children to make it out of poverty. The keen observations made by this particular group of young people reveal a tension undoubtedly experienced by the majority of immigrants to North America over the years: the tensions of attempting to get an economic toehold through hard work in a culture that values leisure and fun to a much larger extent. It is not racism, at least not in the same way that some members of the Euro-Canadian working-class community see Asian people.

The white working-class youth I have had contact with are, for the most part, not a happy lot these days. Those who participated in the research were most vociferous in their complaints about Asian immigration. They put forth a list of grievances that included the familiar refrains of Asian immigrants "using up our tax dollars for welfare," "taking all the jobs," and "driving up real-estate prices." They also complained about having to listen to "Chinese" spoken on the streets instead of English. During the interview of this group I decided to explore this further.

PO: So you've mentioned that you don't like having to hear so many people speaking in a Chinese language on the streets. [They make sounds of agreement.] Would it bother you less if the immigrants came from Europe? [All but one agree.]

Some immigrants are coming from places like Eastern Europe: Hungary, Poland, Yugoslavia, places like that. Most of them don't speak English when they get here. So why would it bother you less?

Diane and Keith: They're white. [A few of them laugh.]

PO: But you would still have the problems you've mentioned before: too few jobs, people going on welfare, not speaking English, those things.

Craig: They're more respectful people, I think.

Diane: They're very polite.

Patrick: Orientals spit a lot. They really do. [Many of them laugh.]

PO: You know, these comments you are making about Asian immigrants used to be said by English and French Canadians about Eastern Europeans and Southern Europeans such as Italians. Now all this has changed and they are accepted.

Keith: Well, I don't know. I'd just rather have Europeans here, any Europeans. At least they can drive. [A few of them chuckle.]

At first glance this exchange seems to demonstrate overt racism against people from Asia, and perhaps this is partially true. Further analysis, however, suggests that fear has been a factor in the development of these racist attitudes. It appears that the white students are more than a little anxious about competing against Asian people, especially the Chinese, when it comes to both academics and procuring employment. I think one of the female students uttered the sentiments of many when she spoke of the Chinese students who "always got A's and B's and they'd gloat about it" and Chinese people who, after job interviews, were hired instead of her. These very stereotypes — that all Chinese youth are excellent students, work exceptionally hard at whatever they do, and never have time for fun — are obstacles to building relationships between the Chinese and European communities of Vancouver.

Rightly or wrongly, the white working-class youth of today are not concerned as much with European immigration because they are not worried about the ensuing "competition" for grades and employment. When put up against a culture they perceive as having a superior work ethic, these same young people begin to develop a fear of working at dead-end jobs and living in poverty. To be sure, their racism may be fuelled by the prospect of falling behind non-white people in economic power and status. After all, Canada's white working class, as in other places, has had a long and painful history of having to contend with exploitation at the hands of capitalists from their own race. Remnants of the white supremacist racial hierarchies of centuries past appear to be still at work in the minds of the white working-class students.

The findings from my research, corroborated by my subsequent classroom experiences, go far to explain the recent rise of "white defensiveness" within British Columbia's working class. That attitude can easily result in ugly behaviour. I recall hearing one of my white students yelling out "Go home ya immigrants!" to a group of younger East Asian students on the grounds of the main school. Another time, a few days after a Vancouver daily printed a one-page article on the findings of my thesis, a student informed me that both he and his mother "were outraged" by my anti-white ideas as reported in the newspaper. Apparently my call for a more "tolerant" society and a recognition that Canada will never return to the way it was were enough to brand me as "a traitor."

That conversation marked the first time that I realized I had come into contact with people from the far-right white supremacist community, as exchanges over the next few months illuminated. It is a difficult task to try and get someone immersed in a supremacist and essentialist philosophy to see otherwise (although I tried). It is for the youth who are beginning to be influenced by the ideas of the new right, including white defensiveness, that I've developed pedagogical ideas that work to counter intolerance. A comparison of the current situation in Canada with that of the Great Depression of the 1930s has been helpful in getting the students to question their original attitudes towards both the unemployed and immigrants. The parallels are strong in that labourers during the 1930s were very reluctant to accept immigrants out of a fear of more competition for scarce employment. I have found that Socratic techniques coupled with Paulo Freire's notion of praxis have been most effective with these white working-class students (Freire 1973). It is clear that a certain class awareness might develop out of this tendency, one that I would hope progressive curriculum could encourage to cross ethnic lines. After all, it is in the interests of the common good to help the white working-class youth realize that they have more in common with their peers from other races than with Euro-Canadian capitalists.

My teaching experiences have illuminated other examples of economic concerns that lead to racial tensions that in turn result in social hierarchies. The wealthy business classes of Hong Kong and Singapore sit atop an East Asian social hierarchy that positions the peasants of mainland China, Vietnam, and Cambodia at the bottom in a social location that makes them vulnerable for labour exploitation. The derogatory view that many First Nations people have towards the white population has everything to do with bitterness at the poverty they have had to endure because of economic oppression and racist laws. Perhaps most important of all, the corporate media's constant fanning of the hot embers of racism serves to protect the wealth of Canada's elite by pitting one race of workers against another. Anyone simply had to gaze at the front page of Conrad Black's *Province* newspaper in the summer of 1999 to witness this process at work as another group of poverty-stricken Chinese people was spotted in an old rusted ship off the B.C. coast. In the midst of all the hysteria this tabloid ran a front-page headline that screamed out that the real problem with Chinese immigration is not with the shiploads of Chinese migrants but rather with the hordes of illegal Chinese people who come in with fake passports from other points of departure. The media-constructed reaction has been predictable: outrage.

What can an educator do about all of this?

I know that for myself, awareness of my own ethnocentric attitudes became the first step towards working to eliminate them. Many non-white students have described episodes in which they felt white teachers were not sensitive to the students' own cultures, implying that ethnocentrism was behind this insensitivity rather than strong racist attitudes. I have also learned about the hidden norms of white privilege in Canadian society, still embedded in much curricula, and this realization is now at the root of my anti-racist pedagogical approach. The most effective way to lessen white hegemonic power includes a collective effort on the part of all the minorities. If they hope to be successful in creating a more liberatory Canadian society, these groups will simply have to forget about the ancient social hierarchies that they have experienced.

I have attempted to modify curricula in social studies and other courses I teach by filling in the gaps in the regular curriculum, which means incorporating the contributions of non-Europeans to Canadian society, reflecting the wishes of Asian, Aboriginal, and Black students. It means highlighting the blatant implementation of white supremacist racial hierarchies during the empire-building period, and explaining how even the education system itself enabled institutional racism to be part of nation-building in Canada. Although the conservative elements in our society resist these kinds of curriculum changes, educators are always in possession of a certain degree of autonomy once the classroom door is closed.

Because very few students entering my classroom are even aware of their working-class status, I have also made labour history and class interests part of my focus. (Even students whose families are on welfare often say they are middle class.) A lack of class awareness can result in an acceptance of middle-class arguments — for cutting taxes and shrinking social programs, for instance — that puts working-class people at an even further disadvantage. This myopia also works to perpetuate and maintain racist attitudes.

The profound significance of the relationship between racism and working-class concerns has altered my approach to anti-racist pedagogy. Working-class students in the high-school courses I teach become more willing to talk about racism after I link it up with economic or material concerns. Anti-racist teaching strategies appear to have been more successful in recent years for me. Numerous Euro-Canadian students who initially exhibited signs of "white defensiveness" have altered their stance to one of understanding that Vietnamese fishers or Indian labourers simply want to feed their children, too. Once first-generation Canadian youth learn about Aboriginal history and the colonial legacy, they understand contemporary Aboriginal issues from a legal, moral, and more compassionate perspective. Moreover, if poverty is framed within a human-rights paradigm, students are much more receptive to discussions around economic inequality. I have tried to develop pedagogy in such a way as to make it more difficult for corporate media to pit one racial group of labourers against another.

I am not so naive anymore to believe that racism would entirely disappear if Canada had a fair and just economy. I do strongly believe, however, that racist attitudes would greatly decrease if this were so. I also believe that working-class students need to develop some knowledge of their class concerns in order to see what they have in common with their peers from other cultural backgrounds. A sophisticated   265 perspective on the concept of power can lead, in some of these young people, to a commitment to fight for social and economic justice.

To these ends, I have also tried to get working-class students to understand the implications of international free-trade deals upon their own futures. When we have discussed aspects of NAFTA and national labour practices within each of the three countries involved, the students have quickly come to understand the ramifications upon their own lives and the lives of all working-class people, especially in Canada. Which is the bigger obstacle to an economically secure future: treaties with Aboriginal people or free-trade deals with poor countries? Are immigrants taking away the jobs of Canada's working class more than profitable transnational corporations that shut down plants here and relocate them in Mexico? What were the World Trade Organization (WTO) protests in Seattle really about?

It has become apparent to me that with the proper information, working-class students of any race are much more likely to want to engage in the political process, to even get out and exercise their civic duty and vote during elections and referendums. Indeed, only a knowledgeable electorate can become responsible enough to create a democracy that has the common good as its goal and not simply the good of those who have the most power in our society. Pride in one's heritage is very important, but we all know it can be extremely hurtful if that same respect is not given to others. To paraphrase an old Chinese proverb: "If we don't change direction we will eventually get to where we are heading." We already live in an intolerant and xenophobic society, so our view of the future can become an extremely frightening image, indeed. The time has come to attempt to create a responsible citizenship, one that has as its main goal the best interests of the common person, regardless of ethnicity, social class, gender, age, or sexual orientation.

We now live in a diverse, postmodern, ever-evolving society. As always, race and social class are inextricably linked together. The public education system has to be a major player in the transformation of Canada into a much more inclusive and positive society for all people. After all, it was one of the crucial instruments for maintaining white hegemony, and it may very well still be. For the most part the education system works to maintain corporate hegemony today. Anti-racist education, of course, is the first step in the transformation. This is why, on the first day of every school year in September, I am always filled with an intense curiosity, almost awe, as I watch the students from myriad cultural backgrounds walk into my East Vancouver class-

room.

"We Are All the Same — Just Because You Are Black Doesn't Matter"

••••••••••••••••••••••••••••••

Gifty Serbeh-Dunn
and Wayne Dunn

I. Gifty

"Are you trying to say that we are all racists?" This question was raised in one of my classes at the University of Victoria after a lecture on race. I immediately tried to defend the person (a Black man) whose lecture had led to this question. Then I realized that it was not my responsibility to defend anybody or even to educate my classmates on the issue of race. Still, I found myself drawn deeper and deeper into a discussion about race. Little did I know how much I would eventually be saddened by the chain of events initiated by that discussion.

The entire discussion, and its aftermath, really took me by surprise. I was a relative newcomer to Vancouver Island, having recently moved from Ottawa, with a quick stop in Stanford, California. In my sixteen months on the island I had never experienced the type of racial discrimination that I had noticed in Ottawa and California — up until this discussion, that is.

While we were discussing the lecture, some of my classmates stated that, as white males, they were beginning to experience 267 "reversed racism" and that political correctness was to blame for all that. Comments like "I am not racist and resent any insinuation that I might be" were bandied about. We heard remarks such as "I am a white, middle-class, professional male and I also feel oppressed. I feel insulted when people like you try to make me feel guilty for being white." I felt they were missing the point. It was obvious that they were taking the issue personally and missing the reality of racism in Canada, missing how it affects people's lives every day. These same classmates, with whom I had been engaging in a wide range of philosophical discussions, were unable to discuss racism. For them it was as if admitting that racism existed in our society somehow made them responsible. They saw it as a personal thing.

What was even harder for me was how their inability to discuss, at least in an education setting, an issue as important as racism made the classroom feel unsafe for me. Soon after the discussion about race, another episode occurred in the same class. This time it was about the importance of culture. Many of my classmates resisted (and resented) any discussion on culture. To them, culture was not something that needed to be discussed in a graduate-level social science program. My classmates were saying, "Culture is not important." One of them said, "I am more interested in business and environment and wish we would not insist on including culture in our discussion." Another said that this culture stuff was a waste of time and money, and since he had paid good money to come to study, he would like to see the culture thing dropped. The final straw in this exchange was when some of my classmates walked out of the classroom as the faculty member attempted to address the importance of culture.

These incidents created a conflict that split the classroom into two groups and made the learning atmosphere very difficult. For the first time in my experience as an African immigrant to Canada, I really felt like an outsider. Something in my core had been touched by those remarks. Until those incidents occurred the three other visible minority students and myself had carried the load of race for the entire class. The class always looked to us for examples on culture and always expected us to address issues of race (which came up often in our program). It was as if we were the only ones with "culture," and the only ones who belonged to a "race." I asked myself why race and culture issues had to be mine and only mine? Why were my colleagues negating my feelings, and why were they unable to see that racism exists?

I tried to reflect on what was happening, to make some sense of it all. Did people make their remarks because they were from Victoria and had never been sensitized to racial differences? Weren't they aware of the Canadian mosaic? Were they aware of multiculturalism? In fact, was our class discussion of globalization for nothing? Was this experience occurring because the people who asked these questions were Anglo-Canadian and had lived all their lives in Victoria, which is predominantly Euro-Canadian? Would people in Toronto, Montreal, and Ottawa ask such questions, even if they had such thoughts?

Dealing with the experience

Those classroom episodes were a powerful experience for me. For the first time in my fifteen years in Canada my skin colour was thrown into my face. I felt that I had to carry the race and culture load for my class because I was Black. My first reaction was anger, which was accompanied by tears. These responses were followed by compassion for my classmates, who were so unaware of the diversity that existed in our society and so closed to the diversity that was right in their class.

I was angry at my classmates for being so unwilling to discuss race and culture that they would walk out, not just on me, but on the instructor who was trying to deal with the issue. I was literally in tears from the frustration of having to face such rudeness and ignorance. I wondered if I had expected too much from my peers. Perhaps my earlier experiences in Canada were positive because people in Ottawa were exposed to more cultural diversity. I wanted desperately to educate my classmates, to tell them that culture is part of every human experience, not just non-whites' experience. I felt it would be a shock for them to realize that culture was not about colour, that whites were not excluded from it. I wanted them to know that they had no need to be afraid of an open discussion about race. Yet at the same time I was angry and resented their ignorance.

After I calmed myself down I decided to try to educate my classmates about the issues. For over a month after the initial discussion I was still not sure if this was the right thing to do. It is not my responsibility to take care of other people's ignorance about race and culture, I thought. Still, it felt right at the time to educate them, and so educate I did. Perhaps I simply wanted others to understand my disgust at how the entire issue was being handled.

I started off by speaking to those classmates who were open enough to listen, without placing any judgement on whether my disgust was valid. I explained why I was offended by our class's inability to have an informed discussion of race and culture. I tried to help them see that it was no different than some of the other issues we regularly discussed and analysed.

269

I explained how the personalization of the discussion on race and the lack of openness to discuss culture illustrate some of the racism ingrained in our society. I talked about how my classmates' fear that they might offend me and the other non-white students was stifling open discussion of theoretical concepts that were a fundamental component of our Master's program. I said that my discomfort with their fear was because they were denying us all the opportunity to get to know each other, and to learn from the situation. I really wanted them to understand and be able to participate in a meaningful discussion on race and culture.

Some of the responses from my classmates were interesting and elucidating, particularly when one of them said, "We're all the same. Just because you're Black doesn't matter." I realized there was a lot more work to do than just explaining my feelings. I was shocked to realize that many of my classmates — professional people living in Canada, one of the most multicultural countries in the world — simply didn't get it. For them, the Canadian mosaic was not much of a reality.

My mind flooded with questions. I asked my classmates, "Isn't the beauty of the country all about the differences of its people? Are we really the same?" I asked my friends, "How can we be the same when visually we look so different from one another? How can I, an African, be the same as you, an Irish immigrant?" I argued, "Our experiences are not the same, our lives are not the same, and by God I am thankful that we are not the same."

My reaction surprised them. I realized that they thought that if they held on to the belief that we were the same then there would be no need for any discussions on race and culture. I persisted in pointing out how I was different from each of them by virtue of being African, a woman, and a recent immigrant to this country. For all these reasons we could never be the same. And it was okay to be different.

More about my "difference"

I was born and raised in Ghana, West Africa. The last-born of nine children, I came to Canada in the early 1980s to visit family friends in Ottawa. I had no intentions whatsoever of staying in Canada, and I looked forward to my return to Ghana. A military coup changed my plans, and I was stuck: an eighteen-year-old girl far away from all my loved ones, with no idea of when I would see them again. Until then I had never been away from family for more than three months at any time.

My father decided that we should take advantage of this opportunity and I should go to school in Canada. In typical Ghanaian fashion, I was left out of this decision. However, despite my fear and homesickness, I was consoled by the promise that I could return and continue with my education in Ghana as soon as things improved. That did not happen, and I ended up with B.A. and M.A. degrees from Carleton University in Ottawa. I planned to return to Ghana with my education and set up a consulting business assisting Canadian businesses with cross-cultural sensitization of their personnel in West Africa. My plans were thwarted again (but happily this time) when I met and married a wonderful Canadian man. We moved to California while he finished a Master's degree at Stanford University, and then we moved to a small community just outside Victoria on Vancouver Island. We still have not ruled out living in Ghana eventually, if only for a few years.

In Ottawa I had lived an active life. I worked as an international student advisor at Carleton University and was an energetic member of the African Canadian community. Within this community the question of identity arose in many of our discussions, but always in the context of our differences as Africans and how we could contribute and make our mark in Canada. In my discussions with Black friends in Ottawa (people who were born in Canada or had immigrated from the West Indies) it surfaced that they believed that my approach to racism and racist activity was too lenient. I had to justify my position with explanations of our different histories. Growing up in Ghana I had never had to face racism, and it took me a few years in Canada to even recognize what racism was. I was aware that sooner or later I would experience it, and I was keen to learn more about this phenomenon from my friends.

I also experienced some frustration because skin colour was often the primary basis for one's identity. Class and gender were often overlooked, even within the African Canadian community. We resented whites lumping all Black people together because of our skin colour, but we were quick to do the same to each other. When I tried to assert my identity as a woman, especially as an African woman, this was seen as an attempt to set myself apart. Perhaps it is odd that the question of sameness rubbed me in such a negative way. People in the African Canadian community accepted difference but did not like to be seen as standing apart from the rest of the community.

The question of "belonging" seldom came up in Ottawa. In my circles difference was often celebrated. In the larger community and in my classes my Africanness was never overlooked. Never, in any of the discussions we had, did anyone refuse to admit that I was different. That is why I was shocked to hear my colleagues in Victoria insist that they did not think I was different. The incidents there caused me to reflect on why the question of "difference" was treated differently in my class in Victoria than it was in Ottawa. Was it because Easterners know how to mask how they feel about difference, or was it because Ottawa is much more multicultural than Victoria? Or did the Ottawa circles I lived in blind me to the realities of how whites viewed difference?

My experiences in Victoria led me to revisit some of the stereotypes I faced in Ottawa. Often I heard and saw in the media and all around me negative information about and images of Africa. For example, I often heard how "backward" Africa must be. (Interestingly, people usually posed this as a question.) I spent a great deal of time explaining Africa. The other stereotype I had to deal with concerned the oppression of African women. I was constantly told that I was very lucky to have the opportunity to be in Canada. When I asked why, I would be told that they did not think African women could leave home. (Was I a refugee?) I was quick to point out that my father's people, the Ashanti, are matrilineal. I tried to explain that the oppression they heard about isn't so straightforward, that Africa is a large continent and its people live in many different situations.

In the middle of the race and culture incident, while I was still extremely upset about it, I called my husband (who was away travelling on business) and told him about my experiences in class. His first reaction was anger — a lot of anger. Then he told me he would be there for me in whatever way I wanted him to be.

II. Wayne

I grew up in a small Northern Saskatchewan community that is, and remains, very racist towards Aboriginal people. Without realizing that there was anything racist about it, I grew up buying into common stereotypes of Aboriginal people. Fortunately, when I was in my early twenties a set of circumstances and a strong-willed Métis friend combined to help me see things differently, and I went on to develop a professional career working with indigenous peoples in Canada and around the world.

When I think of the divide that existed, and continues to exist, between indigenous and non-indigenous peoples in my village, it really amazes me. Our community was on the very edge of the Canadian north and almost everyone liked the outdoors — hunting, fishing, and other outdoor activities. And what did the local indigenous peoples like? Hunting, fishing, and other outdoor activities. Why, then, were attitudes so set and the community so divided? I have asked myself this question often, but cannot find an answer, even today. It is amazing how part of it parallels Gifty's experience. Most people in my village would react angrily and deny the existence of any racism — just as I would have when I was still living there. This is exactly the reaction of Gifty's classmates.

The experience in my wife's class was very different for me. I had never before had to look at the racism in our world and see it as something personal. When Gifty shared her experience and frustration with me I was shocked and angry. Surprisingly, my anger was more at the institution for allowing this to happen than it was at her classmates. We had previously discussed the lack of diversity in the Master's program, and Gifty had mentioned that all of the instructors and guest speakers in the program were white. I found this shocking and shared her frustration at the learning limitations that this created.

My instinct was to challenge the institution and do battle to "right this wrong." Fortunately, I realized that, as much as I loved my wife and was hurt and angry, I had no right to "fix" the situation for her. (Besides, in these situations she is much more capable than I am anyway. My tendency is often to tackle things like this head on and polarize the issue.) I tried to listen empathetically to her and to let her know that, whatever action she decided on, I would support her.

This incident made me realize a number of things. In the two years we had been married our racial difference had been respected and explored but had never been a major concern. We have both lived in a very international world, with friends from all over the world. Racial difference, then, is an everyday reality for us. Our friends, our work, and our play are full of people who are different, racially and otherwise. Our racial difference has never troubled our families; rather, it is a source of joy. Both of our families have been curious: my family has wanted to know more about life in Ghana, and Gifty's family has been interested in how I grew up and how my family lived.

One incident that occurred shortly after our wedding illustrates how comfortable our families were with our different backgrounds. We spent Christmas with my family in Saskatchewan. Gifty is extremely personable, and everyone quickly took to her. My nephew, about six years old at the time, was totally enamoured with her. In February he brought some of his artwork home from school — he had drawn a winter scene, with black snowmen. He assumed that if people could be different colours, so could snowmen.

Suddenly the events in my wife's class in Victoria pushed me out of my safe, secure world. Gifty's experience caused me to face racism and discrimination on a very personal level, and it felt uncomfortable. In retrospect, I realize I was afraid. I was seeing some of the issues our children would have to deal with. I think it was the first time it really dawned on me that our children would probably face similar situations because they have a different skin colour and a different background from others. This scares me, and I realize I'm going to have to do some work to deal with the issue on a personal level — so I can be there to support them.

So what next? We certainly don't intend to let this incident change our minds about living on Vancouver Island. Yet it does make me aware of the racism that we will encounter, and that our children will encounter. I should not have been surprised by the reaction in Gifty's class. After all, this is the same British Columbia that is so polarized around the ongoing Aboriginal treaty negotiations, the same British Columbia where there is a sharp divide between indigenous and non-indigenous peoples. It is the same resource-based economy that is going to have to learn to address some of these issues as successive Supreme Court rulings recognize indigenous rights to resources.

These will be interesting times, and the incident at Gifty's school has helped me to be more prepared. It is up to me to learn more about racism and to think how I will be there for our children when they encounter it.

Nothing in my background prepared me for these issues

I was raised in a little house on a small farm at the edge of the bush in Northern Saskatchewan. When I stood on the porch of my house looking north, the most northerly east-west road was south of me. We were on the edge: if you walked north from our house you would only come across one other farm before reaching the North Pole. Like all of our neighbours, we didn't have indoor plumbing and many other modern conveniences.

Growing up, I was the oldest of three children. In addition to farming, my father fished commercially, logged, and did all sorts of other jobs to try to make ends meet. My mother often ran the farm on her own, with all the help a little son could provide, while my father was off trying to make some cash money. I had two younger sisters. This upbringing really shaped the person I have become. Even though my work puts me in interesting and innovative situations in many countries, I still see myself as a Saskatchewan farm boy with Irish roots.

All this ethnicity and race "stuff" were just not part of the world I grew up in. As a family, and as a community, we did not have much sense of our ethnicity. My father talked about members of his father's family emigrating from Ireland, but there was nothing specific, no names or dates. This made the idea of our origins seem distant, and I certainly didn't have any feeling of connection to Ireland or Irish culture (although I did like the music of the Irish Rovers). My father's mother was born in England and came to Canada as a three-year-old at the turn of the century. But, again, I felt no connection to English culture or heritage on a personal level.

My mother's side of the family was perhaps even more removed from connecting with their ancestral culture and ethnicity. The first I can recall hearing about their ethnic origins was when I was about ten years old, after my mother died and I was told that her family was Ukrainian. I didn't even realize then what a rich cultural heritage that linked me to. Later I was told that there was indigenous ancestry in my mother's family, but I have never been able to confirm or deny this. Then, in about 1992, a first cousin of my mother's arrived in Saskatchewan. He had a lot of knowledge of our family history, and I discovered that my mother's father's family had immigrated from England in the mid-nineteenth century. Later, on a trip to the area of Ontario where her family was from, I found out a lot more about family connections on that side and met a lot of family. I am just now finding out about my mother's maternal family and hope to make contact with them soon.

We had, then, little or no contact with any family members beyond my grandparents, and certainly no connection with the ancestral cultures and heritage of my family's homelands. Nothing in my upbringing prepared me for the issues that surfaced in Gifty's class. In many ways I can empathize with her classmates who see ethnicity and culture as something other people have. That is the dynamic I grew up in too, and one that still influences who I am. I can see that I have some work to do, and some learning ahead of me, as I move through life in a mixed-race family. I want to learn more about my roots and the cultures of my ancestors so I can pass this on to our children. They will be all the richer for knowing the cultural roots of both sides of their family.

III. Gifty

Like Wayne, I do not expect to leave British Columbia any time soon. The magnificent beauty of this place is a sure attraction to me. Additionally, my experience in the classroom has made me doubly attentive to what I see and hear around me. I have also become alert and sensitive to the divide that I see between Aboriginal communities and the white population. The flavour of my interactions with all those I have come into contact with has changed. For example, I am now ready to discuss identity and its meanings and implications with anyone I meet. I have come to realize that the diversity surrounding me in Ottawa led me in one way or another to take those differences for granted.

I now cannot see myself as being engaged in work on Vancouver Island without incorporating cross-cultural awareness as a significant component of that work. Fortunately, the kind of consulting work I am involved in will allow me the flexibility to build in this component. I would like to be known in this area as the person who does not take cross-cultural sensitivity for granted. For me, the importance of assisting people to appreciate and understand the importance of the issues of culture and race has been clearly illuminated.

If I had any doubts about my calling in life, that is no longer the case. In each encounter that I make in this place I now call home, I am quick to establish that the issues of race, culture, and ethnicity are important and should not be secondary to anything else. Indeed, to establish these issues, I have taken to asking people where they come from. I ask the people who tell me they are "from here" where their forbearers came from. Only in that context do I seem able to draw attention to the fact that they too have culture, in the same way as I do. Sometimes, when people from various backgrounds have participated in such a conversation, I often hear about how much they take for granted notions of difference — and, in the end, how much they have come to realize that difference is not simply a matter of having dark skin.

Can Blacks Be Racist? Reflections on Being "Too Black and African"

Henry Martey Codjoe

I am on dangerous terrain here. I am going to discuss a contentious subject: issues of race and racism in Canadian society, particularly as they affect Blacks/African Canadians. Using my own personal experiences and complemented by research on race relations, I intend to probe the meanings of "race" and "racism" and why they are such powerful social forces. I am particularly interested in the charge by some whites that Blacks are and can be racist.

Given their personal experiences and outlook, whites and Blacks have different interpretations of what it means to be racist. Indeed, Blacks and whites do not possess the same experiences because, as David Mura (1999: 97) explains it:

> For some people, the categories of race have caused a whole range of negative experiences. For other people the same categories have enabled them to escape these experiences. For some people the categories of race have excluded them from certain privileges. For others the same categories have availed them of certain privileges. For all people the categories of race have meant their ancestors experienced different histories.

277

Following this premise, I argue that Blacks may be *prejudiced* but cannot be racist, and that the notion of "Black racism" is a contradiction in terms.

Reconstructing my being from African to Black

More than once I have been called a "Black racist" for being "too Black and African" (see Codjoe 1994). How could this be? Well, until I came to Canada from my native Ghana, I had known all my life that I was an African. It was not until I started living in North America that I found I was "Black" (Busia 1998: 274). My identity was *socially constructed* from African to Black. I was told, on many occasions, that I was different. I did not belong. My stay in Canada would be temporary. Canada is a "white man's country." Never mind that "exiles, migrants, immigrants and refugees have turned the [country] into [a] multicultural state" (Busia 1998: 279).

Many a time I was asked when I would go back to Africa, as if Africa was one country where all Black people lived. It didn't matter that I was a Canadian citizen and had lived in Canada for most of my adult life: many years more than many white immigrants. Yet I was not Canadian. I was Black, and Blacks don't belong in Canada. They belong to Africa, and go back they must. Canada is a white country, and to be Canadian means to be white. And so in this dichotomy of race, "Those who are not White are presumed to be recent arrivals and often told to go 'back where they came from'" (Rosenblum and Travis 2000: 16).

Consequently, it was not long before, as a student in the late 1970s and early 1980s, I was socialized into racialized thinking. The sheer power that race held in people's imaginations made me intensely conscious of race and racial difference. Like Randall Robinson, writing in his *Defending the Spirit: A Black Life in America*, I became "obsessively black." Race became "an overarching aspect of my identity." I also believed that Canada "has made me this way. Or, more accurately, White [Canadians] have made me this way" (Robinson 1999: xiii).

That being the case, I embraced my blackness and Africa. I discovered myself as an African like never before. I developed Black consciousness. I would not say I was militant, but I was no longer ashamed of being Black or African. I "emancipated myself from mental slavery," as Bob Marley would say. I almost dropped my name Henry: too European, I thought. I asked my friends to call me Martey, my African name. If the dominant society is going to define me as

Black, then I will do the defining. I will establish the boundaries of my being. The dominant culture will not dispossess me of my being with every glance. They can call me Black, but I will tell you what kind of Black I am. My new identity could be viewed in "a context in which ethnic minorities are articulating the desire to have our voices heard, a desire to celebrate our own signs of difference and validate our stories" (Busia 1998: 273). It is ironic and somewhat embarrassing to admit to myself that I learned more about myself now as an African or a Black person in Canada than I had in my native Ghana.

But alas, my new-found identity was seen as racist. By embracing Africa and espousing Black pride and nationalism I became, for some people, a Black racist — a person who hated white people and Canada. By embracing my blackness, I was perceived to be rejecting everything white. How ungrateful after all that Canada had done for me! How racist of me!

Since then I have always been baffled when I hear the charge of racism levelled against Blacks. Can Blacks really be racist? Is there Black racism, like white racism? Are they the same things? What are we talking about here? It appears that some whites think Blacks are and can be racist. In fact, accusations of "Black racism" or what is now referred to as "reverse racism" have been with us for a long time. Black nationalists like Malcolm X were always accused of being "anti-white." In a 1964 Harvard Law School Forum, Malcolm X was asked the difference between white racism and Black racism — as if the two were synonymous. In more recent times, Beverly Daniel Tatum, an African American psychologist, professor, and author of *Why Are All the Black Kids Sitting Together in the Cafeteria?* (1997), says she is often asked during her workshops on racism whether "people of colour" can be racist.

What is this thing called "race"?

Truthfully, I had not been used to the intractability of race in North America until I came to Canada. As fellow Ghanaian A.P.A. Busia notes: "It has been a hard lesson, because in Ghana nobody notices. In a land where we are 'Black,' that blackness is not significant to a child's mind." Therefore, "When you are born in a land where everyone seems made in your likeness, you do not, as a group, have to learn strategies of self-affirmation and self-love to counter the opposing, culturally dominant force of mirrors in which you don't figure, have no reflection, or are given images of yourself which do not in any way reflect the selves you see inside" (Busia 1998: 269, 273).

So one can imagine how green I was about racial matters during my early years in Canada. I had no idea that race mattered so much, that whites and Blacks were living racially structured lives, and that there existed a racially hierarchical society in which people occupied structural or institutional positions by virtue of their "racial" belonging. It was quite a revelation. I learned very quickly about race. But what is this thing called "race" that has occupied us for so long? Why does race matter so much?

There is consensus among most social scientists today that "race" as we have come to know and use it in society is arbitrarily and socially defined (James 1999). The proposition that race is a "social and cultural construction" has almost become an academic cliché. All the same, an examination of Canadian history shows that what W.E.B. Du Bois once called the "color line" is indeed a social and cultural construction, created to differentiate racial groups and to show the superiority or dominance of one race over another. Indeed, as Rosenblum and Travis (2000: 16-17) note:

> The term *race* first appeared in the Romance languages of Europe in the Middle Ages to refer to breeding stock. A "race" of horses described common ancestry and a distinctive appearance or behavior. *Race* appears to have been first applied to New World peoples by the Spanish in the 16th century. Later it was adopted by the English, again in reference to people of the New World, and generally came to mean "people," "nation," or "variety." By the late 18th century, when scholars became more actively engaged in investigations, classifications, and definitions of human populations, the term "race" was elevated as the one major symbol and mode of human group differentiation employed extensively for non-European groups. . . . [Thus] the idea of race emerged among all the European colonial powers, although their conceptions of it varied. However, only the British in North America and South Africa constructed a system of rigid, exclusive racial categories and a social order based on race, a "racialized social structure."

Pointing out, then, that "race continues to be one of the most salient and significant categories into which we place people in this society," James Jones, in his *Prejudice and Racism* (1997: 3) states, "We create these social categories, place people in them, and then treat members of the categories on the basis of the labels we have affixed to them."

How one is treated in these social categories depends on whether you belong to the "historically advantaged majorities" or the "historically disadvantaged minorities." It does not matter that these categories are "socially imagined and not biologically real categories." But because we continue to act as if these social categories are real and to associate people's colours with their "races," the concept of race has become real in its consequences. Thus, "whether or not 'black' people and 'white' people actually exist is not as important as the fact that human beings behave as if they do" (Allahar 1993: 39). So race becomes important because we make it important. Hence, "From the constructionist perspective, race exists because we have created it as a meaningful category of difference among people" (Rosenblum and Travis 2000: 18). It is a very powerful social force.

Indeed, few issues in our time have possessed such an overpowering impact upon the world as race. All over the world racial divisions, discrimination, and conflict have created problems for societies. In North America, race and its lingering effects of racism continue to be a grave source of advantage and disadvantage. Racism continues to operate under an ideology that justifies the dominance of one race over another (Mura 1999).

So, what do I mean by racism?

For the sake of my argument here, I will employ a number of definitions of racism. Specifically, I refer to racism as "the way that relations between [whites] and [Blacks] are organized such that Whiteness is perceived as normal and neutral while blackness stigmatizes groups and individuals as exceptional, problematic, exotic, or threatening" (Thompson 1997: 10). It presupposes a "belief in the inherent superiority of one race over all others and thereby the right to dominance" (Lorde 1992: 496).

Looking at the concept historically, Manning Marable (1992: 5) adds that racism is "a system of ignorance, exploitation, and power used to oppress African Americans . . . and other people on the basis of ethnicity, cultures, mannerisms, and color." Rooted in European global expansion that began in the late fifteenth century, it is the "ideology that considers a group's unchangeable physical characteristics to be linked in a direct, causal way to psychological or intellectual characteristics, and that on this basis distinguishes between superior and inferior racial groups" (Feagin and Feagin 1996: 7).

This singling out of groups on the basis of real and alleged physical characteristics has been used over time to connote the more common term *race*, and the approach has used colour and other physical characteristics to signify who is "inferior" or "superior." In other words, racism has meant:

281

an ideology promoting an uncritical acceptance, and negative social definitions of a group often identified by physical features (e.g., skin color); and is premised on the belief in the cultural and biological superiority of a particular racial group over others. Insofar as racism is supported by a system of inequality and oppression constructed within societies, it is more than individual; it is structural and institutional." (James 1995: 49)

In this regard, and viewed in the U.S. context, "Racism can be viewed as the socially organized set of attitudes, ideas, and practices that deny African Americans and other people of color the dignity, opportunities, freedoms, and rewards that this nation offers" (Feagin and Vera 1995: 7).

From these definitions of racism we can deduce two significant points: first, the belief of one group to be superior; and, second, the group that believes itself to be superior has the power to carry out its racist behaviour (Solorzano 1997). This it does, as David Wellman points out in his *Portraits of White Racism*, on an "advantage based on race." According to Wellman (1993: 4), "Regardless of its historically specific manifestations, racism today remains essentially what it has always been: a defense of racial privilege." In this regard, Frankenberg (1993b: 54) adds, "It is a position of structural advantage, associated with 'privileges' of the most basic kind, including, for example, higher wages, reduced chances of being impoverished, longer life, better access to healthcare, better treatment by the legal system, and so on."

These points take the position that racism is about institutional power and privilege. In this case, racism is not simply a matter of bigotry or prejudice, and that is where the problem arises. I believe that when whites say Blacks are racist, what they really mean is that Blacks are *prejudiced*. They consider prejudice and racism to be one and the same. I think there is a qualitative difference between the two, and they should not be confused or used interchangeably. What do I mean by prejudice here? I like the definition provided by Jones in his *Prejudice and Racism* (1997: 10). He defines prejudice as "a positive or negative attitude, judgment, or feeling about a person that is generalized from attitudes or beliefs held about the group to which the person belongs." This definition of prejudice is qualitatively different from the other various definitions of racism. If "racism is a system of power as well as of beliefs and actions, [and] through which the power and resources of a given society are distributed unequally and unjustly" (Mura 1999: 102), then it is not the same as prejudice (Codjoe 1998).

Is there such a thing as Canadian racism? You bet there is

What is interesting about the discussion of race relations and racism in Canada is its denial. There is a folk wisdom in Canada that holds the view that "we do not have a Black problem." We love our Black people here. There is no racial hostility. It's those nasty Americans who hate their Black people. As George Elliott Clarke (1998: 100-1) notes, "The most significant difference between Canada and the U.S. is, finally, that America has a race problem. In Canada, the party line goes, there are no racists save those who watch too much American television. Whenever some blatantly racist event transpires, the official line is to deny it." Most Blacks are still puzzled about how Canada has been able to maintain a reputation for tolerance and harmony when it comes to race relations. Even the Economic Council of Canada, in "Economic and Social Impacts of Immigration" (1991), published just before its closure in June 1992, concluded, "There is no significant discrimination against immigrants in general or coloured immigrants in particular" (quoted in Reitz 1993: 32). However, as J.G. Reitz and R. Breton (1994: v) say in the Foreword to their book *The Illusion of Difference: Realities of Ethnicity in Canada and the United States*, "Canadians think of themselves as being more tolerant of racial minorities, more welcoming of newcomers, more respectful of cultural differences than are their neighbours to the south." But, they note, this is more illusion than reality. As Stanley Barrett (1987: 307, 325) notes, "Racism in Canada has been institutionalized. . . . Racism in this country is as deeply rooted as that in the United States." Indeed, as Reitz and Breton contend, there may be only an illusion of difference between Canada and the United States when it comes to race relations. They point out:

> The general cultural differences between Canada and the United States imply differences of tone in ethnic and race relations in the two countries. The Canadian style is more low-key than the American; moreover, Canadians have a conscious tradition of tolerance that Americans do not have. *In terms of their effects on the experiences of minority groups, however, these differences are more apparent than real.* (1994: vi; emphasis added)

Like most Blacks in Canada I have experienced my share of Canadian racism. I have been through — several times — the ugly rite of passage every Black person has to go through in North America: being called a "nigger." These epithets hurt, but the most insidious one is the one called "smiling racism" or "quiet racism" (Chigbo 1989); and they say Canada is well known for this mode of racism because

283

"White Canada imagines itself to be congenial, hospitable, tolerant" (Clarke 1998: 101; see also Chigbo 1989). This racism is the covert type: "Persons making covert, racially biased decisions do not explicitly broadcast their intentions; instead, they veil them or provide reasons that society will find more palatable" (Scheurich and Young 1997: 5). I have heard many Blacks in Canada say they would prefer the American "no holds bared racism in your face" to Canada's "stab me behind my back racism." Whenever I think of my experiences of getting a job in Canada, I couldn't help but agree with the covert nature of Canadian racism.

When I left university to look for a job, I was armed with an undergraduate and two graduate degrees. I thought my job search would be easy. I was wrong. After failing in one province, I moved to another. It was still the same. I was so desperate that I took a job working in a restaurant. By the time I got my first interview for a position that befitted my educational qualifications, I had applied for and received rejection letters from more than two hundred positions. I kept every one of those letters. That period was the most difficult of all the years I have lived in Canada. It was a traumatic experience, one that I will never forget.

My first job was a temporary position. I believed the supervisor who hired me just took pity on me. In those job interviews I did everything that needed to be done. I spent money on polished resumés. I printed them on expensive paper. Maybe I spoke too softly at the interviews. I began to speak louder and clearer. Maybe I didn't look the interviewer straight in the face. I gazed. Maybe my handshake was not strong enough. I squeezed hard. Maybe I wasn't dressed well enough. With some help, I bought an expensive suit. Maybe I didn't ask enough questions. I bombarded my interviewers with questions. Nothing worked. Well, I couldn't help with my accent. That I could not change. What was it then? What was I not doing right? Nonetheless, I persisted.

My break came after two years of unemployment. I will never forget how I got that first full-time, permanent job. I had applied for the position the first time I saw it. It suited me well. It didn't ask for the ubiquitous "Canadian experience." It looked very good, I applied for it, and my application worked. I went for an interview. By that time I had been to so many job interviews that I had become a pro. I eased through the interview, so I thought. I felt good. A week or so later the rejection letter arrived. They had found a suitable candidate. A few days after, I saw the same job ad again. How could that be? Maybe it
didn't work out with the acceptable candidate, I thought. I applied

again. I am sure they recognized my resumé. I was called for an interview. The routine and questions were the same. The interviewers were the same. I felt confident. I had been down this road before. My handshake was unusually firm.

I anxiously awaited the good news this time. It did not come. Another rejection letter. *Tant pis*. Maybe next time. I continued to look. In a week or so, there it was again: the same job ad for which I had been rejected twice. I couldn't believe it. What was going on? So I applied again, though I debated that move this time. I was so desperate, almost two years without work, that I went for it. I thought this time I would not be called for an interview. They had seen enough of me. I was wrong. To my surprise, I was called again for an interview. It was the same supervisor of the unit and the same human resource personnel who met with me. The supervisor jokingly remarked about the number of times we had met.

The interview went fine. When I went home, I did something I had never done before. I wrote a letter to the supervisor. It went something like this:

> You have interviewed me several times for this job. Obviously, you deemed me qualified; otherwise you wouldn't be inviting me for interviews. The job calls for a graduate degree. I have two. You want a Canadian citizen or a landed immigrant. I have Canadian citizenship. True, I don't have experience, but the job says it's an entry one and does not specify much experience. What are you looking for exactly? What is it am I saying at the interview that does not convince you that I can do the job? I know I am qualified to do the job. I can do it. Just give me a chance to prove myself. You can always get rid of me if you think I am not up to it. I beg you to give me a chance to prove myself. That's all I am asking for. Please.

I prayed and mailed the letter. God answered my prayers. I made it. My two-year search for a job was over. When I reported to work the first day, the supervisor told me that it was my letter that finally made him hire me. Apparently, he had agonized over it. There was no doubt in my mind that had I been white, I would have had the job the first or second time. Meanwhile, I knew all my white classmates had landed jobs, even though I had better academic credentials. In fact, some were embarrassed to see me still looking for work. We all knew the reason, but couldn't say.

I know some readers might be sceptical of this story, but my case is not alone. I know many Africans and Black Canadians who have had a difficult time finding good work. These are people with   285 excellent academic credentials, and if it had not been for the colour of their skin they would have quickly become gainfully employed. My own brother, armed with an M.B.A., could not find work; in the end he settled for a job as a dishwasher. Indeed, considerable research and reporting document the racism and discrimination that Black Canadians suffer from in gaining employment, and detail the experiences of the many educated Black and Asian immigrants who end up in lowly jobs (see, for example, Henry 1994; Malarek 1985; Chigbo 1989; Ip 1988; Canadian Press 1994; Canada 1985). The instances of racist hiring practices are endemic in Canadian society. The systemic and substantial barriers to equality in employment are overwhelming.

Ironically, I had to move to the United States, considered by Canadians to be more racist, to get a job as director of a research institute. I know it would have been hard, if not impossible, to get such a job in Canada. My brother, too, had to move to the United States to find a job more commensurate with his graduate business education, and he now works as a vice-president with a major bank in New York City. He tried many times to land a position with a Canadian bank but never did receive an interview. I know many Canadians of African origin who have also moved to the United States and found meaningful work, which is a shame. As Africans, some of us have worked very hard to integrate and become Canadian. Yet we were always racially defined as the "other." No matter how much we tried, it appears that the standards for full membership as a Canadian are still related to whiteness.

Canada's "smiling racism" was with me until the very day I left the country. The realtor who showed our house to prospective buyers quietly hinted that if I wanted my house to sell quickly, I would have to remove all traces of anything that indicated that Blacks had lived in the house: no family pictures, no African art or crafts, everything Black or African must go, and we must be out of the house before he showed the house to prospective buyers. He would call and let us know. No matter what we were doing, we must leave. One time we were late in getting out and we ended up hiding in our minivan in the garage. When he showed the garage, we ducked. It was a shameful and degrading experience. The house sold, but my wife and I never did meet the family that bought it. What this and other experiences taught me is best summed up by L. Steinhorn and B. Diggs-Brown (1999: 78): "What is so corrosive for Blacks is that there is no escaping these racial indignities. No matter how much you've accomplished, no matter how wealthy you may be, no matter how many people you employ, presumptions are made about you that are based solely on the colour of your skin."

You bet there is racism in Canada. Poll after poll has shown that Canadians are not really tolerant of people who are not white, and that, on the contrary, they are a "systematically racist people whose very institutions are exclusive" (Paris 1995). This is well documented (see, for example, Bolaria and Li 1985; Barrett 1987; Cannon 1995; Hill 1981; Canada, House of Commons 1984; James and Shadd 1994; Lewis 1992; James 1999; McKague 1991; Reitz and Bretton 1994; Sher 1983; Sunahara 1981; Henry et al. 1995).

So, is there such a thing as Black racism?

Show me a white Canadian who has to go through what I and many African Canadians go through finding work, and I will tell you there is no such thing as Black racism. When Tatum (1997: 10) is asked in her workshops on race relations, "Can people of colour be racist?" she replies, "The answer depends on your definition of racism." She continues:

> If one defines racism as racial prejudice, the answer is yes. People of color can and do have racial prejudices. However, if one defines racism as a system of advantage based on race, the answer is no. People of color are not racist because they do not systematically benefit from racism. And equally important, there is no systematic cultural and institutional support or sanction for the racial bigotry of people of color. In my view, reserving the term "racist" only for behaviors committed by whites in the context of a white-dominated society is a way of acknowledging the ever-present power differential afforded whites by the culture and institutions that make up the system of advantage and continue to reinforce notions of white superiority.

I also share the view expressed by Feagin and Vera (1995: x):

> What is often referred to as "black racism" consists of judgments made about Whites by some black leaders or commentators to the effect that "no White people can be trusted" or "the White man is the devil." But these critical ideas or negative prejudices are not the equivalent of modern White racism. The latter involves not just individual thoughts but also widely socialized ideologies and omnipresent practices based on entrenched racialized beliefs. The prejudice and myths used to justify anti-black actions are not invented by individual perpetrators, nor are they based on personal experience. These patterns of highly racialized thought are embedded in the culture and institutions of a White-centered society.

287

Whites who say Blacks are racist tend to view or define racism in individual terms and to treat bias among Blacks as if it were fundamentally more fearsome than bias among whites. But this is a weak argument. It is a limited and narrow definition of racism. Seeing racism as a form of prejudice is not sufficient if we correctly conceptualize racism as "institutional and structural," that is, as "a network of traditions, legitimating standards, material and institutional arrangements, and ideological apparatuses that, together, serve to perpetuate hierarchical social relations based on race" (Thompson 1997: 9). This means that it is wrong to restrict our understanding of racism to an individualized arena, because that approach serves as a barrier to a broader and more comprehensive understanding of the phenomenon. Racism is more than a matter of individual prejudice and scattered episodes of discrimination (James 1995; Mura 1999; Feagin and Vera 1995).

Believe me, there is no such thing as Black racism

Deep inside, whites know that Blacks have a hard time, but will not acknowledge it. I am sure my white friends knew that the problems I had finding work had to do with race. Now, don't get me wrong. I have known whites who have also had a hard time finding work. But their experiences pale in comparison to what many African Canadians go through on a daily basis. Sometimes, when I relate experiences of discrimination to white colleagues, they find it hard to believe. I am sure that there are Blacks who make up or exaggerate their personal experiences with racism. But I know it did not take my white classmates two years to find work. Some found work even before we graduated.

Again, the racism most Blacks face is structural and institutional. The barriers that are erected when Africans look for work are prime examples. Let's take the issue of "Canadian experience." Many of us were born outside of Canada and so have no "Canadian experience" when we apply for work. In my case, I came to Canada when I was young. I had never worked before. But when it came time to look for work, I knew my accent would be a problem. In fact, I was told so by many. There was really nothing I could do about it. I have known some African friends who tried very hard to get rid of their African accents. Indeed, some tried so hard it would be difficult to tell they were African if you were speaking to them on the telephone. Yet, they tell me, when they show up for job interviews, employers are shocked to find they are Black, but not before they remark how well they speak

English. It is always a no-win situation. According to Grace-Edward Galabuzi, a Ugandan immigrant and former co-ordinator of the Toronto-based Alliance for Employment Equity, "Blacks suffer from discrimination in employment," but "Africans suffer more than most because of their accent." This structural barrier "is further compounded by the stereotypical image of Africans as primitive and incompetent." Consequently, according to Galabuzi, "The majority end up working at menial jobs because they are excluded from jobs commensurate with their qualifications" (quoted in Chigbo 1989: 438).

I know many whites would not trade places with Blacks. This reminds me of a *Nightline* program I watched several years ago. It was a segment on racial division in America. Whites who moments earlier had denied that racism was a problem finally conceded that being Black might be more difficult than being white. One man remarked, "I'd rather be white. It's easier. I admit that it's easier to be white. I admit that Blacks got a bad hand dealt to them." When the moderator asked them how much compensation they would seek if they were to change from white to Black, one said, "I would take $50 million, then I could live anywhere. I wouldn't have to deal with any racism" (quoted in Berger 1999: 12).

That story goes to show "the value that White people place on their own skins. Indeed, to be White is to possess a gift whose value can be appreciated only after it is taken away" (quoted in Mura 1999: 125-26). Black comedian Chris Rock captured this in a monologue: "There ain't no White man in this room that will change places with me — and I'm rich! That's how good it is to be White. There's a one-legged busboy in here right now that's going: 'I don't want to change. I'm gonna ride this White thing out and see where it takes me'" (Harmon 2000). "Whiteness," as a research respondent told Frankenberg (1993b: 51), is "a privilege enjoyed but not acknowledged, a reality lived in but unknown."

So believe me when I say there is no such thing as Black racism. If we understand racism as structural, then it's difficult to say Blacks can be racist. At the same time, I would be foolish and dishonest to say that some Blacks do not harbour any hostilities towards whites. But to say that whites are as vulnerable to Black prejudice as Blacks are to white racism is stretching it. Those experiences cannot be the same. Race and racism are far more powerful in determining the life chances of Blacks than they are for whites. I can say that Black prejudice or so-called racism towards whites is not pervasive.

I don't believe that as Blacks we have the power and wherewithal 289 to discriminate and oppress whites. Whites who never live through the daily inconvenience and degradation of being Black don't fully and perhaps never will understand how profoundly different the Black daily experience is from theirs. Notes Marian Wright Edelman in her book *The Measure of Our Success: A Letter to My Children and Yours*: "It is utterly exhausting being Black — physically, mentally, and emotionally. . . . There is no respite or escape from your badge of colour" (quoted in Feagin and Sikes 1995: 3). No white person in North America can say with honesty that they have suffered in such ways because of "black racism." Blacks are still far more likely than whites to identify race discrimination as a pervasive problem in North American society. The lengths to which many whites will go to avoid intimate contact with anything Black show how Blacks have been stereotyped and demonized as a people.

The notion of "Black racism" is, therefore, a contradiction in terms. More than most groups in North America, Blacks bear the stigma of "the savage" and "continue to be seen as an inferior species, not only unsuited for equality but not even meriting a chance to show their worth. White immigrants only hours off the boat, while in some cases subjected to scorn, are allowed to assert their superiority to Blacks" (Hacker 1992: 14). This has always been the case.

Blacks don't make up the stories of oppression. They are real. They are not fantasies. But instead of being avoided, or ignored — instead of constantly running up against the brick wall of silence — racism must be acknowledged, confronted, and talked about. There must be understanding and respect for the diversity of Canadian society. There is so much we can all do together as Canadians to make this world a better place for all. To paraphrase Martin Luther King, Jr., we should all be judged by the content of our character and not by the colour of our skins. It may be a dream, but it is a dream worth fighting for.

"Why Are Black People So Angry?" The Question of Black Rage

●●●●●●●●●●●●●●●●●●●●●●●●●●●●

Adrienne Shadd

In *"Where Are You Really From? Notes of an 'Immigrant' from North Buxton, Ontario,"* I deal with the question of identity as an African Canadian — that is, someone of African descent whose ancestry extends back five generations. Written over six years ago, the description of what people go through when they dare to identify themselves as a "Black Canadian" comes across as something of an annoyance (I use the term "psychologically taxing"), just one of the things one routinely has to put up with as a Black and a Canadian. But what are the implications of the Black Canadian constructed as "other," as foreigner, immigrant, or criminal, for those of us who live it every day?

Here I want to look further at the ramifications of this construction of blackness, which go far deeper and are rarely discussed: anger — rage, if you will — how it gets expressed and is sometimes unexpressed, sublimated, or turned inward. I want to look at how rage has and has not become part of this construction of Black identity that we must carry with us.

★ ★ ★

At the "Writing Thru Race" conference in Vancouver in 1994, I encountered, by implication, this very question. The evening sessions of the conference were devoted to readings in which poets, novelists, playwrights, and writers of all stripes treated the audience to their latest musings, published and unpublished. For me these sessions were the most riveting of the conference, offering much that was thought-provoking and passionate to what was already an unprecedented colloquium. One woman read prose entirely in Hindi, so that the audience might hear the beauty of her untranslated tongue. Another writer punctuated his poem with Arabic chants. Yet another woman paid poetic tribute to the Filipino workers who overpopulate the hotel and restaurant industry in low-paying service positions. Many of the Black writers, in prose, poetry, and drama, railed against the sting of racism in their lives.

In the plenary session, when we split into small groups to discuss what might come out of this conference in terms of a political agenda for writers of colour in Canada, one person commented that he was shocked at how angry Black writers were. On his very face you could see a kind of fear of the implications of this anger. Perhaps it was a generalized fear of Black people. I wasn't sure.

At the time I was frankly shocked by his response, especially the sense of fear. Surely, Black people talking about racism and how it made them feel was not any big revelation. Personally, I had not even registered any particular anger on the part of these writers. Were they really that angry, or were they simply describing their experiences of racism and declaring the injustice of it all in a relatively calm and matter of fact way? I hadn't particularly noticed.

When I think about it now, however, I have to admit that Black people are angry. We have always been angry, and we will continue to be angry in a context in which we are made to feel inferior and treated as such. In bygone days anger had to be carefully hidden because it could have tragic life and death consequences. In 1734, for instance, a slave woman named Marie-Joseph Angélique was put on trial for arson in the burning down of the home of her mistress. The fire had gone on to cause the destruction of a good part of the city of Montreal. Angélique had supposedly set fire to the house's attic because she had heard that her mistress wanted to sell her off to the West Indies. During the course of her trial, several witnesses claimed that she had made threats towards her mistress, saying that if she were ever sold, her mistress would repent. Still, nobody actually saw her commit the crime. After two months of testimony and cross-examination of the defendant, Marie-Joseph Angélique was convicted and sentenced to be executed.[1]

I believe that she did utter many of the statements attributed to her, and that she paid with her life because of them. Witnesses were able to paint her as an uppity, angry, vengeful bondswoman capable of arson, based on these alleged statements. The tragic saga of Marie-Joseph Angélique is a classic example of what can happen if rage is exhibited openly. In a judicial system that was generally lenient towards women, she was one of only a few women put to death in all of New France's history (Carrigan 1991: 440-43).

African Canadians learned, over the years, to keep their anger in check. Stanley Grizzle's (1998: 67) memoir of his days as a sleeping-car porter in the 1940s and 50s is typical: "Some porters were a study in controlled anger during their work shifts, always angry. And they would simmer during those shifts — for this was a job where, every day, you were made to feel that you were beneath the passengers." This anger was not visible to the passengers and company management, to be sure, but the porters themselves were aware of it. It was palpable to them. In the eyes of the travelling public they had to appear as professional, courteous, and happy with their position in life. Behind the mask, however, it was a different matter entirely.

With the advent of the Black Power movement in the United States, and the modern-era riots, the image of the happy, carefree "darkie" seems to have been replaced with one far more threatening and recalcitrant. Nowadays, Black youth, especially young men, tend to be portrayed as menacing thugs and criminals, quick to hurt you if you look at them sideways. When a particularly egregious case of racial injustice occurs — often involving police shootings — Blacks are shown on the streets, shouting, with picket signs. The portrayal of the angry Black person seems to have replaced the older stereotypes in the media.

If this is true, then why the shock on the part of the person at the "Writing Thru Race" conference? Perhaps it is an issue of class. Maybe the working-class Black, struggling to make ends meet, is the one expected to be angry, or dispossessed youth, or the homeless, or welfare recipients — Marx's lumpenproletariat. Perhaps these are the people expected to be enraged with the system, surely not the educated, middle class, and successful, and not the writer, whose literary gift has afforded him or her a privileged location in the vertical mosaic of racial/class/gender hierarchy in Canada. Doesn't middle-class position go a long way towards mediating — even eradicating — the more base realities of racism and discrimination?

Absolutely not, argues Ellis Cose in *The Rage of a Privileged Class* (1995). According to Cose, it is precisely the African American middle class, whose educations and achievements should have entitled them to all the rewards and privileges of the American dream, who are particularly angry. Cose interviewed countless highly successful professionals and captains of the corporate world and found that they felt slighted, disrespected, cheated out of opportunities routinely granted their white counterparts, and generally lacking the full entitlements that their educations and careers would lead them to expect.

Here in Canada, it is no different. Among just about everyone I know, the topic of race and racism is never far from our lips, and the anger and resentment are welled deep in our hearts. Several years ago, for instance, I interviewed a woman who had forged a career in nursing in Canada. She was one of the first Black nurses to be allowed to train in a Canadian hospital, and over the years she had moved into a position of relative prominence in the nursing field.[2] Her experiences with racism had been so painful that she could not bear to discuss them with me, and told me so. Those experiences had occurred over thirty years earlier, but Blacks continue to experience some of the same insults and indignities. I know people who have had to lodge grievances with their unions or professional associations, in disputes with their employers. I even had a friend who went to the Human Rights Commission. While the issue of racial discrimination could not always be proven, it was always believed to be a factor in these situations. Even so, no one has yet studied the phenomenon of pent-up rage in the Black community. We have had to rely on our activists, and our writers, to inform the public.

In 1994 writer Dionne Brand issued a collection of essays, *Bread out of Stone*, which target Canadian racism and sexism and the myriad ways in which we, as Black folks, Black women, are subjected to them. The book stands as a brilliantly written collection and chronicle of how an intelligent, perceptive person of colour views the issues, and the pieces are dead-on in their perceptions. Critics, though, were clearly annoyed with the book and did not take kindly to the angry tone of Brand's writing. Philip Marchand of *The Toronto Star* wrote that the essays were "bitterly censorious attacks on her ideological foes" (quoted in Martin 1997: 70). Even Andre Alexis, an African Canadian writer who reviewed the book, decided that the collection was "narrow, ungenerous and self-serving" (Alexis 1995: C19).

But is it not traditionally the writers who feel an obligation to pull back the cloak of oppression — like the magician's cloth — and reveal the injustices for all to see? In speaking of her experiences at a Caribbean Writers Conference at Wellesley College in Massachusetts, Brand (1998: 91) uncloaks some of her impatience at and disdain for how Canadians have viewed her work:

I have plans to talk myself on "Poetry and Politics." . . . It is probably not even necessary to say "poetry and politics" as if these words are distinct, but I've become so used to explaining and explaining their dependency on each other to Canadian reviewers and audiences that I've forgotten that it is unnecessary here. One thing you do not have to do at a Caribbean writers' conference, or perhaps any writers' conference outside Canada, is explain that writers mean to change the world.

Perhaps the real reason that the delegate at the "Writing Thru Race" conference was so shocked by the Black writers' anger is that people do not expect to see Black rage in the Canadian context. It is easier to accept the American or Caribbean Black as angry, but it is just not conceivable in Canada. Other Canadians have so readily bought into this myth of Canada as a multicultural nirvana that, despite everything, so the myth goes, this is a pretty darn great country we live in. There are incidents of prejudice to be sure, but down and dirty racism, embedded in the fabric of the society and its institutions? Not here.

The problem is that historically Canada (that is, its two "founding nations") — in its conquest and near genocide of Aboriginal peoples, its enslavement and oppression of African people, its denial of rights and discrimination against other minorities such as the Chinese and Japanese — has defined itself as a site of white Western (albeit anti-American) Europeanness. Thus, the long history of settlement of African people, for example, and their rightful place as makers of Canada have been denied in favour of a construction of blackness as recent, as "other." As Canadian cultural theorist David Sealy (2000: 98) points out, "The implication of this construction of Canadian identity for hegemonic constructions of Black identity is revealing: it's impossible to be both Black and Canadian at the same time, since Canada is imagined either as a place without Black people, or where the few Blacks there are well-behaved, even apolitical."

In *Under the Gaze: Learning to Be Black in White Society*, Jennifer Kelly (1998: 37) cites Stuart Hall's observation that nation states are not just political entities, but that they also produce meanings from which national identities are shaped. Thus she demonstrates how the Canadian national identity as white and European has been purposefully constructed over time through control of our national myths, historiography, immigration policy, and especially the exclusion of Africans and other peoples of colour from the select group of those considered to be our cultural producers. (Even Canadian jazz great Oscar Peterson achieved international icon status only after

295

touring the United States with the famous U.S. impresario Norman Ganz.)

Thus, for example, Kelly (1998: 37) argues:

> The way in which maps of meanings are constructed often relates to the way in which groups are included or excluded from a nation's history. . . . For African Canadians this idealization [of the nation's past] is reflected in the ways in which certain symbols such as the Underground Railway, protection of the Lion's paw and the guiding North Star came to indicate that the Canadian state was a haven for African Canadians fleeing the U.S.

So, to be more accurate, Black history has not been completely excluded from history textbooks. Rather, the mid-nineteenth-century fugitive slave era has been embraced (and all other history of Black people ignored) precisely because it has enabled the mythmakers to portray Canada as a haven for Black people in that period. After 1865 Black Canadians disappear from view. It is as if they have fallen off their precariously held perch on the edge of a steep Canadian cliff.

Yet Black people remain angry. But at what price? Randall Robinson, a respected lobbyist on African and Caribbean affairs in the United States, has written a memoir that courageously addresses the question of Black rage:

> From slavery, we have sublimated our feelings about white people. We have fought for our rights while hiding our feelings toward whites who tenaciously denied us those rights. We have even, I suspect, hidden those feelings from ourselves. It is how we have survived. Well-educated blacks have even been inculcated with the upper-stratum white distaste for excessive emotionalism. Black folk of my time talk about white people and their predilections at least once daily but never talk about or with anger. It seems unnatural. Where have we stored the pain and at what price? (Robinson 1998: 4)

In Canada Blacks are no less angry than they are in the United States. A part of that anger stems from that widespread notion that we are not supposed to be angry, that race relations are much better here than in the United States. (See the article here by Henry Martey Codjoe, who describes how he and his brother could barely get their foot in the occupational door in Canada. Now one is the director of a research institute in Georgia and the other a vice-president of a bank in New York.)

Blacks in Canada have many other things to be angry about. We are angry about having to fear that our children might be labelled as sub-intellects when they enter any given teacher's classroom. We have all heard horror stories about perfectly intelligent children being misplaced into slow learners' classes for no other reason than the colour of their skin. We are angry about how Africa is depicted in the media: there are never any positive stories about the continent, just the incessant pictures of starving children, warring tribes, and unforgiving landscapes. It is no accident that the stories are rarely presented by Africans themselves, but by the supposed do-gooder white liberals, who never tire of begging for our money to help these poor starving Africans. No one is saying that these projects should not exist, or that they are not beneficial to the children involved. But did anyone ever consider the impact of the images on Black children here? When our children ask us if all Africans are as poor and starving as the ones shown on television, it is a poignant moment for Black parents.

We are angry that studies still show that white job seekers get three times as many job offers as Black job seekers. We are angry that one of the new job ghettos for Blacks has changed from the railroad and domestic service to those annoying customer-service-representative positions. We are angry because of racial profiling — whether this has to do with questionable police shootings of unarmed Blacks, driving while Black, shopping while Black, breathing while Black . . . and we are angry, again, because we are constantly told that we are lucky to live in Canada, where our system respects people of all backgrounds and cultures. We know damn well that this hides a pernicious system of white privilege and white supremacy. Sure, things are certainly better than they used to be, but the anger still "caroms around in our psyches like jagged stones" (Robinson 1998: 4).

For me, it is the white ignorance and denial of systemic racism that galls me the most. Okay, racial injustice is one thing. But this widespread notion that we live in a meritocracy, as a neighbour of mine arrogantly informed me recently, this *really* burns me. What about all the evidence to the contrary: the old boys' network, the glass ceilings, the employment ghettos? If you cannot even see something that is so glaring to me, how can we exist in the same universe? Where is the common ground? And if I express outrage, am I perceived as someone who overreacts or sees racism around every corner?

Generally speaking, anger — specifically Black anger — is constructed as a destructive and futile emotion, to be feared and sublimated at all costs. Bell hooks (1995: 18-19) argues for the positive and constructive force of Black rage:

This one-dimensional misrepresentation of the power of rage helps

297

maintain the status quo. Censoring militant response to race and racism, it ensures that there will be no revolutionary effort to gather that rage and use it for constructive social change. Significantly, contemporary reinterpretations and critiques of Malcolm X seek to redefine him in a manner that strips him of rage as though this were his greatest flaw. Yet his "rage" for justice clearly pushed him towards greater and greater awareness. It pushed him to change. He is an example of how we can use rage to empower.

The profound and transformative power of Black rage is all around us. On a personal level, it can spur us to greater heights of success and achievement. No one can fail to be moved by the story of the 1930s Olympic runner Ray Lewis, who tells the story of two people — one a schoolteacher and the other a coach — in his hometown of Hamilton, Ontario:

> The coach didn't want me on his team, but I ran so fast, he had to put me on, and I became his number one man. The schoolteacher . . . spoke of me in a derogatory manner in front of a whole class in high school. My classmates gathered around me and said that this man had referred to me as a low down dirty nigger scum of the earth. . . . I went to the principal. He did nothing about it. He only had a second class apology. I never told my mother or father about it, because my father was a very good, quiet man. He was a gentleman and a gentle man, and he would have said to me, "Raymond, let's pray about it." And I didn't want to pray, I wanted to go out and kill that son of a bitch.

Yet Lewis, a Canadian school champion at age seventeen, an Olympic bronze medalist in 1932, and a silver medalist at the British Empire Games in 1934, was able to turn these deeply negative and humiliating experiences around through the positive utilization and power of his rage: "So these things made me angry. I was fifteen years old. But every time the gun went off at the start for the next . . . twelve years, I raced against those two men. That's why I have one hundred metals" (Hymn to Freedom 1994).

Collectively, the positive power of rage has meant that Blacks have been on the cutting edge of social change. Let us not forget that it was Blacks, in coalition with Jews, the labour movement, and others involved in social justice, who, in Ontario, spurred the passage of all the fair employment, fair accommodation, and human rights legislation that was passed in the 1950s and 1960s — legislation that today we take for granted (Gairy 1981; Grizzle 1998; Moore 1985; Shadd 1989; Walker 1997). But it was not until we protested unfair treatment in various aspects of our lives — the constructive utilization of rage — that the movement for civil rights in the province was begun. At a book launching in Toronto recently, community activists Akua Benjamin and Keren Braithwaite reminded the gathering that Blacks have been at the forefront of the movement towards equity in Canada. While the language and ideas of employment equity, and so forth, have become the mainstay of the academic and policy elite (leaving aside for the moment the right-wing backlash as represented in the Ontario provincial government and the emergence federally of the Canadian Alliance Party), these concepts, they argued, were introduced and pushed forward by African Canadians and others.

No, it is not Black anger or rage that worries me. Rather, it is the inability to become enraged. It is the turning in on oneself, the feelings of inadequacy or inferiority, the silencing of Black people, especially young Black people, and the channelling of this rage towards destructive activities that concern me. Why do so many young Blacks feel so disaffected? I have been told by more than one young person that neither they nor any of their friends vote in Canadian elections, whether at the federal, provincial, or municipal levels. They simply don't feel there is anything in it for them. And why, too, are disproportionate numbers of Black youth engaged in criminal activities? Again, Robinson (1998: 3-4) grapples with the different ways in which deep-seated anger gets expressed, or sadly misdirected, in the United States: "Hidden deep anger. We don't acknowledge it. We don't direct or aim it. But it is there. Spin the cannon. When it points threateningly outward, even white liberals dismiss us to a perimeter of irrelevance or worse. When it points inward, white conservatives find in our self-hate praiseworthiness."

Does this mean that, in the coming years, today's youth will be increasingly silenced, or, rather, will they be increasingly angry and intolerant of mistreatment? I believe it is our job as Black parents to ensure that our children become angry. We must teach them to recognize unfairness and injustice and to confront and expose those blights every step of the way. Anger must become a normal part of our identity as African people, part of the natural armour we carry around with us. Anything else would be counterproductive, abnormal. This is our particular challenge for the twenty-first century. Yes, I think Black rage is a good thing.

Notes

1 Incendie de Montreal, Procedure criminelle contre Marie-Joseph Angélique, TL4, S1 074-4136, Archives Judiciaires de Montréal, Archives Nationales du Québec, Centre de Montréal. Although a five-year-old niece of the widow de Francheville testified on the very last day of the trial that she had seen Angélique take a scoop of embers up to the attic just before the fire broke out, this testimony must be viewed as highly suspect. Because children are highly suggestible and easily influenced, her appearance at the very end of the two-month trial, after all the other witnesses, and with little else linking Angélique to the crime, is simply not believable.

2 Because of Canada's unofficial policy of racial segregation, until after World War II Blacks could not train as nurses, and Black doctors were denied hospital privileges in several cities. As a result, African Canadians interested in pursuing careers in the medical field were forced to train in the United States at Black colleges, and they usually had to remain in the United States after graduating.

INTERROGATIONS

•••••••••••••••••••••••

STEPHEN PATEL

As if my room were an asylum of memory
where the walls, peppered with ears and hollowed faces
were an audience listening to me.
Loud and in rant
my voice reeking of frustration,
my eyes closing in a fury
remembering familiar choruses,
questions interrogating my body
like a sea of prodding fingers.
There, my voices trembling with rage would say

It's been one too many times I've been asked
What are you? Where are you from?
Too many times I've responded
Canadian, Trinidadian, Indian, a human being.
Maybe I'm an alien, a mix' up misfit
socially misread and categorized incorrectly
shelved, conveniently, in that Other category.
It's been one too many times I've been a fraction
my racial identity never enough,
always a petty portion.
You have a Hindu name. Did you change your given name?

What's the matter? Your first name too complicated for Canadians?
Aren't you Indian? Isn't India your homeland?
What do you know about the West Indies?
Isn't that lucky money? But you're not Chinese.

What are you?
The question surfaces from the vortex of lights
I see rally rags and kaiso tents, tassas, tablas and steel pan
the Nina, Pinta, the Santa Maria
All this, as I tumble onto the shores of Maracas Bay
wielding a cutlass in one hand
a maple leaf in the Other.

So you is a . . .
A dogla Chinee, a English duck or a whitewash ugly ducklin';
a whitenized coolie with good, straight hair
with nappy hair or with a pressed head, a relaxed head.

What is your nationality?
In the Great White North
among the lumpy rapids — the fresh water frenzy:
A refugee, a damn illegal immigrant,
a stupid Paki, or an immigrant for sure.
To the class conscious Canadians:
The doughnut dunking trailer park trash,
an illegitimate citizen packed for the periphery.

What are you?
A taxi driver with an immigrant degree
badgered by: Speak slower.
Is that English you're speaking?
or icantunderstandawordyoujustsaid.

I must be . . .
The idiot who vacuums your office carpets,
who throws your curbside trash away,
who sanitizes your toilets,
who clears your dinner table and washes your dishes,
who pliantly holds your bleached towels while
you absolve your tidy hands of my misfortunes.

What are you?
The massala boy toy pursuing purity
in an arranged marriage;
302   the western professor of the Kama Sutra

unravelling the secrets of Eastern cultures;
the bad John, the saga boy, the baby father,
the oversexed sex machine, the drug dealer
the lazy spliff smoking slacker, the bank robber,
the good ball-player, the clean-cut doctor, the mathematician.
What did you take in school? You look like a science major.

Back in my room, I gain my voice, and I speak
back to your ears peppered along my asylum walls.
Do you know what I am?
Can you hear what I am before you see me?
Is rage my constant monologue?
Will I ever be able to stare at your hollowed faces without
a barrage of questions?
Will I ever escape your colonizing imagination,
your insults, your laughters?

It's been one too many times
I haven't been Indian enough, Black enough;
certainly I've never been Chinese enough,
neither Trinidadian enough, nor Canadian enough.
When will you be able to look at me
beyond the straightness of my hair,
the darkness of my skin, the thickness of my eyebrows,
the roundness of my face, or the angles of my eyes.
When will this interrogation stop?

REFERENCES

Alexis, Andre. 1995. "Taking a Swipe at Canada." *The Globe and Mail*, Jan. 7, 1995.

Allahar, A.L. 1993. "When Black First Became Worth Less." *International Journal of Comparative Sociology*, 34,1-2: 39-55.

Anderson, Benedict. 1983. *Imagined Communities*. New York: Verso.

Anderson, Grace and David Higgs. 1976. *A Future to Inherit: The Portuguese Communities of Canada*. Toronto: McClelland & Stewart.

Anzaldua, Gloria. 1987. *Borderlands/La Frontera: The New Mestiza*. San Francisco: Aunt Lute Books.

Apple, Michael. 1993. "Series Editor's Introduction." In *Race, Identity and Representation in Education*, ed. C. McCarthy and W. Crichlow. New York: Routledge.

Armstrong, Luanne. 1992. "Being White." *Tessera*, 12 (Summer).

Arnold, Rick, Bev Burke, Carl James, D'Arcy Martin, and Barb Thomas. 1991. *Educating for a Change*. Toronto: Between the Lines.

Asian Dub Foundation (rock band). 2000. *Community Music*. London: London Records.

Azoulay, Gibel Katya. 1997. *Black, Jewish and Interracial: It's Not the Color of Your Skin but the Race of Your Kin, and Other Myths of Identity*. Durham, N.C.: Duke University Press.

Bannerji, Himani. 1995. "But Who Speaks for Us? Experience and Agency in Conventional Feminist Paradigms." In *Thinking*

Through: Essays on Feminism, Marxism, and Anti-Racism. Toronto: The Women's Press.

Bannerji, Himani, Linda Carty, Kari Dehli, Susan Heald, and Kate McKenna. 1991. *Unsettling Relations: The University as a Site of Feminist Struggles.* Toronto: Women's Press.

Barbosa, Manuel. 1978. *Luta Pela Democrácia nos Açores.* Coimbra, Portugal: Centelha.

Barndt, Deborah. 1993. "Putting Ourselves into the Picture: Recovering History through Images and Stories." Unpublished notes for talk to Critical Pedagogy Series. Toronto: Ontario Institute for Studies in Education (OISE), Feb. 17.

Barrett, S.R. 1987. *Is God a Racist? The Right Wing in Canada.* Toronto: University of Toronto Press.

Barth, Frederik. 1969. *Ethnic Groups and Boundaries.* Prospect Heights, Ill.: Waveland Press.

Bawumia. M. 1995. "Racism and Economic Development." *Review of Human Factor Studies,* 1,1: 91-98.

Berger, M. 1999. *White Lies: Race and the Myths of Whiteness.* New York: Farrar, Straus, Giroux.

Bergeron, Léandre. 1971. *The History of Quebec: A Patriote's Handbook.* Toronto: NC Press.

Bolaria, B.S. and P. Li, eds. 1985. *Racial Oppression in Canada.* Toronto: Garamond Press.

Bourdieu, Pierre and Terry Eagleton. 1992. "Doxa and Common Life." *New Left Review,* 191: 111-21.

Bramble, Maxine. 2000. "Being Me in the Academy." In *Experiencing Difference,* ed. C.E. James. Halifax: Fernwood Publishing.

Brand, Dionne. 1998. *Bread out of Stone.* Toronto: Vintage Canada.

Breitman, G., ed. 1965. *Malcolm X Speaks: Selected Speeches and Statements.* New York: Ballantine Books.

Britt, D. 2000. "Gore Manager's Dig Contained Kernel of Truth." *The Washington Post,* Jan. 21: B01.

Brodkin, Karen. 1998. *How Jews Became White Folks and What That Says about Race in America.* New Brunswick, N.J.: Rutgers University Press.

Busia, A.P.A. 1998. "Re:Locations — Rethinking Britain from Accra, New York, and the Map Room of the British Museum." In *Multicultural States: Rethinking Difference and Identity,* ed. D. Bennett. New York: Routledge.

Canada. 1985. *Employment Equity: A Response to the Abella Commission of Inquiry on Equality in Employment.* Ottawa.

Canada. House of Commons. 1984. *Equality Now! Report of the Spe-*

cial Committee on Participation of Visible Minorities in Canadian Society. Ottawa: Queen's Printer.

Canadian Press. 1994. "Educated Immigrants End up in Lowly Jobs." *The Edmonton Journal*, July 31: A8.

Cannon, M. 1995. *The Invisible Empire: Racism in Canada*. Toronto: Random House of Canada.

Carrigan, Owen. 1991. *Crime and Punishment in Canada: A History*. Toronto: McClelland & Stewart.

Cherney, Elena. 1998. "Who Is a Jew? City's Jewish Community Is an Island of Tradition in a Sea of Assimilation." *The Gazette* (Montreal), May 2: B1-B2.

Chigbo, O. 1989. "Land of 'Smiling Racism': Canada's Image as a Racially Tolerant Society Is a Myth." *West Africa*, March 20-26: 438.

Christensen, C.P. and M. Weinfeld. 1993. "The Black Family in Canada: A Preliminary Exploration of Family Patterns and Inequality." *Canadian Ethnic Studies*, 25,3: 26-44.

Clarke, G.E. 1998. "White Like Canada." *Transition*, Issue 73, 7,1: 98-109.

Codjoe, H.M. 1994. "Black Nationalists Beware! You Could Be Called a Racist for Being 'Too Black and African.'" In *Talking about Difference: Encounters in Culture, Language and Identity*, ed. Carl E. James and Adrienne Shadd. Toronto: Between the Lines.

____. 1998. "Race and Economic Development: Some Historical and Contemporary Perspectives." *Review of Human Factor Studies*, 4,2: 88-113.

Cose, Ellis. 1995. *The Rage of a Privileged Class*. New York: Harper-Perennial.

Creese, Gillian. 1999. *Contracting Masculinity: Gender, Class, and Race in a White-Collar Union, 1944-1994*. Toronto: Oxford University Press.

Daniels, R. 1999. "Hating Whitey: The Myth of Black Racism." www.black-collegian.com/african/Whitey1299.shtml.

Davis, Mike. 1999. "Magical Urbanism: Latinos Reinvent the US Big City." *New Left Review*, 234: 3-43.

De Figueiredo, Antonio. 1975. *Portugal: Fifty Years of Dictatorship*. Middlesex, U.K.: Penguin Books.

De Melo, João. 1991. *Gente Feliz com Lágrimas*. Lisboa: Dom Quixote.

D'Souza, D. 1995. *The End of Racism: Principles for a Multicultural Society*. New York: The Free Press.

Elliott, Jean Leonard and Augie Fleras. 1993. *Unequal Relations: An*

Introduction to Race and Ethnic Dynamics in Canada. Scarborough, Ont.: Prentice- Hall.

Errante Antoinette. 2000. "But Sometimes You're Not Part of the Story: Oral History and Ways of Remembering and Telling." *Educational Researcher*, 29,2: 16-27.

Essed, Philomena. 2000. "Dilemmas in Leadership: Women of Colour in the Academy." *Ethnic and Racial Studies*, 23,5: 888-904.

Feagin, J.R. and C.B. Feagin. 1996. *Racial and Ethnic Relations.* 5th ed. Upper Saddle River, N.J.: Prentice-Hall.

Feagin, J.R. and H. Vera. 1995. *White Racism: The Basics.* New York: Routledge.

Feagin, J.R. and M.P. Sikes. 1994. *Living with Racism: The Black Middle-Class Experience.* Boston: Beacon Press.

Fentress, J. and C. Wickham. 1992. *Social Memory.* Oxford: Blackwell.

Foster, Cecil. 1996. *A Place Called Heaven: The Meaning of Being Black in Canada.* Toronto: HarperCollins.

Frankenberg, R. 1993a. *White Women, Race Matters: The Social Construction of Whiteness.* Minneapolis: University of Minnesota Press.

____. 1993b. "Growing up White: Feminism, Racism and the Social Geography of Childhood." *Feminist Review*, 45: 51-84.

Frederickson, G.M. 1997. "America's Caste System: Will It Change?" www.nybooks.com/nyrev.WWWfeatdisplay.cgi?1997102368R.

Freire, Paulo. 1973. *Pedagogy of the Oppressed.* New York: Seabury.

Frye Jacobson, Mathew. 1995. *Special Sorrows: The Diasporic Imagination of Irish, Polish, and Jewish Immigrants in the United States.* Cambridge, Mass.: Harvard University Press.

____. 1998. *Whiteness of a Different Colour: European Immigrants and the Alchemy of Race.* Cambridge, Mass.: Harvard University Press.

Gikandi, Simon. 1996. *Maps of Englishness: Writing Identity in the Culture of Colonialism.* New York: Columbia University Press.

Gilman, Sander. 1994. "Dangerous Liaisons: Black Jews, Jewish Blacks, and the Vagaries of Racial Definition." *Transition*, 64: 41-52.

Gilroy, Paul. 1993. *Black Atlantic: Modernity and Double Consciousness.* Cambridge, Mass.: Harvard University Press.

Globe and Mail, The. 1976. "Even PQ Stunned by Victory." Nov. 16: A1.

Goldberg, D.T. 1997. *Racial Subjects: Writing on Race in America.*

New York: Routledge.

Goulbourne, Michelle. 1993. "Perceptions of Schooling, Self-Structure and Depression: A Study of Immigrant and Non-immigrant African-Canadian Adolescents." Unpublished paper, Department of Sociology, McMaster University, Hamilton, Ont.

Graveline, Fyre Jean. 1998. *Circleworks: Transforming Eurocentric Consciousness*. Halifax: Fernwood Publishing.

Grizzle, Stanley. 1998. *My Name's Not George: The Story of the Brotherhood of Sleeping Car Porters: Personal Reminiscences of Stanley G. Grizzle*. Toronto: Umbrella Press.

Haas, Jack and William Shaffir. 1991. *Becoming Doctors: The Adoption of a Cloak of Competence*. Greenwich, Conn.: JAI Press.

Hacker, A. 1992. *Two Nations: Black and White, Separate, Hostile, Unequal*. New York: Charles Scribner's Sons.

Haig-Brown, Celia. 2000. "Moving into Difference (with Echo)." In *Experiencing Difference*, ed. C.E. James. Halifax: Fernwood Publishing.

Hall, Stuart. 1990. "Cultural Identity and Diaspora." In *Identity, Community, Culture and Difference*, ed. J. Rutherford. London: Lawrence Wishart.

____. 1991. "The Local and Global: Globalization and Ethnicity." In *Culture, Globalization, and the World World-System*, ed. A. King. Binghampton, N.Y.: SUNY.

Harmon, A. 2000. "A Limited Partnership — How Race Is Lived in America." www.nytimes.com/library/national/race/061400harmon-net.html.

Henry, F. 1994. *The Caribbean Diaspora in Toronto: Learning to Live with Racism*. Toronto: University of Toronto Press.

Henry, F., C. Tator, W. Mattis, and T. Rees. 1995. *The Colour of Democracy: Racism in Canadian Society*. Toronto: Harcourt Brace & Company, Canada.

Hill, Donna, ed. 1981. *A Black Man's Toronto: The Reminiscences of Harry Gairey*. Toronto: Multicultural History Society of Ontario.

hooks, bell. 1992. *Black Looks: Race and Representation*. Toronto: Between the Lines.

____. 1995. *Killing Rage: Ending Racism*. New York: Henry Holt.

Hymn to Freedom. 1994. Part III, *Ontario: A History Buried*. Documentary film, Almeta Speaks Productions.

Ignatieff, Noel. 1995. *How the Irish Became White*. New York: Routledge.

Ip, G. 1988. "Jobless Doctor Taking Case to Rights Panel." *The Globe and Mail*, Dec. 29.

Iseke-Barnes, Judy. 2000. "En/Countering Stereotypes, and Gathering in Educational Institutions." In *Experiencing Difference*, ed. C.E. James. Halifax: Fernwood Publishing.

James, Carl E. 1994. "The Paradox of Power and Privilege: Race, Gender and Occupational Position." *Canadian Woman Studies Journal*, 14,2 (Spring): 47-51.

____. 1995. "Reverse Racism": Students' Response to Equity Programs. *Journal of Professional Studies*, 3,1.

____. 1999. *Seeing Ourselves: Exploring Race, Ethnicity and Culture.* Toronto: Thompson Educational Publishing.

____, ed. 2000. *Experiencing Difference*. Halifax: Fernwood Publishing.

James, Carl E. and Adrienne Shadd, eds. 1994. *Talking about Difference: Encounters in Culture, Language and Identity.* Toronto: Between the Lines.

James, Joy. 1993. "Reflections on Teaching: Gender, Race, and Class." *Feminist Teacher*, 5,3: 9-15.

Jones, J.M. 1997. *Prejudice and Racism.* 2nd ed. New York: McGraw-Hill.

Jordan, June. 1989. *Moving Towards Home: Political Essays.* London: Virago Press.

Joseph, Gloria I. and Jill Lewis. 1981. *Common Differences: Conflicts in Black and White Feminist Perspectives.* Boston: South End Press.

Karamcheti, I. 1995. "Caliban in the Classroom." In *Pedagogy: The Question of Impersonation*, ed. J. Gallop. Bloomington: Indiana University Press.

Kelly, Jennifer, 1998. *Under the Gaze: Learning to Be Black in White Society.* Halifax: Fernwood Publishing.

Laube, E. 1998. "From the Publisher." In *Stand! Race and Ethnicity: Contending Ideas and Opinions*, ed. B. Mori. Madison, Wis.: Coursewise Publishing.

Lewis, S. 1992. *Consultative Report on Race Relations.* Toronto: Ontario Ministry of Citizenship.

Li, Peter. 1994. "A World Apart: The Multicultural World of Visible Minorities and the Art World of Canada." *Canadian Review of Sociology and Anthropology*, 31,4: 365-91.

Lorde, Audre. 1984. *Sister Outsider: Essays and Speeches.* Trumansburg, N.Y.: The Crossing Press.

____. 1992. "Age, Race, Class, and Sex: Women Redefining Difference." In *Race, Class, and Gender: An Anthology*, ed. M.L. Anderson and P. Hill Collins. Belmont, Cal.: Wadsworth Publishing.

Malarek, V. 1985. "Study Reveals Racist Hiring Practices." *The Globe and Mail*, Jan. 22: 1.

Marable, M. 1992. *Black America*. Westfield, N.J.: Open Media.

Martin, June Roland. 1994. "Methodological Essentialism, False Difference, and Other Dangerous Traps." *Signs: Journal of Women in Culture and Society*, 19,3: 630-57.

Martin, Sandra. 1997. "Being Dionne." *Toronto Life*, March.

McIntosh, Peggy. 1989. "White Privilege: Unpacking the Invisible Knapsack." *Peace and Freedom*, July/August.

___. 1995. "White Privilege and Male Privilege: A Personal Account of Coming to See Correspondences through Work in Women's Studies." In *Race, Class and Gender: An Anthology*, ed. M.L. Anderson and P. Hill Collins. Belmont, Cal.: Wadsworth Publishing.

McKague, Ormand, ed. 1991. *Racism in Canada*. Saskatoon: Fifth House Publishers.

McKee, Christopher. 1996. *Treaty Talks in British Columbia: Negotiating a Mutually Beneficial Future*. Vancouver: UBC Press.

Moore, Donald. 1985. *Don Moore: An Autobiography*. Toronto: Williams-Wallace.

Morrison, Toni. 1992. *Playing in the Dark: Whiteness and the Literary Imagination*. Cambridge, Mass.: Harvard University Press.

Mura, D. 1999. "Explaining Racism to My Daughter." In *Racism Explained to My Daughter — With Responses from W. Ayers, L.D. Delpit, D. Mura, and P. Williams*, ed. T.B. Jelloun. New York: The New Press.

Ng, Roxana. 1987. "Immigrant Women in the Labour Force: An Overview of Present Knowledge and Research Gaps." *Resources for Feminist Research/Documentation sur la récherche féministe (RFR/DRF)*, 16,1.

___. 1994. "Sexism and Racism in the University: Analyzing a Personal Experience." *Canadian Woman Studies*, 14,2: 41-46.

Norquay, Naomi. 1993. "The Other Side of Difference: Memory-Work in the Mainstream." *Qualitative Studies in Education*, 6,3: 241-51.

___. 1998. "Family Immigration (Hi)stories and the Construction of Identity." *Curriculum Studies*, 6,2: 177-90.

Omi, Michael and Winant, Howard. 1993. "On the Theoretical Status of the Concept of Race." In *Race, Identity and Representation in Education*, ed. C. McCarthy and W. Crichlow. New York: Routledge.

Ortega, Julio. 1984. *Poetics of Change: The New Spanish-American Narrative*. Austin: University of Texas Press.

Page, Joanne, ed. 1992. *Arguments with the World: Essays by Bronwen Wallace*. Kingston: Quarry Press.

Paris, E. 1995. "Adapting to Canada and Racism." *The Globe and Mail*, March 4.

Phoenix, A. 1997. "'I'm White, So What?' The Construction of Whiteness for Young Londoners." In *Off White: Readings in Race, Power and Society*, ed. M. Fine et al. New York: Routledge.

Porter, John. 1969. *The Vertical Mosaic: An Analysis of Social Class and Power in Canada*. Toronto: University of Toronto Press.

Portuguese Interagency Network (PIN). 1993. "Employment Equity in Ontario, Bill 79." Submission to the Standing Committee on the Administration of Justice. Toronto, Aug. 27.

Pratt, Minnie Bruce. "Identity: Skin Blood Heart." In *Rebellion: Essays 1980-1991*. Ithaca, N.Y.: Firebrand Books, 1991.

Raby. D.L. 1988. *Fascism and Resistance in Portugal: Communists, Liberals and Military Dissidents in the Opposition to Salazar, 1941-1974*. Manchester: Manchester University Press.

Race & Class. 1999. 41,1-2.

Razack, Sherene. 1993. "Storytelling for Social Change." In *Returning the Gaze: Essays on Racism, Feminism and Politics*, ed. Himani Bannerji. Toronto: Sister Vision Press.

Reagon, Bernice Johnson. 1983. "Coalition Politics: Turning the Century." In *Home Girls: A Black Feminist Anthology*, ed. Barbara Smith. New York: Kitchen Table/Women of Color Press.

Reitz, J.G. 1993. "Statistics on Racial Discrimination in Canada." *Policy Options*, March.

Reitz, J.G. and R. Breton. 1994. *The Illusion of Difference: Realities of Ethnicity in Canada and the United States*. Toronto: C.D. Howe Institute.

Renan, Ernest. 1945. "Qu'est-ce qu'une nation?" In *E Renan et l'Allemagne*, ed. E. Bure. New York: Brentano's.

Rich, Adrienne. 1986. "Notes Toward a Politics of Location (1984)." In *Blood, Bread and Poetry*. New York: W.W. Norton & Co.

Robinson, R. 1999. *Defending the Spirit: A Black Life in America*. New York: Plume Books.

Roman, Leslie. 1993. "White Is a Color! White Defensiveness, Postmodernism, and Anti-Racism Pedagogy." In *Race, Identity and Representation in Education*, ed. C. McCarthy and W. Crichlow. New York: Routledge.

____. 1997. "Denying (White) Racial Privilege: Redemption Discourses and the Uses of Fantasy." In *Off White: Readings in Race, Power and Society*, ed. M. Fine et al. New York: Routledge.

Rosenblum, K.E. and T.C. Travis. 2000. "Constructing Categories of Difference." In *The Meaning of Difference: American Constructions of Race, Sex and Gender, Social Class, and Sexual Orientation*, ed. K.E. Rosenblum and T.C. Travis. 2nd ed. Boston: McGraw-Hill.

Scheier, Libby, Sarah Sheard, and Eleanor Wachtel, eds. 1990. *Language in Her Eye: Writing and Gender — Views by Canadian Women Writing in English*. Toronto: Coach House Press.

Scheurich, J.J. and M.D. Young. 1997. "Coloring Epistemologies: Are Our Research Epistemologies Racially Biased?" *Educational Researcher*, 26,4: 4-15.

Schoem, David, ed. 1991. *Inside Separate Worlds: Life Stories of Young Blacks, Jews and Latinos*. Ann Arbor: University of Michigan Press.

Schucter, Charles I. and William V. van Pelt, eds. 1992. *Speculations: Readings in Culture, Identity and Values*. Englewood Cliffs, N.J.: Blair Press.

Sealy, David. 2000. "'Canadianizing' Blackness: Resisting the Political," in *Rude: Contemporary Black Canadian Cultural Criticism*, ed. Rinaldo Walcott. Toronto: Insomniac Press.

Shadd, Adrienne. 1999. "Institutionalized Racism and Canadian History: Notes of a Black Canadian." In *Seeing Ourselves: Exploring Race, Ethnicity and Culture*, ed. C.E. James. Toronto: Thompson Educational Publishing.

Ship, Susan Judith. 1994. "But What Is Your Nationality?" In *Talking about Difference: Encounters in Culture, Language and Identity*, ed. Carl E. James and Adrienne Shadd. Toronto: Between the Lines.

Silva Magazine (inaugural issue) 1996/1997. "Editorial: Silva: What's in a Name? A Canadian Original." Winter.

Sivanandan, A. 1990. *Communities of Resistance: Writings on Black Struggles for Socialism*. London: Verso.

____. 1982. *A Different Hunger: Writings on Black Resistance*. London: Pluto Press.

Sleeter, Christine. 1993. "How White Teachers Construct Race." In *Race, Identity and Representation in Education*, ed. C. McCarthy and W. Crichlow. New York: Routledge.

Small, S. 1994. *Racialized Barriers: The Black Experience in the United States and England in the 1980s*. London: Routledge.

Solorzano, D.G. 1997. "Images and Words That Wound: Critical Race Theory, Racial Stereotyping, and Teacher Education." *Teacher Education Quarterly*, Summer: 5-19.

Spence, Lynette. 1999. *Routes to Rootes: Exploring Questions of Race, Identities and Knowing with "Black" Young Women*. M.A. thesis. Toronto: Graduate Studies in Education, York University.

Srivastava, Aruna. 1997. "Antiracism Inside and Outside the Classroom." In *Dangerous Territories: Struggles for Difference and Equity in Education*, ed. L. Roman and L. Eyre. New York: Routledge.

Steinhorn, L. and B. Diggs-Brown. 1999. *By the Color of Our Skin: The Illusion of Integration and the Reality of Race*. New York: E.P. Dutton.

Stern, Leonard. 1998. "Who Is a Jew? Definition of Jew Is Emerging as One of Israel's Most Treacherous Issues." *The Gazette* (Montreal), May 2: B1-B2.

Sunahara, A.G. 1981. *The Politics of Racism: The Uprooting of Japanese Canadians during the Second World War*. Toronto: James Lorimer and Company.

Tator, Carol, Frances Henry, and Winston Mattis. 1998. *Challenging Racism in the Arts: Case Studies of Controversy and Conflict*. Toronto: University of Toronto Press.

Tatum, Beverly D. 1992. "Talking about Race, Learning about Racism: The Application of Racial Identity Development Theory in the Classroom." *Harvard Educational Review*, 62,1: 1-24.

____. 1997. *"Why Are All the Black Kids Sitting Together in the Cafeteria?" And Other Conversations about Race*. New York: Basic Books.

Thompson, A. 1997. "For: Anti-Racist Education." *Curriculum Inquiry*, 27,1: 7-44.

Tilly, Susan A. 2000. "Provincially Speaking: 'You Don't Sound Like a Newfoundlander.'" In *Experiencing Difference*, ed. C.E. James. Halifax: Fernwood Publishing.

Tomic, Paty and Ricardo Trumper. 1992. "Canada and the Streaming of Immigrants: A Personal Account of the Chilean Case." In *Deconstructing a Nation: Immigration, Multiculturalism and Racism in '90s Canada*, ed. Vic Satzewich. Halifax: Fernwood Publishing and Social Research Unit, Department of Sociology, University of Saskatchewan.

Torres, Rodolfo D., Louis Miron, and Jonathan Xavier Onda, eds. 1999. *Race, Identity, and Citizenship: A Reader*. Cambridge, Mass.: Blackwell.

Vallières, Pierre. 1971. *White Niggers of America*. Toronto: McClelland & Stewart.

Walker, Alice. 1988. *Living by the Word*. San Diego: Harcourt, Brace, Jovanovitch.

Walker, James W. St. G. 1997. *"Race," Rights and the Law in the Supreme Court of Canada: Historical Case Studies*. Toronto and Waterloo: Osgoode Society and Wilfrid Laurier University Press.

Weis, Lois and Michelle Fine. 1996. "Narrating the 1980s and 1990s: Voices of Poor and Working-Class White and African-American Men." *Anthropology and Education Quarterly*, 27,4: 493-516.

Wellman, D.T. 1993. *Portraits of White Racism*. 2nd ed. Cambridge: Cambridge University Press.

Werbner, Pnina and Tariq Modood, eds. 1997. *Debating Cultural Hybridity*. London: Zed Books.

West, Cornel. 1993. *Race Matters*. Boston: Beacon Press.

Williams, Patricia. 1991. *The Alchemy of Race and Rights: Diary of a Law Professor*. Cambridge, Mass.: Harvard University Press.

Willamson, Janice. 1992. "Jeanette Armstrong: What I intended Was to Connect . . . and It's Happened." *Tessera*, 12 (Summer).

Willinsky, John. 1998. *Learning to Divide the World: Education at Empire's End*. Minneapolis: University of Minnesota Press.

Willis, Paul. 1977. *Learning to Labour*. Farnborough, U.K.: Saxon House. www.scifi.com/bionics/.

Yon, Daniel. 1995. "Identity and Differences in the Caribbean Diaspora: Case Study from Metropolitan Toronto." In *The Reordering of Culture: Latin America, the Caribbean and Canada*, ed. A. Ruprecht and C. Taiana. Ottawa: Carleton University Press.

Contributors

Luis M. Aguiar is a second-generation Portuguese Canadian who teaches in the Department of Sociology, Okanagan University College, Kelowna, B.C. He teaches courses in "race" and ethnicity, the sociology of labour, globalization, and cultural studies. He has researched and published scholarly articles on immigrant workers in the garment industry in Montreal, and immigrants in the cleaning industry in Toronto. His research includes the political mobilizations of "immigrant" building cleaners in Toronto and, with a team of two colleagues, an investigation of "whiteness" in the Okanagan Valley.

Guy Bédard is associate professor in the Department of Political Science at the Université du Québec à Montréal, where he teaches courses in methodology, statistics, and political sociology. He also lectures and conducts research on impact assessment at the Université du Québec à Chicoutimi. His Ph.D. work focused on the "national question of Quebec."

Lillian Blakey is a third-generation Canadian of Japanese origin. She was born in 1945 in rural Alberta, where her parents went after they were forced to leave British Columbia during the Second World War. In 1952 her family moved to Toronto. As an art teacher Blakey has used art with students to assist them in developing positive self-identity. She has also worked as a program leader responsible for equity in the former North York Board of Education in Toronto, where she assisted teachers and students to be more inclusive in their approach to art. She now works as a school literacy co-ordinator in the Toronto District School Board.

Henry Martey Codjoe was born in Ghana, West Africa, and in 1974 emigrated to Canada, where he later became a Canadian citizen. He is director of institutional research and planning and adjunct assistant professor of social science at Dalton State College in Georgia. Before moving to the United States, he lived in Quebec, Ontario, and Alberta.

Angèle Denis is a sociologist working under the guise of a bureaucrat. She concentrates on fiction and diary writing.

Sabra Desai is a human rights and equity activist educator and researcher who has worked in the field of equity and organizational change from an integrated anti-racism feminist perspective for over fifteen years in Canada. As part of her international assignments she has worked in Ethiopia, Guyana, and South Africa. She teaches in the School of Social and Community Services, Humber College of Applied Arts and Technology, Toronto.

Wayne Dunn grew up on a mixed farm in a small northern Saskatchewan community and now lives in Mill Bay, Vancouver Island, where he has a consulting business. He holds a Master of Science in Management degree from the Stanford University Graduate School of Business and has worked with First Nations communities throughout Canada, the United States, and the Americas, assisting them in areas of business and economic development. He has also worked with resource companies and agencies such as the United Nations Agencies and the World Bank, assisting them to work more effectively with Indigenous peoples and local communities.

Camille Hernández-Ramdwar teaches at York University, Toronto, in humanities and Caribbean studies, and she is completing her Ph.D. at the University of Toronto. Her writing has been published in numerous anthologies, including *Mercury Retrograde, . . . But Where Are You Really From? Stories of Identity and Assimilation in Canada* (1997), and *Miscegenation Blues* (1994).

Lawrence Hill is the author of the novels *Any Known Blood* (1997) and *Some Great Thing* (1992), as well as *Women of Vision: The Story of the Canadian Negro Women's Association* (1993) and the children's history book *Trials and Triumphs: The Story of African Canadians* (1993). He is at work on "Black Berry, Sweet Juice," a memoir about growing up of mixed race in Canada. He lives in Oakville, Ont.

Nicholas Anthony Hurley is an artist and computer technician who lives in Barbados. He does his artwork on a part-time basis. His work has been influenced mainly by Japanime and video games, Jim Lee, Stephen Platt, and Nick Manabat.

Stan Isoki was born in a Japanese internment camp in Lemon Creek, B.C. His family emigrated to postwar Japan after World War II and returned to Canada in 1951. He retired from the North York Board of Education after thirty-two years and now teaches in the Faculty of Education, York University, Toronto.

Carl E. James teaches in the Faculty of Education and the School of Social Work, York University, Toronto. A former youth worker with a background in sociology, he works in areas of race, ethnicity, culture, social class, anti-racism, urban education, practitioner research, and Caribbean studies. He is the author of *Seeing Ourselves: Exploring Race, Ethnicity and Culture* (1999) and editor of *Experiencing Difference* (2000), and is also researching the experiences of second- and one-and-a-half-generation Caribbean Canadian youth living in Toronto.

Kai James is a first-year student in engineering science at the University of Toronto. He has worked as a recreational leader and a human rights assistant. His interests include writing poetry, playing basketball and chess, and listening to hip hop music.

Marlene Jennings was born in Longueuil, Quebec. Her father was an African American and her mother a Franco-Manitoban. A lawyer by training, and a community activist and volunteer for many years, she is a Liberal Party Member of Parliament and the first Black Quebecker to be elected to the House of Commons from Quebec. She is intensely interested in issues of social justice and has sponsored private members' bills on banning the cosmetic use of pesticides, quashing the treason conviction of Louis Riel, and establishing indicators for wellness in Canadian society.

Ivan Kalmar is an associate professor in the Department of Anthropology, University of Toronto. His early work showed how features of Inuit grammar are impossible to understand without reference to the   319 practice of speaking within an Inuit cultural context. Later he examined the difficulties that ensue in translating official and semi-official government documents into the Inuit language. The need to reflect on the translator's background in judging a translation led him to the parallel problem of the anthropologist's dependence on his or her own cultural origins, and he began work on his own secular Jewish background. His latest work concerns orientalism and the Jews, dealing with the cultural consequences for nineteenth-century Jews of having been considered an oriental people settled in the West. His research extends from North America to France, Italy, and the regions of erstwhile Austria-Hungary.

Didi Khayatt is an associate professor in the Faculty of Education, York University, Toronto, and the director of the York Centre for Feminist Research. In the past she was co-co-ordinator of the bilingual Women's Studies Programme, Glendon College, York University, and a secondary school teacher. She holds a Ph.D. in sociology of education and has published in the areas of gender, race, sexuality, and social class.

Arun Mukherjee did her graduate work in English at the University of Saugar, India, and came to Canada as a Commonwealth Scholar to do graduate work at the University of Toronto. She has taught at several universities in Canada. She is an associate professor at York University, Toronto, and teaches courses in postcolonial and minority Canadian literatures. Her books include *Oppositional Aesthetics: Readings from a Hyphenated Space* (1995), *Postcolonialism: My Living* (1998), and *York Stories: Women in Higher Education* (2000). She edited *Sharing Our Experience* (1993), an anthology of autobiographical writings by Aboriginal women and women of colour. She also does research on postcolonial literatures, particularly postcolonial literary theory and postcolonial pedagogy, South Asian Canadian literature, and feminist literary theory.

Paul Orlowski has taught in B.C. high schools, primarily in polyethnic working-class neighbourhoods and has focused on advocacy for marginalized groups, especially those living in poverty. He also teaches pre-service teachers of social studies at the University of British Columbia, Vancouver, where he emphasizes issues of representation, hegemony, and corporate media control of discourse. His doctoral research examines how "whiteness" has been constructed and operates in the British Columbia context.

Gottfried Paasche is master of Winters College, York University, Toronto. Together with Prof. Joaquin Kuhn of the University of Toronto he is working on translating the writings of the German pacifist and anti-militarist Hans Paasche and on a book of four German families spanning the first half of this century. He has also helped to produce a video, *Silent Courage: Maria Therese von Hammerstein and Her Battle against Nazism*.

Stephen Patel is a mixed-race Canadian who embraces much of his Caribbean heritage. He recently returned from Japan, where he taught English for six months, and he remains committed to raising awareness of racism and other forms of oppression.

Valerie Bedassigae Pheasant is a member of Potawatomie Nation. She is originally from Wikwemikong and is now a member of the Whitefish River First Nation — a political affiliation. She is a graduate of the Ontario Institute for Studies in Education/University of Toronto.

howard ramos was born and partly raised in Toronto, then moved to Manitoba, and now lives in Montreal, where he is a Ph.D. student at McGill University. He is working on completing his thesis on Aboriginal mobilization in Canada and examining issues of ethnicity, race, and identity. He has also taught in the area of television and society and works on short stories of "everyday" life.

Leslie Sanders teaches in the School of Arts and Letters, Atkinson Faculty of Liberal and Professional Studies, York University, Toronto. She is the author of *The Development of Black Theatre in America* (1998) and of numerous articles on African American and African Canadian literature.

Robert Edison Sandiford is the author of *Winter, Spring, Summer, Fall: Stories* (1995) and two volumes of comics erotica, *Attractive Forces* (1997) and *Stray Moonbeams* (forthcoming), both illustrated by Seattle artist Justin Norman. A Canadian of Barbadian descent, he divides his time between Canada and Barbados, where he is the arts and entertainment editor of *The Nation* newspaper.

Gifty Serbeh-Dunn came to Canada from Ghana in her late teens and finished high school in Canada. She lives in Mill Bay, Vancouver Island, where she is active in community work and works in her husband Wayne's consulting business. She has worked as the international student advisor at Carleton University, Ottawa, and as a consultant with the Canadian International Development Agency and various private consulting firms. Her work has included assignments in Africa, the United Kingdom, and North America. She holds M.A. degrees in Canadian studies (Native studies) from Carleton University, and conflict analysis and management from Royal Roads University in Victoria, B.C. Her recently completed thesis "Healing Wounds: Sustained Dialogue in the Cowichan Valley" deals with the role of identity in cross-cultural conflict.

Adrienne Shadd is a freelance researcher, writer, and editor living in Toronto. She is the co-author of *'We're Rooted Here and They Can't Pull Us Up': Essays in African Canadian Women's History* (1994) and co-editor of *Talking about Difference: Encounters in Culture, Language and Identity* (1994).

Susan Judith Ship is an independent consultant and policy analyst. She has taught courses in women and politics at the University of Ottawa and has published in the area of gender, politics, ethnicity, and race. She has conducted research and training in First Nations and Inuit community health, and developed educational materials for community health representatives. She has been active for many years in developing innovative community-based cross-cultural and anti-racism education programs for children using the performing and visual arts.

Katalin Szepesi was born and raised in Toronto and now lives in North Dakota. Educated at York University, Toronto, she taught with the former North York Board of Education before going into missionary training.

Barb Thomas was born in England and emigrated to Canada as a baby. She is an activist, facilitator, and writer, with extensive experience in anti-racism work and popular education. She has worked with various organizations in Canada, the Caribbean, and Southern Africa to train social change educators and promote equity and democratic organizational change. For ten years she was a program co-ordinator of the Cross Cultural Communication Centre, Toronto, and she was also a co-founder of the Doris Marshall Institute for Education and Action. She recently job-shared as the National Education Co-ordinator of the Service Employees International Union. She is the author of

Multiculturalism at Work: A Guide to Organizational Change and has co-authored a variety of other publications, including *Educating for a Change* (1991) and *Combatting Racism in the Workplace: A Course for Workers.*

Pui Yee Beryl Tsang is a writer, historian, and community worker. Raised in Vancouver, she now lives in Toronto.

Lori Weber teaches English at John Abbott College, Ste-Anne-de-Bellevue, Quebec. In her Canadian literature classes she introduces students to the unknown bits and pieces of their country's history and its rich social fabric. She lived and taught in Atlantic Canada for several years, first in Nova Scotia and then in St. John's, Newfoundland. She grew up in Montreal, in the multicultural neighbourhood of Park Extension, which is still the backdrop for most of her writing and probably always will be. She has published poetry and short fiction in various Canadian journals and anthologies.